PSYCHOLOGY AND HEALTH SERIES

Edited by Donald Marcer
Department of Psychology, University of Southampton

During the last 20 years the behavioural sciences have come to play an increasingly important part in the training of doctors, nurses and other health professionals. Not surprisingly, this shift of emphasis in education has been accompanied by a minor deluge of textbooks, all concerned with the relationship of psychology to health. Though many of these books are excellent, the range of subject matter that most of them seek to encompass necessarily means that many complex issues cannot be covered at anything other than a superficial level.

This series consists of individual texts, each dealing in some depth with a particular issue in which health professionals and psychologists have a shared interest. Though most are written by psychologists with an established academic record, they are aimed primarily at practising professionals. With this in mind, the contributing authors have all had experience in teaching students or members of the medical and other health professions and, with very few exceptions, have worked in a clinical setting. They are thus well suited to fulfil the brief that is common to all the books in this series: that is, while the theoretical basis of the issue under discussion must be spelt out, it must be done in such a way that it enables readers (be they doctors, nurses, physiotherapists, etc., or students) to practise their professions more effectively.

Understanding Stress

IN PREPARATION

Breaking Bad News?
Giving diagnoses to patients
Ian Robinson

Understanding Stress

A PSYCHOLOGICAL PERSPECTIVE FOR HEALTH PROFESSIONALS

Valerie J. Sutherland
and
Cary L. Cooper

Manchester School of Management,
University of Manchester, Institute of Science
and Technology

CHAPMAN & HALL
London · New York · Tokyo · Melbourne · Madras

Published by Chapman & Hall, 2-6 Boundary Row, London SE1 8HN

Chapman & Hall, 2-6 Boundary Row, London SE1 8HN, UK

Blackie Academic & Professional, Wester Cleddens Road,
Bishopbriggs, Glasgow G64 2NZ, UK

Chapman & Hall, 29 West 35th Street, New York NY10001, USA

Chapman & Hall Japan, Thomson Publishing Japan, Hirakawacho
Nemoto Building, 6F, 1-7-11 Hirakawa-cho, Chiyoda-ku, Tokyo 102,
Japan

Chapman & Hall Australia, Thomas Nelson Australia, 102 Dodds
Street, South Melbourne, Victoria 3205, Australia

Chapman & Hall India, R. Seshadri, 32 Second Main Road, CIT East,
Madras 600 035, India

First edition 1990
Reprinted 1992, 1993

© 1990 Chapman & Hall

Typeset in 10/12pt Times by Leaper & Gard Ltd, Bristol
Printed in Great Britain by St Edmundsbury Press Ltd, Bury St
Edmunds, Suffolk

ISBN 0 412 33930 7

A catalogue record for this book is available from the British Library
Library of Congress Cataloging-in-Publication Data available

To the memory of a dear friend and colleague, Bob Davies, who died of cancer, July, 1988. A sad and premature loss of a creative and inspired mind.

Contents

Preface

The costs of stress to the individual, industry and society are well documented and responsible for a high toll on our combined productivity and health. By some, stress is viewed as a 'third wave plague', while others regard it as the 'whipping boy' – blamed for all our ills and wrongs. To put these extremist views into a more rational perspective, it is important that we understand stress. This is the first objective of the book. For example, we need to be able to differentiate between stress and distress; to identify sources of stress and the consequences of exposure to stress; and to understand how individual differences affect our responses to stress.

All individuals would benefit from an increased understanding of the concept of stress, but for the health professional the potential gain is two-fold. Firstly, it is important that health professionals understand stress in order to manage their own lives and to work effectively and efficiently. This becomes crucial in a work environment that is increasingly difficult as a result of restructuring, staff shortages and financial cut-backs, etc. Some of the problems that might exist for certain occupational health groups are thus described and illustrated with research evidence. Secondly, the health professional needs to understand the concept of stress in relationship to patient and client care. That is, how stress might be implicated in disease and health disorders.

However, it is not enough simply to recognize stress, and so the informed health professional needs to know about the techniques and interventions available for the management of stress, both from a self-help approach and for the guidance of others. These are explained in the final part of the book. In the long term we hope that 'stress management' will be viewed as 'preventive medicine' and that this book will encourage this aim. As our interest in preventive medicine continues to develop, the concept of stress management will occupy an important position in the health care and well-being of contemporary society.

VJS
CLC

1

An Introduction to Stress and Health

To the individual whose health or happiness has been ravaged by an inability to cope with the effects of stress, the costs involved are only too clear. Whether manifested as minor complaints of illness, serious ailments such as heart disease, or social problems such as alcoholism and drug abuse, stress-related problems exact a heavy toll. In addition, it has long been recognized that a family suffers indirectly from the stress problems of one of its members — suffering that takes the form of unhappy marriages, divorces, and spouse and child abuse. But what price do organizations and nations pay for a poor fit between people and their environments? Only recently has stress been seen as a contributory factor to the health costs of companies and countries. But as studies of stress-related illnesses and deaths show, stress is imposing a high cost on our combined productivity and health.

It is increasingly apparent that an interdisciplinary approach to health is necessary and, perhaps, vital. Much is to be gained by the co-operative effort of the biological, psychological and medical disciplines, rather than maintaining the sharp divisiveness that has previously existed between the purely medical/physical sphere of medicine and the social-emotional aspects of well-being. Within this brief introductory chapter, the relevance of incorporating a psychological perspective to the stress-health relationship is presented, together with the objectives of the book. The chapter concludes with a summary of the contents that follow.

We believe that several factors have converged to necessitate the need for this multidisciplinary approach to health and well-being. Health care is no longer considered solely as 'disease-cure'. This conceptual shift towards health, rather than disease, means that work of a preventive nature is being carried out. However, to be successful, this requires a more substantial change in the philosophy which underlies medical training. Indeed, some very important steps in this direction are being undertaken, but other factors may bring change more forcefully.

For example, the contemporary understanding of health promotion means that:

1. Health is more than the absence of disease. It embraces the concept of quality of life and a state of complete physical, mental and social well-being (WHO, 1984). Although this definition has been criticized for being idealistic and too vague, it has prompted others to try and clarify the situation. Ahmed *et al.* (1979) suggest that wellness and illness should take account of the roles that the individual is expected to play, i.e. able to function effectively in both familiar and occupational roles. Therefore, health is viewed as a desirable state in order to fulfil role obligations.

2. It seems to be accepted that physical health and mental health are intricately interwoven, and so health is dependent, in part, on how people think, feel and act (Thorensen and Eagleston, 1984). As these authors suggest: 'the obvious connection between physical well-being and mental status, including social and emotional factors, typically has not been reflected in ... how people are cared for ...'. However, more importantly, not enough attention has been paid to this factor in our understanding of the onset and development of disease and illness.

3. An extension of the last point reintroduces a return of a holistic or integrated approach in health care. The very basis of early Hippocratic medicine embraced the concept of homeostasis and a need to take account of the lifestyle of the individual, both at work and at home, in order to discover the underlying cause of the symptoms. Therefore, it is suggested that we need to adopt a model that recognizes the reciprocal and dynamic influences of what might be termed: mind, body and spirit (Thorensen and Eagleston, 1984). Figure 1.1 shows the potential interactions between physiological, cognitive, behavioural and environmental factors that might influence health outcome, and also indicates why the search for causation in terms of simple linear models is essentially futile. Cognitive, behavi-

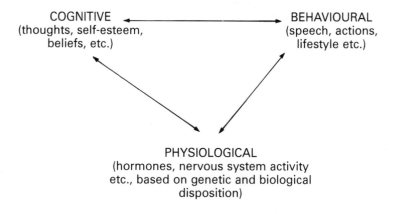

Figure 1.1 The interactive nature of factors in the health outcome model.

oural, physiological and environmntal processes must be taken into account in the understanding of the aetiology, development and treatment of disease and ill-health.

4. Improved health status is linked to changes in personal lifestyle practices that are known risk factors for disease. The killer-diseases in contemporary society are the chronic disorders such as heart disease and cancer, and are both associated with the interactive effects of lifestyle, physiological predisposition and environmental variables. As Knowles (1977) declared; 'Over 99% of us are born healthy and made sick as a result of personal misbehaviour and environmental conditions.' Therefore, the behavioural sciences and in particular psychology, have an important role to play in helping people to alter potential risk-factor behaviours such as smoking, drinking, sedentary lifestyles, poor eating habits and exposure to chronic stress.

5. From this approach to health and well-being, the inter-disciplinary field known as behavioural medicine has emerged. However, Matarazzo (1980) suggests that this should be extended to incorporate a vision of behavioural health, which highlights the notion of personal responsi-

3

bility for ones' own health and a commitment to maintaining health and preventing illness through self-directed and social activities. Ever-decreasing funds are offered to take care of an ever growing and ageing population, and thus alternatives to a medical model must be sought. Therefore, a preventive approach to health care, which places the responsibility for maintaining well-being on the individual becomes an attractive option. The statistics that show significant reductions in deaths due to cardiovascular disease are impressive (a 28% decrease in the USA between 1970–1980), but they say little for any decrease in morbidity. As Thorensen and Eagleston (1984) point out, coronary bypass surgery has become a popular 'cure' for cardiovascular disease, with a typical cost of over $35 000 per operation. Fewer people are dying from this disorder, but many still suffer prematurely and are forced to retire early from the workplace and/or the obligations of society. Clearly, it is necessary to focus more on primary prevention, which should include health education and behavioural health programmes, in order to help individuals help themselves. Wallack and Winkleby (1987) describe three dimensions to primary preventive strategies: (a) 'health protection' is extended to all and is a passive rather than an active approach (e.g. clean water supplies, pasteurized milk etc.); (b) 'disease prevention' identifies people at risk for particular problems and provides specific services for them (e.g. genetic counselling, pre-natal immunization and stress reduction); and finally, (c) 'health promotion' which focuses on people who are basically healthy and attempts to provide skills and information to maintain health and well-being (e.g. not smoking, moderate drinking, exercise, low-fat diets etc.). However, these authors believe that insufficient attention is paid to the social and physical environment as determinants of health and social well-being. For example, in 'drinking and driving' behaviour it may not be enough to only educate the individual on the negative aspects of this behaviour and expect it to change. It is also vitally important to consider the social and physical environment in which the behaviour takes place. Thus, the underlying causes or sources of the behaviour should be identified and dealt with. This idea is not really new because even after the tubercule bacillus microbe was isolated in the laboratory, it was still necessary to understand that environmental factors such as poor nutrition and housing affected host resistance to this disease (Dubos, 1959). In this instance, linking biological, physiological, psychological and environmental agents provided the knowledge to ultimately, and mostly, eliminate the illness in the developed world. In the long-term, this approach may increase our understanding of the incidence of other diseases and how they might be affected by interventions (Wallack and Winkleby, 1987).

6. Finally, it must be acknowledged that a strictly medical-model approach alone may be limited in preventing illness. The following definitions emphasize a need to incorporate both social and environmental factors. Disease is a specific, destructive process or disorder in an organism and an alteration in bodily function; however, illness can exist whether or not disease is present. Although illness is usually assumed to be caused by disease, there is increasing speculation that the causal pathway is reciprocal (Rogers *et al.*, 1979).

A model of health which embraces physiological, behavioural, cognitive and environmental factors might be termed biopsychosocial (Schwartz, 1982). It is within such a framework that an insatiable interest in the topic of stress and the relationship between stress–strain and ill-health has proliferated over the past few decades. Unfortunately, this popularity has not always been beneficial, in that the subject of stress tends to be blamed for all conditions and ills, and/or may be trivialized and not treated seriously. In addition, since many disciplines have embraced the subject, including the biological, social and behavioural sciences, some conflict exists in that there is no agreed definition of stress. Therefore, it is the main objective of this book to provide an understanding of what the psychologist means by stress. Since more than 1100 scientific articles relating to stress, or its effects in biological and social systems (stress disorders and psychological stress) appeared in the 1985 edition of the *Cumulated Index Medicus* (Hinkle, 1987) it would appear that the medical profession has accepted a need to increase its awareness of stress and how it might be implicated in the health and well-being of the individual.

AIMS

Our first objective is to provide a comprehensive psychological perspective on stress for all those individuals working within a health-care setting. The second objective is to provide some understanding on how stress might affect the behaviour, health and performance of health-care providers themselves. The aim is basically two-fold, therefore; 1. to increase the knowledge base of health-care professionals about stress and its relationship to well-being among the patients and individuals that they treat and deal with; and; 2. to enable professionals to understand the sources of stress, their impact on illness and the stress-related problems associated with their own particular occupation.

SUMMARY OF CONTENTS

The contemporary view of stress is that it is not automatically bad, or even to be avoided at all costs. For this reason, there is a need to define, identify, measure and optimize stress; this rationale also provides the structure which appears in the chapters that are to follow. Figure 1.2, a model of stress, provides further illustration of the various aspects that must be considered in the stress equation. This is comprised of the sources of stress that might exist in the environment, which together with the individual's personal characteristics, lead to stress symptoms or outcomes. In Chapter Two stress is defined and the origins of stress-research are described in order to provide a basis for the understanding of the interactive nature of the phenomenon.

In Chapter Three the nature of stress is presented in detail. Six basic categories of potential sources of stress which may exist in the work environment, or in relationship to the work and home interface, are reviewed. Although this assumes that most people are in some form of paid employment, it must also be acknowledged that the unemployed and/or those who do not engage in paid employment have their own specific stress-related problems — these will be dealt with as appropriate. Chapter Four applies to all individuals, because it is concerned with individual differences in response to stress. As already mentioned, situations are not inherently stressful and there are numerous personal factors which might make an individual more or less vulnerable to stress.

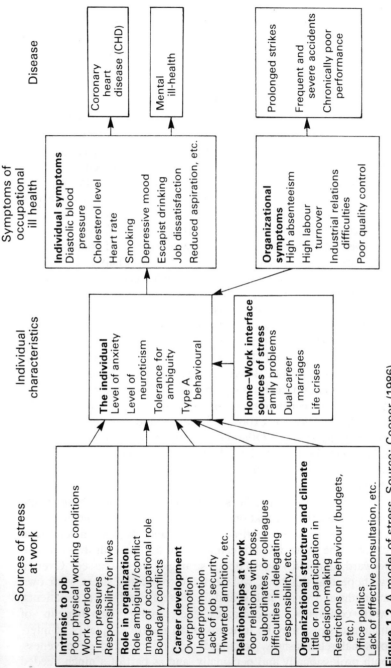

Figure 1.2 A model of stress. Source: Cooper (1986).

Sources of stress at work

Intrinsic to job
Poor physical working conditions
Work overload
Time pressures
Responsibility for lives

Role in organization
Role ambiguity/conflict
Image of occupational role
Boundary conflicts

Career development
Overpromotion
Underpromotion
Lack of job security
Thwarted ambition, etc.

Relationships at work
Poor relations with boss, subordinates, or colleagues
Difficulties in delegating responsibility, etc.

Organizational structure and climate
Little or no participation in decision-making
Restrictions on behaviour (budgets, etc.)
Office politics
Lack of effective consultation, etc.

Individual characteristics

The individual
Level of anxiety
Level of neuroticism
Tolerance for ambiguity
Type A behavioural

Home—Work interface sources of stress
Family problems
Dual-career marriages
Life crises

Symptoms of occupational ill health

Individual symptoms
Diastolic blood pressure
Cholesterol level
Heart rate
Smoking
Depressive mood
Escapist drinking
Job dissatisfaction
Reduced aspiration, etc.

Organizational symptoms
High absenteeism
High labour turnover
Industrial relations difficulties
Poor quality control

Disease

Coronary heart disease (CHD)

Mental ill-health

Prolonged strikes
Frequent and severe accidents
Chronically poor performance

Included in this review are personality traits and behaviour patterns, such as extraversion, neuroticism, Type A coronary prone behaviour, locus of control and the 'hardy' personality — other personal conditioning variables discussed are internal (e.g. age, sex, race) or external factors to the individual (e.g. diet and social setting etc.). Although these moderator variables are reviewed by category, the interactive nature of these factors must not be overlooked. Individual response to stress is dependent on a complex network of 'givens' that include; personality, personal history, needs, wants and the coping strategies adopted. Therefore, stress is understood in terms of an interactive process model, not a static situation, but a dynamic process in which time plays a vital role. The complexity of this issue serves to highlight some of the problems that are inherent in stress research and the difficulties involved in understanding the symptoms and outcomes of exposure to a stressor agent. However, in Chapter Five these potential negative consequences of mismanaged stress are considered in terms of physical, psychological and behavioural outcomes. Costs to the individual, industry and society are presented. A review of some of the proposed stress–health relationships is included such as heart disease, gastrointestinal disorders, diabetes mellitus, allergies and skin disease, cancer, autoimmune diseases and mental ill health. Behaviours that may also have a direct, or indirect effect on health are also discussed (i.e. cigarette smoking and alcohol consumption) in addition to a review of the relationship between exposure to stress and increased accident-vulnerability at work. Other costs to the organization and industry might include absenteeism, high labour turnover, job dissatisfaction, poor productivity and performance; these issues conclude the chapter.

In Chapter Six, specific studies of stress among those in the various health occupations are reviewed, and includes the ambulance service, dentists, doctors and nurses. In the final chapter, the strategies and techniques of dealing with stress are put forward, and individual coping strategies are discussed. Overall, we hope that this book will help you to identify stress, your own strengths and vulnerability, and for those around you (i.e. patients, work colleagues, subordinates and family). The benefits of managed stress may be in terms of an improved quality of interpersonal relationships, enhanced performance and effectiveness, both professionally and personally, and as part of a much needed preventive interdisciplinary strategy in health and well-being for the 21st century.

If we can begin to think of the relationship of stress and health holistically, as Kornhauser (1965) did in the 1960s, we are on the right track:

> Mental health is not so much a freedom from specific frustrations as it is an overall balanced relationship to the world, which permits a person to maintain a realistic, positive belief in himself and his purposeful activities. Insofar as his entire job and life situation facilitate and support such feelings of adequacy, inner security, and meaningfulness of his existence, it can be presumed that his mental health will tend to be good. What is important in a negative way is not any single characteristics of his situation but everything that deprives the person of purpose and zest, that leaves him with negative feelings about himself, with anxieties, tensions, a sense of lostness, emptiness and futility.

2

Understanding Stress — A Historical Perspective

THE ORIGINS OF STRESS RESEARCH

From the introduction, it is implied that potential stressors exist in our environment that may have adverse consequences in terms of cost to the individual, the organization and society. However, this statement makes an immediate, but not totally correct assumption about the nature of stress, because it implies that stress is what happens to people i.e. stress is assigned the role of independent variable. This issue is central to the problems of conceptualization and definition of stress. Historically, the concept has been defined as both the independent and the dependent variable (Cox, 1985) thus wide discrepancies exist in the way that stress is viewed and operationalized. The effect is compounded by the broad application of the stress concept to medical, behavioural and social science research over the past 40–50 years. Each discipline has investigated stress from its own unique perspective, adopting either a stimulus-based (stress as the independent variable) or response-based (stress as the dependent variable) model as a guideline. This is dictated by the objectives of the research and the intended action resulting from the findings. The stimulus-based approach views stress as a disruptive environmental agent, whereas the response-based model views stress in response to these agents. Response may be at the physiological, psychological and/or behavioural level.

The purpose of a clear conceptualization and definition of stress is to provide a guideline for study. From these propositions can be set down. This chapter briefly describes the historical origins and the early approaches to the study of stress, the weakness of the 'simple' models adopted and the evolution of the contemporary 'interactive' model of stress.

Stress as the dependent variable — a response-based model of stress

When asked to provide alternative words to the term stress, associations are usually in the form of response-based meaning (i.e. strain, pressure, tension). The layman readily identifies with the phrase, being-under-stress, because it is not always possible to see stress, only its consequences. A response-based approach to stress, in seeking to define an intangible phenomenon, views it in terms of the dependent variable (i.e. a response to disturbing stimuli). Thus, the main conceptual domain is the manifestation of stress. Figure 2.1 explains diagrammatically this response-based model of stress.

Origins of response-based definitions are found in medicine and usually viewed from a physiological perspective; a logical stance for a discipline trained to diagnose and treat symptoms but not necessarily causes.

John Locke, the seventeenth century physician and philosopher, proposed that intellectual functioning, emotion, muscle movement and the behaviour of internal organs are the product of sensory

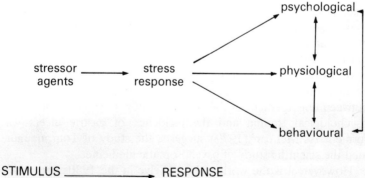

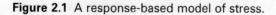

Figure 2.1 A response-based model of stress.

11

experience processed by the brain. From these early notions, the field of physiology gradually developed; the links were established between life experiences, emotions and the importance of hormone and chemical actions in the body. Emotional stress as causal in ischaᵣmic heart disease was proposed by Claude Bernard as early as 1860, with Osler identifying the high incidence of angina pectoris with the hectic pace of life of Jewish business men in 1910. In the 1930s, the psychoanalyst, Franz Alexander and Flanders Dunbar (1943) a physician, reported on the relationship between personality patterns and constitutional tendencies to certain organic disorders (i.e. the psychosomatic theory of disease) (Warshaw, 1979). Claude Bernard was also the first to suggest the idea that the internal environment of a living organism must remain fairly constant despite exterior changes. This notion of stability or balance was developed and described as homeostasis by Walter Cannon. In systems theory, this would be known as dynamic equilibrium, that is, the co-ordination of physiological processes maintains a steady state in the organism (Cannon, 1935). Natural homeostatic mechanisms normally maintain a state of resistance, but are not able to cope with unusually heavy demands because under homeostatic principles there is a finite supply to meet demands.

The earliest reports of systematic study on the relationship between life events and bodily response is probably attributed to Wolf and Wolff (1943, reported by McLean, 1979). Their observations and experiments with a patient, 'Tom', provided the opportunity to observe changes in stomach activity in response to stressful conditions. Wolf and Wolff were able to document changes in blood flow, motility and secretion with feelings of frustration and conflict. Sadness, self-reproach and discouragement were found to be associated with prolonged pallor of the stomach mucosa and a hypo-secretion of acid. Hostility and resentment were associated with a high increase in gastric secretion and acidity. From this work, our understanding of the relationship between engorgement of the stomach lining, lowered resistance to psychological trauma and the incidence of gastric ulcers was formed. As McLean (1979) suggests, the study of Tom inaugurated the scientific study of psychosomatic medicine.

However, it is the work of Hans Selye in the 1930s and 1940s that really marks the beginning of a response-based approach to the study of stress. In 1936, Selye introduced the notion of stress-

12

related illness in terms of the general adaptation syndrome (GAS) suggesting that, 'stress is the non-specific response of the body to any demand made upon it …'(Selye, 1956). Selye's focus was from a medical perspective (i.e. that all patients whatever the disease, looked and felt sick). This general malaise was characterized by loss of motivation, appetite, weight and strength. Evidence from animal studies also indicated internal physical degeneration and deterioration. According to Selye, '… the apparent specificity of diseases of adaptation is ascribed to conditioning factors, such as genetic predisposition, sex, age, learning and diet etc.' Response to stress was deemed to be invariant to the nature of the stressor and followed a universal pattern.

Three stages of response are described within GAS (Figure 2.2). The alarm reaction is the immediate psycho-physiological response, when the initial shock phase of lowered resistance is followed by counter shock. At this time, defence mechanisms are activated forming the emergency reaction known as the 'fight or

Key: 1 Shock;
      2 Countershock;
      3 Resistance;
      4 Collapse.

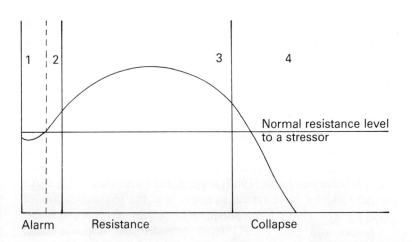

Figure 2.2 General adaptation syndrome. Source: Selye (1956).

flight' response (Cannon, 1935). Increased sympathetic activity results in the secretion of catecholamines, which prepare the body physiologically for action; for example, heart rate and blood pressure increase, the spleen contracts, blood supplies are redirected from the skin and viscera to provide an improved blood supply to the brain and skeletal muscle. Glucose stored as glycogen in the liver is released to provide energy for muscular action, the blood coagulation process is enhanced and the supply of blood lymphocytes increased to combat potential injury and infection. In evolutionary terms, the response was adaptive and vital for survival, but in contemporary society and especially sedentary occupations, it has become disadvantageous and deleterious. Man is denied both the aggression release and the physical activity necessary to quickly remove the build-up of hormone and chemical secretions. The second stage is resistance to a continued stressor, and where the adaptation response and/or return to equilibrium replaces the alarm reaction. If the alarm reaction is elicited too intensely or too frequently over an extended period, the energy needed for adaptation becomes depleted, and the third stage, exhaustion, collapse or death, occurs. Resistance does not go on indefinitely, even when given sufficient energy, because 'every biological activity causes wear and tear ... it leaves some irreversible chemical scars which accumulate to constitute signs of ageing' (Selye, 1983). Although the non-specificity concept of stress-related illness and the GAS had far-reaching influence and significant impact on our understanding of stress, they have been challenged (Lacey, 1967; Mason, 1971; cited Cox, 1985). Research indicates that responses to stimuli do not always follow the same pattern. They are stimulus-specific and dependent on the type of hormonal secretion. For example, anxiety-producing situations are associated with adrenalin, whereas noradrenalin is released in response to aggression producing events. Also, the approach does not address the issue of psychological response to stress, or that a response to a potential threat may, in turn, become the stimulus for a different response. The model is too simplistic. As Christian and Lolas (1985) suggest, the framework of the GAS is still valid for some typical stressors (e.g. the physical factors of heat and cold) but it is not adequate to explain psychosocial stress.

Kagan and Levi (1971) have extended the response-based model of stress to incorporate psychosocial stimuli as causal factors in stress-related illness. Response is viewed as the product of an interaction between the stimulus and the psychobiological programme of the individual (i.e. genetic predisposition and experience or learning). The term interaction is used here as 'the propensity to react in accordance with a certain pattern' (Kagan and Levi, 1971). Since this model also incorporates the concept of feedback, it cannot be considered a simple, stimulus-response model. An additional problem associated with the response-based approach is that stress is recognized as a generic term, which subsumes a large variety of manifestations (Pearlin *et al.*, 1981). Therefore, disagreement exists regarding the real manifestations of stress, and the level in the organism or system which most clearly reflects the response; is it in the single cell, in an organ or throughout the entire organism ... biochemical, physiological or emotional functioning ... at the endocrine, immunological, metabolic or cardiovascular (level) ... or in particular diseases, physical and psychological' (Pearlin *et al.*, 1981). Identification or clarification of this issue is problematic, because the findings of replication research are likely to be confounded. Individuals adapt to any potential source of stress and so the response will vary over time (e.g. in the assessment of noise on hearing and performance).

Although the word stress usually has negative connotations, Selye (1976) emphasizes that stress reaction is not automatically bad, neither can it be avoided, because being alive is synonymous with responding to stress. It is necessary for motivation, growth, development and change, that is, stress is viewed here as eustress. But unwanted, unmanageable stressor situations are damaging, and so, stress becomes distress. The identification of potential sources of stress is the central theme of the stimulus-based model of stress.

Stress as the independent variable — a stimulus-based model of stress

Historically, this approach which links health and disease to certain conditions in the external environment can be traced back to Hippocrates, in about the fifth century, BC. It was the belief of the Hippocratic physician that characteristics of health and disease are conditioned by the external environment (Goodell *et al.*, 1986). The rationale of this approach is that some external force impinges on the organism in a disruptive way. It is also suggested that the word stress derives from the Latin word stringere, to bind tight. The stimulus-based psychological model of stress has its roots in physics and engineering, the analogy being that stress can be defined as a force exerted, which results in a demand or load reaction which causes distortion. Both inorganic and organic substances have tolerance levels. If these are exceeded, temporary or permanent damage occurs. The aphorism, 'it is the straw that breaks the camel's back' is a view consistent with the stimulus-based model of stress. An individual is perpetually bombarded with potential stressor sources in the environment but just one more apparently minor or innocuous event can alter the delicate balance between coping and the total breakdown of coping behaviour. Figure 2.3 represents this model of stress which treats a potential stressor as the independent variable.

Rapid industrialization provided the initial impetus for this approach, and much of the early research into blue-collar stress

*S = stimulus
*R = response

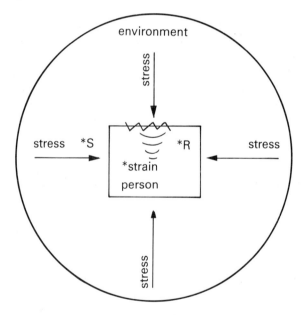

Figure 2.3 A stimulus-based model of stress.

aimed to identify sources of stress in the work environment, in order to provide optimal working conditions. Considerable attention was paid to physical and task circumstances (i.e. heat, cold, noise, social density). Within this model of stress, workload, in terms of both overload and underload conditions were understood (i.e. the inverted U hypothesis; see Chapter three). However, it is now realized that purely objective measures of environmental conditions are inadequate. Individual differences, variability in tolerance levels and expectations, account for the fact that two individuals exposed to exactly the same situation, might react in completely different ways. This is a major weakness of the model. In fact, Lazarus (1966) states that no objective criterion is good enough to describe a situation as stressful, only the person experiencing the event can do this. Although the model has limited use, it has some appeal in organizations seeking to identify common stressor themes or patterns that might affect the majority of the workforce; but rarely (and ill-advisedly) would this intervention be carried out successfully without exhaustive consultation with the personnel concerned.

Industrialization brought many problems associated with physical and task-related sources of stress. Poor working conditions caused diseases such as tuberculosis and pneumonia and led to early death. Legislation, health and safety requirements have resolved many of these unsatisfactory working conditions but contemporary industrialization and new technology bring different problems; new diseases, psychological ill-health and different types of accidents. Our expectations for quality of life have brought a new meaning to the concept of health. It is not only absence of disease or infirmity, but a state of physical, mental and social well-being (WHO, 1984). Well-being is a dynamic state of mind, characterized by reasonable harmony between a worker's ability, needs, expectations, environmental demands and opportunities (Levi, 1987). Thus, an interactive or transactional model of stress, which considers the stressor source, the perception of the situation and the response, is the most useful approach for providing guidelines for the study of stress.

An interactive model of stress

Figure 2.4 details this approach, which incorporates both the

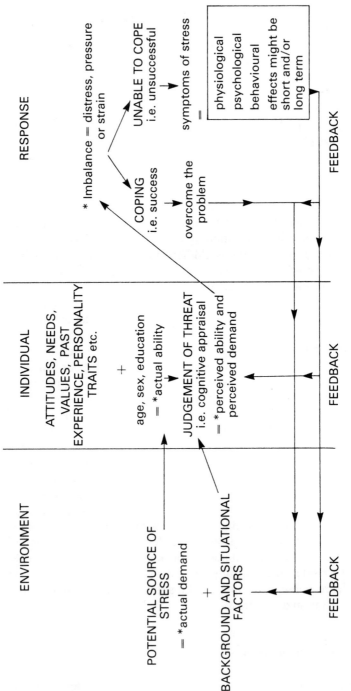

Figure 2.4 Stress perception: an interactive model.

response-based and the stimulus-based models. Within the proposed framework, five major issues are considered:

Cognitive appraisal

Stress is a subjective experience contingent upon perception of the situation, that is, 'stress is not simply out there in the environment' (Lazarus, 1966).

Experience

The way a situation or event is perceived depends on familiarity with the situation, previous exposure, learning and training (i.e. actual ability). Related to this is the concept of reinforcement, that is, past success or failure.

Demand

Pressure or demand is the product of actual demand, perceived demand, perceived ability and actual ability. Needs, desires, and immediate arousal level all influence the way that a demand is perceived.

Interpersonal influence

A potential source of stress is not perceived in a social vacuum. The presence or absence of others, that is, background and situational factors, influence the subjective experience of stress, response and coping behaviour. This can have both negative and positive effects. Other people can be a source of distraction, irritation or unwanted arousal, but they may also provide supportive networks, help to increase self-esteem, provide confirmation of values and a sense of personal identity. Through the process of vicarious learning, increased awareness and an understanding of potential consequences are also gained.

A state of stress

This is the imbalance between perceived demand and perceived ability to meet that demand. The processes that follow are the coping process and the consequences of the coping strategy applied; thus, the importance of feedback at all levels is specified in this model. Successful coping restores imbalance, but unsuccessful coping results in the manifestation of symptoms of exposure to stress. The response may produce either short-term stress manifestations (i.e. maladaptive coping which includes: light another cigarette, 'need' a drink, take a sleeping pill) or long-term effects, such as heart disease or ulcers. However, short-term consequences can also be causal in long-term stress-related illness (i.e. the link between cigarette smoking and lung cancer). Within this model, accidents could be either short-term or long-term manifestations of exposure to stress. As McGrath (1976) suggests, stress must be perceived and interpreted by the individual. It is also necessary to perceive that the potential consequences of successful coping are more desirable than the expected consequences of leaving a situation unaltered. The individual who chooses to use palliatives, views this short-term immediate response (escape!) as less costly or more personally desirable, than altering the demand. It may, of course, not be possible to actually alter the demand at the level of the individual concerned (e.g. the individual forced to work night shifts because no alternative is available, perceived or actual).

Within the interactive model of stress, it is necessary to consider all three conceptual domains of the stress process:

1. Source of stress;
2. Mediators of the stress response;
3. The manifestation of stress.

Situations are not inherently stressful, but are potentially stressful.

PERSON-ENVIRONMENT FIT

The interactive model of stress provides a basis for the person-environment fit approach to the understanding of stress at work (French, 1973; Cooper, 1981). Fit is assessed in terms of the desired and actual levels of various job conditions. The main problem with this approach is that it infers some static situation, whereas in reality response to stress and potential stressor situations are dynamic processes. However, the model is useful where certain personality traits are relatively stable. For example, Kahn *et al.* (1964) found that the introvert under stress from role conflict will tend to reduce contact with other people and will further aggravate work colleagues by appearing to be too independent. Role senders, attempting to define the role will increase their efforts, thus adding to the strain. Therefore, the introvert's coping strategy of defensive withdrawal is ultimately maladaptive. An understanding of such differences between introverts and extraverts can help to avoid potentially stressful situations. Kahn *et al.* have also identified differences between rigid and flexible personality types. Rigid people tend to avoid conflict; they rely on compulsive work habits and show increased dependence on authority figures when under threat. Flexible people respond primarily by complying with work demands and seeking support from peers and subordinates. This compliance can lead to overload problems and reliance on those of equal or lower rank does not help the situation because it is the superior who sets out the work expectation. Thus, the rigid and the flexible types create potential, but very different problems, and may ultimately be more suited for some jobs than others. The problems associated with this line of research are referred to in Chapter 4 on moderators of the response to stress.

STRESS — THIRD WAVE PLAGUE OR WHIPPING BOY?

The development of interactive models of stress are indicative of the complexity of the concept but in reality they actually oversimplify the problem. As Schuler (1980) says, 'it is too all encompassing a phenomenon, too large to investigate'. Yet this has not deterred research interest into the phenomenon. However, the current level of interest and popularity of the idea of stress is not all good. Some organizations adopt a response-based model of stress which allows them to transfer responsibility and view the problem of stress as inherent to the person. Thus, they introduce an intervention which aims to help employees cope with stressor situations but which does nothing to actually reduce or eliminate the origin of the stress. Others may respond only to the stimulus-based model and attempt to make changes without taking account of the needs of individuals (i.e. they only spend resources on the hardware of the organization). Stress is casually blamed for all our ills and seen as the cause of all our problems. The laymen readily and easily identifies with the concept and is eager to know more.

21

Thus, the complexities become over-simplified and are in danger of being trivialized. However, there is an extensive body of research working to redress this balance. Sophisticated techniques allow us to obtain data on biochemical, neuroendocrine and electrical systems of the body and with the aid of computer-based, statistical analysis we are able to investigate many parameters and variables at any one time. This also means that both subjective and objective measures of stress and stress response can be incorporated into a longitudinal study, and so the questions of cause and effect are slowly being resolved.

Gradually, we are beginning to understand why and when stress is harmful; why some people cope and thrive better than others exposed to apparently the same circumstances, and finally, how people might be taught to cope with a source of stress that cannot be eliminated or reduced.

Understanding potential sources of stress that exist in the environment is the focus of Chapter 3. First, an acceptable definition of stress will be established.

DEFINITIONS OF STRESS

Therefore, an understanding of stress is in terms of an interactive process model — a dynamic process in which time plays a vital role. It is thus very apparent that simple dictionary definitions of stress are inadequate when seeking to define and conceptualize psychosocial and occupational stress. However, it is observed that dictionary definitions have evolved to embrace changes in the use of the expression. For example, in the seventeenth century, stress (derived from Latin) was used to mean 'hardship, straits, adversity or affliction' (*Shorter Oxford English Dictionary*, 1933). In the eighteenth and nineteenth centuries, the use of the word stress changed to indicate 'strain, pressure, force or strong effort'. This was intended to include terms relating to the laws of physics and engineering, in addition to person or person's organs and/or mental powers (Hinkle, 1973). Within the field of physics, stress referred to an object's resistance to external pressure, and this model was borrowed by the social sciences. However, as Cox (1985) indicates, the engineering analogy is too simplistic, 'we have to accept some intervening psychological process which does mediate the outcome ... stress has to be perceived and recognized by man. A machine, however, does not have to recognize the load or stress placed upon it.' More recent dictionary definitions actually associate the term stress with disease; 'suffered by managers, etc; subject to continual stress' (*Concise Oxford Dictionary*, 1984, New Edn). More recent medical dictionary definitions incorporate both a response-based and a stimulus-based approach to stress. For example, *Steadman's Medical Dictionary* (1982, 24th edn) defines stress as:

1. The reactions of the animal body to forces of a deleterious nature, infectious, and various abnormal states that tend to disturb its normal physiologic equilibrium.
2. The resisting force set up in a body as a result of an externally applied force.
3. In psychology, a physical or psychological stimulus which, when impinging upon an individual produces strain or disequilibrium.

The *Encyclopedia and Dictionary of Medicine, Nursing and Allied Health* (Miller and Keane, 1978, 2nd Ed.) suggests that stress is:

'the sum of all the non-specific biological phenomena elicited by adverse external influences including damage and defence. Stress may be either physical or psychologic, or both. Just as a bridge is structurally capable of adjusting to certain physical stresses, the human body and mind are normally able to adapt to the stresses of new situations. However, this ability has definite limits beyond which continued stress may cause a breakdown, although this limit varies from person to person ... for example, peptic ulcers may result from prolonged nervous tension in response to real or imagined stresses in people who have a predisposition for ulcers!'

However, within our conceptualization of stress, person-environment fit also acknowledged that 'underload' can be a powerful stress agent. So, we must also incorporate Levi's (1987) definition of stress as poor-fit, that is, 'the interaction between, or misfit of, environmental opportunities and demands, and individual needs and abilities, and expectations, elicit reactions. When the fit is bad, when needs are not being met, or when abilities are over- or undertaxed, the organism reacts with various pathogenic mechanisms. These are cognitive, emotional, behavioural, and/or physiological and under some conditions of intensity, frequency or duration, and in the presence or absence of certain interacting variables, they may lead to precursors of disease.' This definition is consistent with a contemporary interactive approach to the study of stress. Implicit in Levi's definition is the view that stress can have both negative and positive consequences. That is, stress can be a motivator to growth, development and adaption; it is challenge and variety — it can be the spice of life (Selye, 1956). Therefore, a distinction must be made between stressors that cause distress and those which result in eustress, (i.e. the positive stress response) because stress is inevitable, distress is not (Quick and Quick, 1984).

This is particularly important in the work environment, where Beehr and Newman (1978) define job stress as:

'a situation wherein job-related factors interact with a worker to change (i.e. disrupt or enhance) his or her psychological and or physiological condition such that the person (i.e. mind or body) is forced to deviate from normal functioning. This definition also serves to define what we mean by 'employee health'; namely a person's mental and physical condition. We are referring to health in its broadest sense — the complete continuum from superb mental and physical health all the way to death. Note that we are not excluding the possibility of beneficial effects of stress on health.' (p. 670).

Understanding potential stressor sources and moderators of the response to stress are basic to the distinction between eustress and distress. These issues are the topics of Chapters Three and Four.

3

The Nature of Stress

Although the contemporary approach to understanding stress embraces an interactive viewpoint (i.e. stress is in the eye of the beholder) it is necessary to be aware of potential stressors in the environment. Thus, the aim of this chapter is to assess the nature of stress. Evidence from a growing body of research suggests that six major categories of stress may be identified. Since a high proportion of the population are engaged in paid employment outside the home and most research tends to focus on occupational stress, five of these categories are concerned with work stress (Figure 3.1).
These include:

1. Stress in the job itself; stressors intrinsic to the job include workload, poor physical conditions, low decision making latitude, etc;
2. Role-based stress; associated with role conflict, role ambiguity and responsibility;
3. Relationships with others (i.e. superiors, colleagues and subordinates); interpersonal demands are potential stressors.
4. Career development; including under or over promotion and lack of job security.
5. Organizational structure and climate; this includes restrictions on behaviour and the politics and culture of the organization as sources of stress.

Although a significant amount of stress research has focused on white-collar occupations, shop floor blue-collar studies indicate that these classifications may be applicable to the labour force as a whole (Cooper and Marshall, 1978). Every job has potential stress

Intrinsic to job
Too much/too little work
Poor physical working conditions
Time pressures
Decision making etc.

Role in organization
Role conflict/ambiguity
Responsibility for people
No participation in decision
making etc.

Career development
Over promotion/under promotion
Lack of job security
Thwarted ambition etc.

**Organizational structure/
and climate**
Lack of effective consultation
Restrictions on behaviour
Office politics etc.

Relations within organization
Poor relations with boss
Poor relations with colleagues
and subordinates
Difficulties in delegating
responsibility etc.

Individual Manager
Personality
Tolerance for ambiguity
Ability to cope with change
Motivation
Behavioural pattern

Boundary

Organizational

**Organizational interface
with outside**
Company v. family demands
Company v. own interests etc.

Figure 3.1 Sources of managerial stress. Source: Cooper and Marshall (1978).

agents but each will vary in terms of the degree of stress experienced from these five factors. For example, stressors intrinsic to the job are more likely to feature as stress agents among blue-collar workers than among professional groups. Therefore, stress sources will be defined by the nature of the job. However, it is also important to acknowledge that stress in the workplace cannot be fully understood unless reference is made to sources of life stress. These include:

1. The interface between home and work, which refers to the relationship between work demands and family or social demands, (i.e. the stressors that overspill from one life arena into the other);
2. Life cycles and life events.

Each of these categories will be examined separately, but it is important to realize that stressor categorizations are not necessarily discrete entities, and that response to stress is an interactive, dynamic process. However, a classification system does provide a useful framework for a review of sources of occupational/psychosocial stress and the stress response.

FACTORS INTRINSIC TO THE JOB

Within this category, it is necessary to include the physical demands and the task requirements of a job. These intrinsic to the job sources of stress have been a focus of research attention for many years in shopfloor studies. Early blue-collar investigations aimed to identify the links between physical conditions and productivity (Munsterberg, 1913; Roethlisberger and Dickson, 1939), and the importance of relationships between emotional/ social factors, performance and health were soon realised. The significance of 'subjective reactivity' to physical environmental factors also evolved from the Hawthorne studies (Roethlisberger and Dickson, 1939). Kornhauser (1965) found that unpleasant working conditions, the necessity to work fast, to expend a lot of physical effort and working excessive and inconvenient hours were related to poor mental health.

The physical demands of our surroundings and the distress caused by noise, vibration, extremes of temperature (including humidity and inadequate ventilation) lighting, hygiene factors and climate will be reviewed first followed by task demands, which include shiftwork/nightworking, workload (including new technology and working long hours/overtime) repetitiveness, monotony underload and boredom, and the experience of risk and hazard as potential stress agents. Indeed, Cooper and Marshall (1978) suggest that most job descriptions include task and physical factors that at some time can be sources of stress. Thus, the aim of this approach in understanding stress at work is: 1. to identify potentially harmful conditions in order to improve the quality of working life; 2. to identify those individuals best suited to the job conditions, (i.e. to maximize person-environment fit).

Noise

Jones (1983) suggests it is difficult to overstate the importance of sound to our well-being. Language and communication enriches human culture. However, our concern is unwanted sound; this defines a sound as noise (Jones, 1983). Exposure to noise can impede hearing ability and may be problematic, in that the detection of a wanted sound is masked. For example, an accident may occur if warning sounds are not observed (Poulton, 1978). The extent to which noise is a source of stress, causing an increased level of arousal and psychological imbalance, is still debated. Ivancevich and Matteson (1980) suggest that excessive noise (approximately 80 decibels) on a recurring, prolonged basis, can cause stress. However, noise operates less as a stressor in situations where it is excessive but expected, than in those circumstances where it is unpredictable or unexpected. In addition, change in noise levels rather than absolute levels are potentially more stressful.

The main psychosocial impact of excessive noise and other physical demands, is to reduce worker tolerance to other stressors and to adversely affect motivation (Smith *et al.*, 1978). Therefore, the impact is additive, not primary. In spite of this observation, noise is reported by many groups of blue-collar workers as a harmfully perceived stressor; for example, in the UK steel industry (Kelly and Cooper, 1981) and by blue-collar workers in Finland (Koskela *et al.*, 1973; cited ILO, 1986). Unpleasant working conditions due to noise (and other factors intrinsic to the job) were a significant predictor of job dissatisfaction among workers on drilling rigs and platforms in the North Sea (Sutherland and Cooper, 1986) and on an offshore installation in Norwegian waters (Hellesøy, 1985).

Many studies have observed the relationships between noise in the workplace and productivity and noise and rate of error (Broadbent and Little, 1960). Of particular importance is the factor of noise in increasing vulnerability to accidents. Kerr (1950) found mean noise levels correlating significantly with accident frequencies but not accident severity, among 12 000 employees on one site. Cohen (1974; 1976) found accidents to be more frequent in noisy areas (95 decibels or above) particularly among the younger and less experienced workers; with the introduction of ear defenders producing a significant reduction in accident rates. Two health hazards are linked with exposure to noise in the environment. Firstly, the risk of occupational deafness and secondly, that as a source of stress, noise increases arousal levels and might cause some psychological imbalance. However, it appears that personality characteristics also mediate the response to noise as a source of stress. Lader (1971) suggests that those at risk from noise are those who habituate more slowly than normal and who are often characterized by anxiety. The importance of understanding personality characteristics, individual differences and susceptibility to noise are described by McKennell and Hunt (reported by Cox, 1985).

Although noise can be expressed in objective, physical terms (and it is necessary to consider many aspects of noise in the workplace, for example, intensity, variability, frequency, predictability and control) reaction to noise is ultimately a subjective experience (Kummer, 1983). Often the task itself (usually acting as a dependant variable) is also a source of stress, thereby confounding measurement even further. Exposure to noise is associated with reported fatigue, headaches, irritability and poor concentration. Behavioural consequences are in terms of reduced performance, lowered productivity rates and accident occurrence. Social behaviour is also influenced; for example, a reduction in 'helping behaviour', a more extreme or negative attitude to others, more open hostility and overt aggression (Jones, 1983). Thus, there are implications for impoverished relationships in the environment as a consequence of imposed isolation due to excessive noise (and/or the need to wear ear protectors) or poor interpersonal interactions resulting from an accumulation of physical frustration and tensions (Keenan and Kerr, 1951).

Vibration

This is acknowledged as a major source of stress resulting in elevated catecholamine levels and alterations to psychological and neurological functioning (Selye, 1976). Health hazards include nausea, loss of balance and fatigue. Vibrations from rotary or impacting machines could be problematic, for example, in steel casting (Kelly and Cooper, 1981). It also applies to work involved with pneumatic drills, riveting hammers, aircraft propellers, helicopters, etc. Vibrations that transfer from physical objects to the body may adversely affect performance; hands and feet are particularly vulnerable, but the annoyance factor is also a major psychological consideration. In the offshore environment, on drilling rigs and platform installations, vibration is a potential stressor. Although the workers claim that you get used to it, unpleasant working due to vibration and disturbance in the living accommodation were rated as significant stressors by 37% and 27% of workers, respectively. The long-term effects of this exposure are not known (Sutherland and Cooper, 1986).

Temperature, ventilation and humidity

Physiological response to thermal conditions varies greatly between workers and within the same individual from one occasion to the next (Ramsey, 1983). The factory environment is frequently characterized as too hot, too cold, too stuffy, too draughty etc. and thus creates both physical and attitudinal problems (Smith *et al.*, 1978). Work demanding critical decisions, fine discrimination and performance of fast or skilled action is impaired by thermal stress. Manual dexterity is reduced in a cold environment and may be a factor in accident occurrence, due most likely to reduced sensitivity, slowed movement and interference from protective clothing, rather than the loss of impaired cognitive ability (Surry, 1968). The subjective report of thermal comfort is all important. The inability to personally control one's physical environment could also be a significant factor in the perception of thermal comfort. As Ramsey suggests, there seems to be a correlation between comfort and an individual's performance on perceptual motor tasks.

Noise, fumes and heat were the most commonly reported problems among casters in the steel industry (Kelly and Cooper, 1981). Most frequently mentioned by Norwegian workers on offshore platforms were the draughts, uncomfortable temperatures and the dry humid air (Hellesøy, 1985). More dissatisfaction was expressed about overheated working conditions (25%) than about the cold (12% of the respondents). The general effect of working in overheated conditions is a negative reaction to one's surroundings and, as already stated, the effect therefore becomes interactive, and additive. Smith *et al.* (1978) state that this may result in lowered tolerance to other stressors and affect worker motivation. The presence of these sources of stress uses up some attention capacity (Hockey, 1970) and therefore limits the capacity to attend to task-relevant information.

Lighting

The relationship between lighting, illumination levels and production was the concern of the Hawthorne Studies (Roethlisberger and Dickson, 1939). Adequate illumination is an obvious factor associated with safe working. Poor lighting and glare leads to eye strain, damaged vision, headaches, visual fatigue, tension and frustration, because the task may be more difficult and time consuming (Poulton, 1978). Many work environments require constant artificial lighting. Therefore, it is important that a workplace creates a pleasant environment which facilitates performance and promotes safety.

Hygiene

Too many of the world's workforce are employed where hygienic conditions are poor and exposure to accidents and disease causes a constant threat to health (ILO, 1986). Shostak (1980) reports blue-collar grievances of generally neglected working conditions, and the double standard that exists. The all-glass lavish front offices are compared to the noise, lack of windows and air conditioning in dirty factories and workshops. Workers in the steel industry describe dirty, dusty conditions, the poor accommodation provided for rest periods and the lack of toilet facilities nearby (Kelly and Cooper, 1981). These features of the physical environment were rated as high stressor variables among steel casting crews. A clean and orderly place of work is important for both safety and hygiene reasons and for the morale of the workforce, especially where a situation is already acknowledged as hazardous.

31

Climate

In the USA a nationwide sample of workers polled in 1971 rated unpleasant working conditions the third source of discontent (compensation rated first; health and safety hazards second). As Shostak (1980) states 'part of the problem is native to the setting, as in outdoor work'. Thus, the worst thing is the weather and the need to work outside in all conditions. This affects many blue-collar occupational groups, including construction sites, dockyards, highways, seafaring, agricultural work, etc. Unpleasant climatic conditions affect physical well-being, morale, motivation, and vulnerability to accident involvement. If work routines and environments cannot be altered, then adequate protective clothing is vital and attempts to address morale and motivational problems should be considered in alternative ways. While it may be impossible, impractical or unnecessary to modify or eliminate the impact of some aspects of stress associated with the physical demands of a job, it is vital to understand the stress situation from a total perspective before any changes can or should be made. It is also necessary to realize that task demands may also be potential sources of stress.

Shiftwork

It is estimated that 20% of the working population in Europe and North America is working some form of shift system (Tasto and Colligan, 1978; reported by Monk and Tepas, 1985) not by choice, but of necessity. Despite considerable research effort, it is not possible to make overall generalizations regarding the 'best' shift system, but it is clear that shiftwork represents a major source of stress for many occupational groups. Shiftworkers complain more frequently of fatigue and gastrointestinal troubles than day-workers (Rutenfranz *et al.*, 1977) and the impact of shiftworking on eating habits may be responsible for gastrointestinal disorders (Smith *et al.*, 1982). Influences are both biological and emotional, due to circadian rhythm disruption of the sleep/wake cycle, temperature pattern and adrenalin excretion rhythm. For example, Cobb and Rose (1973) found that air traffic controllers had four times the prevalence of hypertension and more mild diabetes and peptic ulcers than a non-shift working control group of US Air

Force personnel. Monk and Folkard (1983) state that shiftwork is a common aspect of contemporary society that must be consciously coped with. They believe that there are three factors which have got to be right for successful coping with shiftwork; sleep, social and family life and circadian rhythms. These factors are interrelated, so that a problem with one can negate the positive effects of success achieved in the others.

Singer (1985) reports 487 different shiftwork systems operating in Europe, including permanent, rotating and continuous shift patterns, some of which demand nightworking. Ultimately, roster designs aim to maximize the positive effects and minimize the negative impact of shiftwork on health and social life caused by the disruption to circadian rhythms. Evidence from research in France (Reinberg; cited by Singer, 1985) suggests that certain individuals with steeper adrenalin curves than normal, are those who tolerate shiftwork best. That is, those with a pattern of very high adrenalin levels during the day and very low levels at night. The 'steeper' rhythm is less vulnerable to distortion and the rationale is that non-adaptation is better than partial adaptation. Akerstedt's (1977) study of railroad workers supports this observation. Three weeks of daywork were followed by three weeks of nightworking. Very little adjustment in the pattern of adrenalin excretion was observed after three shifts of nightwork, with adrenalin remaining high during the day when the workers should be sleeping. Even after three weeks of nightworking, no significant adjustment was observed. Akerstedt (1977) suggests that high adrenalin levels may be the source of disrupted sleep patterns. In spite of the observation that some people may be physiologically better suited to shiftwork, many workers have no choice. Therefore, Knauth and Rutenfranz (1982) suggest that rapidly rotating shift systems with few nightshifts in succession may be best (i.e. less circadian rhythm disruption). Disturbance of nocturnal sleep leads to daytime fatigue and sleepiness impairs motivation and vigilance, thus affecting safety at work. Lavie *et al.* (1982) found that industrial workers ($n = 1502$) complaining about their sleep, had significantly more work accidents, repeated work accidents and significantly more sick days per work accident. Furthermore, complaint of daytime sleepiness was related to multiple work accidents, independent of age and physical effort required at work. Although it must be acknowledged that observed daytime sleepiness can be symptomatic of narcolepsy or breathing disorders, this behaviour may also be a response to stress associated with reduced mental well-being (i.e. symptoms of depression and somatic anxiety). Individuals forced to work night-shifts or an early morning shift suffer from sleep disturbance in that the quantity and quality of their sleep differs as a consequence of shift working (Tilley *et al.*, 1982). Daytime sleep is both more fragile and unstable than nocturnal sleep. Although the night-shift worker may be able to take cat-naps to catch up on sleep loss, 'sleep debt' accumulates over a seven day period, to the extent that the worker has effectively lost the equivalent of at least one night's sleep. However, Selye (1976) suggests that individuals do habituate to shiftwork and it becomes physically less stressful with time.

Workload

Task factors intrinsic to the job include the concept of workload as a potential source of stress. Both overload and underload are acknowledged as stressors. The curvilinear relationship between the amount of work and health and performance is explained in terms of the Yerkes-Dodson Law (Yerkes and Dodson, 1908) the inverted-U hypothesis. Two further distinctions of workload are identified: quantitative overload/underload results from the employee being given too many or too few tasks to complete in a given period of time; qualitative overload/underload is when the individual does not feel capable of doing or able to do the given task, or the task does not utilize the skills and/or potential of the worker (French and Caplan, 1973). Figure 3.2 shows the relationship between performance and underload/overload demand. Within these categories it is necessary to understand that the impact of new technology can affect both overload and underload and that the pressure of both quantitative and qualitative overload can result in the need to work excessive hours, which is an additional source of stress.

Quantitative overload

Both physical and mental overload, that is, simply having too much to do, is a potent stressor at work. Having to work under time pressure in order to meet deadlines is an independent source of stress. Studies show that stress levels increase as difficult dead-

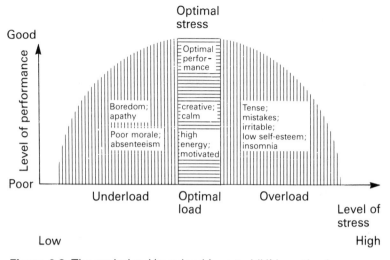

Figure 3.2 The underload/overload inverted 'U' hypothesis.

lines draw near. An association between objective, quantitative overload and cigarette smoking, a risk factor in coronary heart disease and cancer, was observed by French and Caplan (1970). Among British tax inspectors, both quantitative and qualitative overload predicted high levels of anxiety and depression (Cooper and Roden, 1985). Linked to the concept of overload is the issue of workpace. Rate of working has been shown to be a significant factor in blue collar ill-health, especially when the worker is not able to control the pace (Frankenhaeuser and Johansson, 1986). In a national survey in the USA Margolis *et al.* (1974) found that quantitative overload was significantly related to a number of symptoms or indicators of stress — poor work motivation, low self-esteem, absenteeism, escapist drinking and an absence of suggestions to employers.

Quantitative underload

Underload may also affect one's psychological well-being. Boredom in the daily work routine, as a result of too little to do, may result in inattentiveness. This is potentially hazardous if the employee fails to respond appropriately in an emergency (Davidson and Veno, 1980). Work underload was identified as a significant source of stress among crane operators, with boredom and

35

lack of challenge as significant predictors of raised anxiety, depression and reported job dissatisfaction (Cooper and Kelly, 1984). Lack of stimulation may be potentially more damaging at night when the individual could have difficulty adjusting to the change in sleep pattern but does not have enough work to keep alert (Poulton, 1978). Both work overload and underload may also result from an irregular flow of work, which is not under the control of the worker. This is not restricted to paced assembly lines; many outdoor occupations are paced by climatic conditions and a variety of jobs are controlled by the dictates of seasonal demands and/or market needs. Certain workers, such as air traffic controllers, firemen and pilots must deal with long periods of inactivity and the need to spring into action when a crisis occurs.

Qualitative overload

There is evidence that qualitative overload as a source of stress is significantly linked to low levels of self-esteem, although the evidence is based solely on white-collar occupations. However, qualitative overload may be perceived by the blue-collar worker promoted to a supervisory capacity on the grounds of superior work performance but who has no past experience of supervision of others or work delegation. A good, reliable worker is placed under considerable stress because the skills to do the new job are lacking. The stress situation may be compounded if the individual has to take disciplinary action against a previous co-worker.

Qualitative underload

This may be as damaging as overload in that an individual is not given the opportunity to use acquired skills, or to develop full potential ability. However, it is important to remember that this situation will only be experienced as stressful, if needs do not match expectations. For example, research evidence indicates that graduate recruits are likely to suffer qualitative underload. Following a stimulating university environment, they often enter employment with high expectations that are not realized. This manifests itself in reported job dissatisfaction, poor motivation and high labour turnover (Hall, 1976). As with quantitative underload, boredom and shifts or lapses in attention may have serious consequences. Also, the individual feels that she/he is not getting anywhere, and is powerless to show perceived and/or actual skills and talent. Udris (1981; cited by ILO, 1986) suggests that qualitative overload is associated with dissatisfaction, tension, low self-esteem, whereas qualitative underload is linked to dissatisfaction, depression, irritation and psychosomatic complaints.

Working long hours

The experience of both quantitative and qualitative overload may result in the need for an individual to work excessive hours. Simply having too much to do in the normal working day or shift, leads to overtime working. In addition, the worker who struggles to do a job that is too difficult is likely to take more time to finish the task and may need to work extra hours in order to complete the job to a satisfactory standard.

A link between working long hours and stress and ill-health has been established. Breslow and Buell (1960) observed a relationship between the number of hours worked and death from coronary heart disease (CHD). The study of light industry workers in the USA found that subjects of less than 45 years of age but working more than 48 hours per week, had twice the risk of death from CHD, compared to similar individuals working 40 hours or less a week. In addition, a study of 100 young coronary patients showed that 25% of them had been working at two jobs and an additional 40% had worked for more than 60 hours or more a week (Russek and Zohman, 1958). Working long hours also has an overall impact. The individual spends less time in social relationships and so the benefits of social support as a buffer in a stressful job are reduced. However, it must be acknowledged that some individuals regard work and working long hours as a psychological haven and a means of escape from the pressures of home and family and indeed unsatisfactory personal relationships. The stress associated with workload is complex. French and Caplan (1973) suggest that both quantitative and qualitative load produces many different symptoms in addition to psychological and physical strain (i.e. job dissatisfaction, job tension, lowered self-esteem, threat, embarrassment, high cholesterol levels, increased heart rate, skin resistance and more cigarette smoking). Cooper and Marshall (1978) also emphasize that objective workload should not be viewed in isolation. It is necessary to consider perceived

37

demand and ability, in relation to the individual's actual capacity and personality. Although all reasonable steps should be taken to improve the quality of working life; the stress experienced in a situation, the overall job and life satisfaction and the well-being of the individual need to be considered in relation to expectation, needs and the level of social support identified. Thus, the blue-collar worker employed on a paced assembly line may report dissatisfaction with the job but does not display the typical manifestations of response to stress because the job is viewed as purely instrumental to the goals of a satisfactory way of life outside.

New technology

In a rapidly changing work environment, skills may quickly become obsolete. In addition, the need to constantly become familiar with new equipment and systems may pose a threat to the individual. Unless adequate training is provided, potentially stressful situations may develop when new technology is introduced into the workplace and the individual feels unable to do the given task. These pressures of keeping up with new technology are also experienced by business executives and managers (Cooper, 1974). Although computer utilization in personnel departments has increased from 2% to 68% in the past 20 years, use by personnel managers is still modest (Hall and Torrington, 1986). Many managers are still wary of computerized systems. They feel threatened and do not appreciate their usefulness — because they have not received adequate training.

An additional source of stress in a rapidly changing work environment, related to overload, is having a boss schooled in the 'old way'. The new employee, trained in the latest methods and perhaps educated to a higher standard in order to compete in a keen job market, may experience overload stress if adequacy of supervision is questionable. Confidence and respect in the ability of those responsible for the efficient and safe operation of a system or plant, are vital to good interpersonal relationships at work. Introduction of new technology may expose a supervisor to conflict and the experience of qualitative overload, threaten the subordinate with overload because supervision is perceived as inadequate and ultimately adversely affect the quality of relationships in the workplace.

Repetitiveness and monotony

New technology and the increasing automation of industry can lead to the simplification of work and repetitive jobs that are potentially stressful in terms of workload. Although a hectic work-pace is stressful, work that is dull, repetitive and monotonous is equally detrimental to the individual's physical and mental well-being (Kornhauser, 1965). For example, Kritsikis *et al.* (1968) observed a high incidence of angina pectoris among industrial workers employed on a conveyor line system. Recent research using unobtrusive monitoring of heart rate and blood pressure demonstrates that the heart rate of medical nurses was sensitive to emotional stress, whereas the response among truck assembly-line workers was a function of the physical work and activity (O'Brien *et al.*, 1979). In addition, Salvendy and Knight (1983) used on-line monitoring of blood pressure to demonstrate that industrial workers in machine-paced tasks did not display any greater stress-response risk than in self-paced tasks. They state that CHD risk is a complex equation of individual characteristics (age and person-ality), perceived stress level in the job environment and the inter-action between all these factors. Use of physiological monitoring may help to discover the extent to which stress is implicated as a cause of these prominent killers in modern society. However, the perception of stress and psychological response is also critical, for example, Broadbent and Gath (1981) found an association between reported levels of job dissatisfaction and somatic symptoms among assembly-line workers — those engaged in paced work reported more anxiety and depression.

Lack of stimulation, under-utilization of skills and boredom characterizes many blue-collar occupations. Benyon and Blackburn (1972) report the feelings of tension resulting from boredom among workers on a packing-line system. The work provides no sense of achievement or satisfaction. The job stress associated with passive, low skill demands, lack of variety, repeti-tiveness, and low decision latitude factory work also spills over into leisure time and negatively affects life outside of work (Gardell, 1976; cited by ILO, 1986). Lack of stimulation may also be dangerous; Cheliout *et al.* (1979) found a high incidence of de-activation episodes among electronic assemblers (monitored by continuous electro-encephalography, over the entire day). The theta rhythm observed, referred to as micro-sleep, is indicative of the boredom and tedium experienced by the workers and may be responsible for accident occurrence.

Various programmes of job enlargement, job enrichment, job rotation, increased participation in decision-making and shared ownership may be introduced to alleviate some of these problems but they also create separate problems and different sources of stress in the work environment, for example, disruption to social relationships, role ambiguity and status incongruence.

Exposure to risk and hazard

The risk and hazards associated with certain occupations may be a source of stress. Blue-collar workers in the USA rated health and safety hazards as a highly significant source of job discontent (Wallick, 1972). Various occupational groups are identified as high-risk in terms of physical danger, for example, police officers, mine-workers, soldiers, prison personnel, firefighters and workers on oil and gas exploration and production installations (Davidson and Veno, 1980; Kalimo, 1980; Elliott, 1985). These workers may be in a constant state of arousal, ready to react immediately. The resulting adrenalin rush, muscle tension and respiration changes might be a threat to long-term health. However, it is not known if the special risks associated with these occupations are perceived as sources of stress by the competent and trained employee. However, it is possible that a continued emphasis on the need for safety in a hazardous environment might be a greater source of stress. Bohemier (1985) suggests that it is human nature to avoid thinking about danger or death in a hazardous or risky environment and that it is necessary to block out some of the realities which the worker must otherwise continually face. As Cherry (1974) suggests in a study of high-building iron workers; 'many workers learn to combine a hard-boiled veneer about job hazards with abiding private anxieties'.

Various studies indicate that some workers do perceive the risk and hazard associated with the job as a source of stress. Casters in the steel industry and crane operators acknowledge the dangers of the job (Kelly and Cooper, 1981; Cooper and Kelly, 1984); awareness of the dangers and the consequences of making a mistake were significant predictors of depression and anxiety among crane operators. In a Norwegian study, 36% of offshore platform personnel felt unsafe about helicopter transport; 34% felt unsafe about evacuation facilities and 24% were concerned about the risk of fire and explosion (Hellesøy, 1985). Risk of exposure to certain chemicals is frequently reported as one of the most harmfully perceived stressors among blue-collar workers (ILO, 1986). This includes the inhalation of vapours, dust and exposure to chemicals that are irritants to the skin. Adequate protective clothing is vital but training and education are equally important in reducing the stress associated with working in a potentially hazardous environment. The perceived adequacy of medical facilities and the ability to cope with an emergency situation will mitigate the potentially stressful risk situation. In addition, fear and worry about potentially harmful environments and/or suspicion about unknown effects can be sources of distress and, in some instances, the latter might be more detrimental. The risk and hazard associated with many occupations cannot be changed but the perception of risk can be reduced by training and education. Anxious, obsessional and phobic workers are less motivated to work, have low morale and are more vulnerable to accidents. In the long term, they may suffer the consequences of stress-related illness, including heart disease and ulcers.

Travel

Many individuals are faced with the pressures associated with a long journey at the start and finish of each working day. Others engage in travel as part of the job. Traffic jams, delays in public transport and the need to travel in poor weather conditions can be an added strain and challenge to face. In addition to the frustration, tension and irritation often experienced, the already time-pressured individual is forced to spend even less time in social and family activities. This was a significant stressor reported by managers in the construction industry (Sutherland and Davidson, 1989; Langford, 1988). The burden of guilt is increased if tiredness and exhaustion prevents the individual from satisfactory interaction with family and friends. Thus, the stress associated with travel related to the job tends to be additive in that it exacerbates other stressor sources (i.e. it is part of the stress chain) (Kelly and Cooper, 1981).

In general, our understanding about the stress associated with the physical demands of work is extensive, although less is known about the stress of task demands, particularly workload. The way in which the various factors intrinsic to the job interact to form stress chains and how perception of a stressor and/or demand might be meaningfully measured, remain significant problems in stress research. Task demands of a job are associated with the role of the individual in the organization. This stress category is discussed next.

ROLE STRESS

Within the organization, certain behaviours and demands are associated with the role fulfilled. However, dysfunction may occur at two different levels (Kahn *et al.*, 1964) and be a major source of worker stress, that is, role conflict (conflicting job demands) and role ambiguity (lack of clarity about the task). Rizzo *et al.* (1970) suggest that role conflict and role ambiguity are related to job dissatisfaction and inappropriate organizational behaviour. The issue of responsibility associated with the role of the individual will also be included within this category of potential stressors.

Role conflict

Role conflict exists when an individual is torn by the conflicting demands of other members in the organization; doing tasks that are not perceived to be part of the job; or by being involved with a job that conflicts with personal values or beliefs. Stress is caused by the inability to meet various expectations or demands. Van Sell *et al.* (1981) and Kahn *et al.* (1964) found that individuals who suffered more role conflict had lower job satisfaction and higher job tension. Role conflict is also related to physiological stress (French and Caplan, 1970). Telemetry recordings of male office workers illustrated that increased heart rate and feelings of tension about the job were strongly related to reported role conflict. Miles and Perreault (1976) identify four different types of role conflict:

1. Person-role conflict. The individual would like to do the task differently from that suggested by the job description.
2. Intrasender conflict. This happens when a boss communi-

cates expectations which are incompatible, e.g. the individual receives an assignment without sufficient personnel to complete the task successfully.

3. Intersender conflict. The individual is asked to behave in such a manner that one person will be pleased with the result, while others will not be.

4. Role overload. The individual is assigned more work than can be effectively handled.

Role overload has already been discussed; although it would seem intuitive that blue-collar workers would be stressed by the other types of role conflict described, very little evidence supports the notion. For example, the data from a large-scale study of Kibbutz members (Shirom *et al.*, 1973) indicates that there are differences between occupational groups. They found that occupations requiring greater physical exertion (e.g. the agricultural workers) did not show the pronounced relationship between role conflict and role ambiguity and abnormal electrocardiographic readings found among sedentary occupational groups. In addition, Kotlarska *et al.* (1956; cited by ILO, 1986) in Poland, found a much higher incidence of hypertension among elementary shool teachers and bank clerks exposed to conflicting situations and overload of responsibility, compared to miners and labourers. These findings suggest that blue-collar workers may suffer less from the interpersonal dynamics of the organization but more from the physical working conditions (Kasl, 1978). However, these studies do not report psychological response to role conflict. Kasl also states that correlations between role conflict, ambiguity and job satisfaction are strong, while correlations with mental health measures tend to be weak and that personality traits are an important determinant of response to role conflict. It is possible that the blue-collar worker might experience stress from intersender conflict. While satisfying the demands of one superior, or department, another may be displeased, for example, working in a manner to meet production needs could incur reprimand from a safety officer (and vice versa). Role conflict is a more serious problem for the individual working at organizational boundaries (Cooper and Marshall, 1978). Although supervisors or middle managers are more likely to develop ulcers than shopfloor workers (Margolis *et al.*, 1974) because they occupy boundary roles, many blue-collar workers deal with the public, or play a role in a trade union and thus find themselves in a potential stressful boundary-role situation.

Gowler and Legge (1975) have investigated the stress associated with role conflict among managerial personnel. As they suggest, all social positions or roles are upheld with given duties and certain rights. Often the job may incorporate several role sets and these may influence the individuals behaviour, feelings and values. Conflict may occur between different role sets (i.e. between work and the home environment), or within a given role such as manager, for example, conflict may arise when the individual is required to satisfy the policy demands of the organization in addition to protecting the interests of his subordinates. Studies have also shown that personality variables are important mediators in the response to role conflict. Those individuals described as rigid versus flexible in style, and anxiety prone, tend to react to a role-conflict situation in a more extreme manner (Warr and Wall, 1975).

Role ambiguity

An additional source of stress may be present in the workplace when an employee does not have adequate information in order to carry out the task; or does not understand or realize the expectations associated with that particular role. Stress arising from unclear goals and/or objectives can ultimately lead to job dissatisfaction, lack of self-confidence, feelings of futility, a lowered sense of self-esteem, depression, low motivation to work, increased blood pressure and pulse rate and intention to leave the job (Kahn et al., 1964; French and Caplan, 1970; Margolis et al., 1974).

There are a wide range of situations which can create role ambiguity — the first job, a promotion, a transfer, a new boss, a new company or changes in an existing structure (Ivancevich and Matteson, 1980). In times when many jobs are disappearing from manufacturing and heavy industry, career change is often of necessity, not by choice, for some occupations. Each industry has its own technical language, jargon and colloquialisms, which serve to exclude, confuse and isolate a new employee. Unless training is provided to overcome these problems, the uninitiated (although skilled) employee could be exposed to a stressful situation, vulnerable to error and accident involvement. Training to be in the new environment is needed, not necessarily training to do the task. This is likely to be a significant problem for the contract worker in industry, who may work in many different settings in a short period of time.

Responsibility

Responsibility is identified as a potential stressor associated with one's role in the organization. Distinction is made between responsibility for people and responsibility for things (budgets, equipment etc.) with the former acknowledged as significantly more likely to lead to cardiovascular disease (French and Caplan, 1970). However, it should also be noted that lack of responsibility may also be stressful, if the individual perceives this as work underload. For some workers, responsibility for other people's lives and safety is a major source of stress. For example, the crane driver is aware of the consequences of a mistake (Oproek, 1983; Cooper and Kelly, 1984). The offshore drilling crew also recognize the consequences of making a mistake, the need to work as a team and to watch over the new employee. A mistake by the petroleum engineer on the rig can result in a blow out or explosion, which could cause large-scale injury or death, including the total loss of the drilling rig itself (Sutherland and Cooper, 1986). Responsibility for people's safety and lives was also a major factor in predicting risk of heart disease among air traffic controllers (Crump *et al.*, 1980).

Being responsible for other people's work and performance also demands that more time is spent interacting with others. Doll and Jones (1951) demonstrated that foremen and executives had more than the expected rate of duodenal ulcers, whereas various unskilled and non-supervisory groups had ulcer rates as expected. Various studies support this finding but it is also necessary to consider the informal networks within an organization. Responsibility for other people may be self-imposed, in order to feel safe and secure. As one rig worker declared (about new, young workers) 'you feel obliged to 'educate' them ... because it might be my neck as well as theirs' (Sutherland and Cooper, 1986). In a study of 1200 managers in the UK, Pincherle (1972) found links between physical stress, age and the level of responsibility. Increased risk of CHD was associated with age and responsibility for others. However, it is necessary to acknowledge that being responsible for others may be synonymous with overload, role conflict and ambiguity; but, too little responsibility may also be a source of managerial stress. Payne (1981) suggests that managers do not automatically perceive pressure negatively. He found that certain potential strains were rated as both demand and satisfaction. Although this approach may help to clarify the relationships that exist between stressors and mental and/or physical health states, longitudinal studies are still needed to assess the long-term effects of working under high demand conditions, even though they appear to be perceived positively in the short-term. This issue of responsibility as a source of stress leads to the consideration of relationships at work as potential stressors.

RELATIONSHIPS AT WORK

Selye (1974) suggests that having to live with other people is one of the most stressful aspects of life. Good relationships between members of a work group are considered a central factor in individual and organizational health. Poor relationships at work are defined as having 'low trust, low levels of supportiveness and low interest in problem solving within the organization'. Mistrust is positively related to high role ambiguity, which leads to inadequate interpersonal communications between individuals, and psychological strain in the form of low job satisfaction, decreased well-being and feelings of being threatened by one's superior and colleagues (Kahn *et al.*, 1964; French and Caplan, 1973).

Supportive social relationships at work are less likely to create the interpersonal pressures associated with rivalry, office politics and competition (Lazarus, 1966). McLean (1979) suggests that social support in the form of group cohesion, interpersonal trust and liking for a supervisor is associated with decreased levels of perceived job stress and better health. Inconsiderate behaviour on the part of a supervisor appears to contribute significantly to feelings of job pressure (Buck, 1972; McLean, 1979) and close supervision and rigid performance monitoring can also be stressful. In addition, when the workload and work pressure are perceived to be higher, the relationship between the supervisor and employee suffers (Smith *et al.*, 1981). The nature of superior–subordinate interaction was referred to in the discussion on workload and new technology. It is also necessary to understand that the supervisor, or boss with a technical or scientific background, may regard relationships at work as low priority. Their orientation is towards things not people (Cooper and Marshall, 1978) and so consideration for working relationships is viewed as trivial, molly-coddling, petty, time-consuming and an impediment to doing the job well. Contemporary managers must learn to delegate and govern by participation. As Gowler and Legge (1975) indicate, participatory management can create potentially stressful situations, for example, a mismatch of formal and actual power, resentment of the erosion of formal power, conflicting pressures to be both participative and to meet high production standards and subordinates' refusal to participate.

Poor working relationships among co-workers in an organization is a potential source of stress at work; but as work group cohesiveness increases, anxiety about work-related matters decreases. Relationships among co-workers can provide valuable social support and this can ease job strain. French and Caplan (1973) found supportive relationships at work mediate the effects of job strain on cortisone levels, blood pressure, glucose levels and the number of cigarettes smoked. High labour turnover and absenteeism within an industry is disruptive to working relationships. Levels of morale and productivity may be adversely affected. An offshore oil and gas industry study of 'roustabouts' and 'roughnecks' (unskilled and semi-skilled workers) indicates the importance of maintaining fully manned, stable work crews (Livy and Vant, 1979). This investigation found that the work itself was a major cause of job satisfaction and a factor in retaining motivated employees. Teamwork was rated as the most important quality necessary for the job. Although feelings of security and confidence may be generated by the sense of belonging to a stable work crew, the reverse can apply, as Sartre (1944) suggests: 'hell is other people'. The interpersonal demands and the social pressures which arise from social system relationships at work may be potential sources of stress (Quick and Quick, 1984). These interpersonal pressures can be caused by abrasive personalities, leadership style, group pressure, social density and status incongruence.

Abrasive personalities

Some individuals in the organization may unwittingly cause stress to others because they ignore the interpersonal aspects of feelings and sensibilities in social interaction. Levinson (1978b) labels these individuals 'abrasive personalities'. They are usually achievement oriented, hard driving and intelligent but function less well at an emotional level. The need for perfection, the preoccupation with self and the condescending, critical style of the abrasive personality induce feelings of inadequacy among other workers. As Levinson suggests, the abrasive personality as a peer is both difficult and stressful to deal with; but as a superior, the consequences are potentially very damaging to interpersonal relationships and highly stressful for subordinates in the organization.

Leadership style

As already mentioned above, leadership style is a potential source of stress at work for employees. Lewin *et al.* (1939) document the effects of exposure to an authoritarian style of leader. The scientific, technical manager, oriented to things rather than people, may also adopt an interactive style which is stressful to subordinates. They are less likely to engage in a participative form of leadership or appreciate that feedback on performance and recognition for effort are also beneficial to the superior-subordinate relationship. Reaction to an authoritarian style of leader varies; tensions may be expressed by outward calm, passive, repressive attitudes, which will manifest physiologically as elevated blood pressure, or there might be an overt display of aggression and conflict. This latter behaviour may be cathartic for the individual, but is not appropriate in the workplace, and would be a stressful situation for co-workers.

Group pressure

Benefits of the work group are well documented (Smith *et al.*, 1982). Individual needs for affiliation are satisfied and the group offers social support to the worker, which is a source of strength. However, both formal and informal groups in the organization put considerable pressure on an individual to conform to group norms, which may concern production rates, status and style of relationships, etc. A stressor situation develops if the values, beliefs and behaviour of the individual are suppressed (Quick and Quick, 1984) and Laing (1971) suggests that these interpersonal group pressures cause various psychological and behavioural disorders. Roethlisberger and Dickson (1939) indicated the power of informal group norms in controlling behaviour in the work environment. Social influence can affect productivity rates and attitudes to work and safety, which could be detrimental to both the individual and the organization.

Social density

Research evidence suggests that there is an association between crowding and psychological stress, which leads to an increase in both contagious and non-contagious illness (Cox *et al.*, 1982). Where individuals do not have adequate workspace, work performance suffers, increased blood pressure is observed and job dissatisfaction is reported (Evans, 1979). However, each individual has varying needs for interpersonal space and distance; it may be perceived as too much, or too little. A source of social stimulation to one individual may be perceived as aggravation and annoyance to another, for example, crane drivers report the isolation of work in the cab (Cooper and Kelly, 1984); and the need for casters in the steel industry to wear ear defenders isolated them from their peers and restricted conversation (Kelly and Cooper, 1981). International interpreters report the stress associated with the need to share an interpreting booth with an incompatible colleague (Cooper and Davies-Cooper, 1983). This stressor outcome was manifest in the form of job dissatisfaction and poor mental well-being. As Quick and Quick (1984) suggest: 'A balance in social density is desirable'.

Little is known about individual differences and the reaction to violation of personal space and territory, yet this is important where individuals work and/or live together in close proximity for long periods of time. Although the concept of burnout (i.e. the stress associated with a high degree of contact with others) is normally applied to professional occupations, there is also a need to understand burnout in terms of the blue-collar worker. The consequences are equally important to all occupational groups. Hartman and Pearlman (1982) define three components of being burned out: emotional and/or physical exhaustion; lowered job productivity; and over depersonalization. Behavioural response includes increased absenteeism, high labour turnover and drug abuse.

Status incongruence

Status and social esteem of workers in society varies greatly and is related to skill level, professional and technical competence, educational background and the value placed on a particular industry. For example, Shostak (1980) believes that, overall, the general public devalue manual work when measuring its standards against the dimensions used in assessing a job (i.e. money, power, prestige, the nature of work and amount of job prerequisites (e.g. schooling)). Although this may be a potential stressor for the individual, within every organization status incongruence may also exist by virtue of one's job category, nationality etc. and when the individual believes or perceives that status expectations are not met. For example, Philbert *et al.* (1975) report the problems of the heterogeneous population of a pipe-laying barge, living and working in confined conditions for long periods of time. Disparity of status according to nationality, and/or category of task performed, were identified as potential problems. Incongruence between actual status at work and what the worker believes it should be, can lead to stress and frustration, especially when status is lower than expectations demand. Stress and insecurity will also be experienced by the individual who perceives that the status position assigned to a job is higher than perceived rightful entitlement.

The introduction of participative styles of management and the use of quality circles could expose more employees to stress associated with status incongruence, if the systems are not introduced carefully. Increasingly more individuals could also be exposed to perceived status incongruence due to the current trend of using a flexible contract-labour force. A situation may arise where two individuals will work side-by-side, doing exactly the same work but in no respect equal in terms of status within the organization. A 'them' and 'us' situation develops, where even the permanent staff feel threatened and insecure, and this can lead to frustration, job dissatisfaction, reduced well-being and increased vulnerability to accidents.

CAREER STRESS

This category of potential stressors includes job insecurity, over-promotion, under-promotion and thwarted ambition. Individuals suffering from career stress often show job dissatisfaction, burnout, poor work performance and unsatisfactory interpersonal relationships at work (Ivancevich and Matteson, 1980).

Job insecurity

Fear of job loss and the threat of redundancy are common features of working life. Jobs in manufacturing and heavy industry are disappearing and the subsequent rise in the number of jobs in the service sector are more likely to provide employment for women (especially part-time) and school leavers. Job insecurity may also be related to the introduction of new technology. Automation simplifies jobs because machinery does the work of many people. Added to the threat of unemployment is the stress associated with 'job deskilling'. Cakir et al. (1979) found that when the qualification level of a job was changed after automation, the workers complained of monotony, even though the job was not repetitive. In addition, the use of contract labour in many industries may add to this burden of job insecurity. However, if the contracted employee 'selects in' to this form of employment and has no expectations regarding job security and/or promotion prospects, then these situations will not be perceived as stressful.

Threat of job loss is a potent source of stress associated with several serious health problems, including ulcers, colitis and alopecia (Cobb and Kasl, 1977) and increased muscular and emotional complaints (Smith et al., 1981). The morale and motivation of the workforce is affected, with subsequent negative impact on productivity and efficiency. Indirectly, fear of job loss and insecurity in times of high unemployment adversely affects both the individual and the organization. A keen, competitive job market may threaten the quality of peer relationships at a time when social support is of particular importance. The stress associated with feelings of insecurity may otherwise be reduced by the buffering effect of good supportive relationships at work; and this may be broken down, if the workforce perceives that competition is necessary to retain a job. Other individuals may stay in a job that is disliked or unsuitable, because no alternative for change

51

exists. A study of personnel working for one offshore oil/gas contractor in the North Sea showed that 41% of workers reported the stress of feeling trapped into offshore work because no suitable onshore work was available (Sutherland and Cooper, 1986). This could lead to job dissatisfaction and reduced mental well-being.

Finally, the stress associated with the need to change and/or retrain is also likely to manifest at a time of life when the individual is most vulnerable. An individual under the strain of impending job loss realizes that in middle age, learning seems to take longer, energy is more scarce, opportunities are less and the threat of a keen, younger workforce competing for jobs are formidable obstacles. Fear of rejection and rejection itself, are damaging to morale, self-esteem and confidence. Overall, the perception of stability in the organization and employment affects the well-being of employees. In times of instability, poor conditions are tolerated — exposure to long hours, arduous conditions, stressful travel arrangements — all add to the stress chain (Kelly and Cooper, 1981) with one condition exacerbating another.

Career status

Margolis *et al.* (1974) found that the ability to use and develop skills were significant predictors of self-esteem. Therefore, the individual with career aspirations will feel thwarted if these expectations are denied. The chronic frustration of an incongruent state will have deleterious consequences for both the individual and the organization. Disruptive behaviour, poor morale and poor quality interpersonal relationships are associated with the stress of perceived disparity between actual status within the organization and expectations. Hellesøy, *et al.* (1985) identified limited career opportunity as a problem creating frustration and reduced motivation among offshore platform workers in Norway: 29% were dissatisfied with promotion opportunities and a further 33% expressed neither satisfaction nor dissatisfaction, suggesting that they had no expectations regarding promotion. This is an important observation. Under-promotion will only be a source of stress when expectations are not realized. For example, Arthur and Gunderson (1965) found that promotion lag in a military environment was significantly related to psychiatric illness and job dissatisfaction. In this highly structured hierarchical environment, with clearly defined career paths, a state of incongruence is evoked when individuals do not fulfil expectations. Certain occupational groups may be at risk from work underload and underpromotion; for example, graduates entering a managerial career (Hall, 1976) and women managers. Davidson and Cooper (1981) found that women are more likely to be clustered at the lower levels of most organizations, even though they are often considerably more qualified than their male counterparts of similar management level.

The stress associated with over-promotion has already been mentioned in terms of overload. Low self-esteem is experienced by the overworked individual who has been promoted too soon. In addition, conferred status on the basis of ability alone, does not protect the individual from feelings of status incongruence. If perceived ability and status does not match conferred status, the promoted employee will experience stress. However, it is suggested that too little responsibility can be as damaging as too much. Lack of promotion prospects is a potential source of stress for the individual who has successfully mastered a job but does not gain recognition in the form of advancement. Lack of stimulation and challenge and the inability to develop skills, will add to the stress of being passed over for promotion. Brook (1973) describes case studies of individuals showing behavioural disorders ranging from minor psychological symptoms and psychosomatic complaints to more serious mental disorders as a result of over- or under-promotion.

However, as Hall (1976) suggests, there are three distinctive career stages. Needs, expectations and values will vary as a function of career stage. In the early years of a career when the individual is in the establishment phase, there are strong needs for gaining recognition and safety. In the next stage of advancement, the individual is less concerned with fitting in than with gaining mastery of the organization. Finally, there is a levelling off period as a plateau is reached and the career stage reaches the point of maintenance. The experience of stress would thus be mediated according to career phase, for example, the quality of relationships with superiors and peers will change — in the early years good relationships with the boss will be a major concern, but in the advancement phase, co-worker relationships may deteriorate if they are perceived as a threat to promotion prospects. In addition, a preoccupation with the job during advancement might have a disruptive effect on family life during important developmental years (Davidson and Cooper, 1981). Therefore, while stress factors exist for all individuals, valence and subsequent health and well-being outcomes will vary according to career stage.

ORGANIZATIONAL STRUCTURE AND CLIMATE

Cooper and Marshall (1978) describe this category of stress in terms of being in the organization and the threat to freedom, autonomy and identity that this imposes. Four factors are proposed (Landy and Trumbo, 1980); autonomy, structure, reward and consideration orientation. Thus, the organization has a personality to the extent that these factors may be seen as the way in which the organization treats its members. How employees perceive the culture, customs and climate of the organization are important in the understanding of potential sources of stress resulting from being in the organization. Satisfaction or dissatisfaction are ultimately related to the perception and evaluation of structure and climate. For example, Friedlander and Greenburg (1971) found that perceived organizational supportiveness was the significant predictor of success in the evaluation of a training programme. The way in which the programme was presented was as important as the content. Stress factors identified within this category mainly focus on the amount of job involvement or participation on the part of the employee, and the concept of social support.

Lack of participation in the decision-making process, lack of effective consultation and communication, unjustified restrictions on behaviour, office politics and no sense of belonging are identified as potential stressors. Lack of participation in work activity is associated with negative psychological mood and behavioural responses, including escapist drinking and heavy smoking (Caplan et al., 1975a). Increased opportunity to participate results in improved performance, lower staff turnover and improved levels of mental and physical well-being (Margolis et al., 1974). Participation should also extend to worker involvement in the improvement of safety in the workplace; this will help to overcome the apathy among blue-collar workers, which is acknowledged as a significant factor in the cause of accidents (Robens et al., 1972). Karasek (1979) supports these suggestions; a six-year prospective study demonstrated that job control (i.e. intellectual discretion) and work schedule freedom were significant predictors of risk of CHD. Restriction of opportunity for participation and autonomy results in increased depression, exhaustion, illness rates and pill consumption. Feelings of being unable to make changes concerning a job and lack of consultation, are commonly reported stressors among blue-collar workers in the steel industry (Kelly and Cooper, 1981) among offshore operators and drilling personnel in Norway (Hellesøy, 1985) and by contractor personnel on rigs and platforms in the UK and Dutch sectors of the North Sea (Sutherland and Cooper, 1986). Poor organizational climate, job insecurity and the relationship with the organization were all significant predictors of low mental well-being among executives (Cooper and Melhuish, 1980).

Participation in the decision-making process increases investment in the organization, helps to create a sense of belonging and improves communication channels. Related to participation and the sense of belonging is the concept of social support, which mediates the impact of stress. Social support may be classified as interpersonal (based on the individual's relationship) or institutional (from general social and communal systems)(ILO, 1986). The personality of the organization, therefore, plays a part to the extent that an environment is created in which the employee may or may not perceive a sense of belonging. The feeling of attachment and security which is perceived in a supportive environment is critical to the perception of mastery over situations (Thoits, 1982). Several schemes exist which attempt to overcome the stress associated with the rigid structure of the organization, lack of autonomy and consideration and inequitable reward systems. The introduction of autonomous work groups, quality circles, representation on the board, profit share schemes and share ownership aim to improve organization structure and climate, and the quality of working life, but are not without their own problems.

In the first part of this chapter various categories of work stress have been considered. The purpose of describing potential stressor factors at work is twofold:

1. Organizations need to define, identify and measure stress in the workplace before changes can be made.
2. If pressures and strains exist that cannot be eliminated, individuals need to be aware of any risks that exist and how they can best cope with potentially harmful situations.

Nevertheless, to fully understand occupational stress and response to potential stressors in the workplace, it is necessary to adopt a holistic approach and also consider life stress (i.e. extra-organizational demands). By acknowledging that events in one area of life may spill-over into another (i.e. work – home, home – work) a more accurate picture of the vulnerable, at-risk individual may be assessed. This is not only restricted to understanding the consequences of negative spill-over. A satisfying home or social life may buffer the individual against the harmful impact of a high-strain, high demand job; or an enjoyable, rewarding working environment may help the individual cope with an unhappy home life. This is termed the home–work interface situation.

THE INTERFACE BETWEEN WORK AND HOME

Included in this category are all the personal life events which might have an effect upon an individual's performance, efficiency and adjustment at work (Bhagat, 1983) and must be taken into account when assessing sources of occupational stress. Issues concerning the family (Pahl and Pahl, 1971; Handy, 1978; Hall and Hall, 1980), life crises (Dohrenwend and Dohrenwend, 1974; Cooper and Marshall, 1978), financial difficulties, conflicting personal and company beliefs, and the conflict between organization and family demands, may all put a strain on the individual at work, in the same way that stress at work may spill-over and have a negative impact on family and personal life. However, it should be acknowledged that personal life events (i.e. in the form of social support) may reduce the impact of organizational stressors. (This will be discussed in Chapter four in the individual differences section).

Burke and Greenglass (1987) suggest that there is a need for a greater understanding of the reciprocal relationship between work and home domains. Research evidence indicates that job and life satisfaction are influenced by the demands and conflicts of home and family life. Negative life changes (e.g. divorce, bereavement) are related to lower levels of satisfaction with supervision, pay and the work itself, whereas positive life changes are related to satisfaction with promotional opportunities (Sarason and Johnson, 1979). Guest and Williams (1973) report findings on the effects of overseas relocation among executive families; it was observed that overall satisfaction with the assignment was influenced by the job itself and the adjustment of the executives' wives to the foreign environment. Knowledge that a spouse or partner is unhappy may affect performance and safety in a hazardous work environment. This is termed negative emotional spillover (Evans and Bartolomé, 1984). Various researchers have indicated the importance of a supportive partner in a managerial career; for example, Gowler and Legge (1975) coined the term 'hidden contract', in respect of the managerial wife and career success.

Relationships between work and family

Various factors may affect the relationships between work and family, and family and work. The job itself may elicit and reinforce certain personality characteristics; the need for power/responsibility and the Type A workaholic disposition can cause conflict in the home domain. The stress and strains of a job may spill over into family life and life events, or life changes may spill over into work time. Job structure can place constraints on the amount of time spent with the family and the need to engage in shift working may affect the quality of those relationships. Indeed, the decision to take a particular job and/or sustain it, may be affected by family and family commitments. Shimmen (1962) found that attitudes to shift work were influenced by whether the spouse could adjust to being alone at home at night. Evans and Bartolomé (1984) believe that work has a much stronger influence on family than vice versa. Only extreme life events seem to affect work life (e.g. divorce, death of partner). Thus, feelings generated about work determine the quality of the relationship and not the reverse (i.e. work satisfaction and stress dictates the nature of the relationship).

Much of the research work into this area has focused on managerial and professional groups and tends to neglect blue-collar occupations (especially for women). However, empirical evidence does indicate that the home/work interface is a significant source of stress for both women and men but differences exist as a function of gender (Davidson and Cooper, 1983).

LIFE CYCLES AND LIFE EVENTS

Each stage of an individual's life cycle may present a different source of stress or pressure. It is important to realize that at certain stages of life or career there are going to be times when each of us may not function to full capacity, are unproductive and even disruptive to those around us. An awareness of the existence of possible high-risk situations or vulnerable periods of life should help us to adopt a positive attitude to coping and managing, rather than a negative stance. The individual who is made to feel a failure, unable to cope, will become defensive and less likely to seek help or admit that help is needed. Signs of not coping (e.g. sleeplessness or tension) should be regarded as an indication that perhaps life-event pressure needs to be managed in a different way. The consequences of mismanaged stress are well documented. Numerous studies have shown predictive relationships between life strains and health outcomes, including death and disability due to heart disease, diabetes and psychiatric disturbances. Bhagat (1983) suggests that life strains increase the likelihood of anxiety and depressive symptoms and so the individual finds it difficult to maintain the psychological stamina needed for job involvement. Ultimately, the effects are in terms of reduced job performance and job satisfaction. Behavioural response might include tardiness, absenteeism, withdrawal from the job, escapist drinking or use of other palliatives with long-term adverse effects. The following section highlights some of the life events that are potentially harmful because they bring change that disrupts one's equilibrium. Such changes can dramatically alter the structure of life and relationships and a person's outlook on life.

Relocation

Changes in the economy and labour market have increasingly forced more workers to relocate to stay in employment. It is estimated that managers in the UK change jobs about once every three years. Blue-collar workers completely change both career and location as their jobs in heavy industry and manufacturing are replaced by service sector employment. Some individuals need to remain geographically mobile in order to stay in employment (e.g. in relatively short-term contract work). This may require relocation of the family or the need to work away from the home and family for extended periods of time. Although some individuals thrive and cope with this way of life, for many others the experience is stressful and traumatic. If this happens, it becomes a 'lose-lose' situation for all concerned — the individual, the family, the organization and the local community — because close ties are not established or developed (Packard, 1972; Cooper, 1981).

A study of the stress and strain of job transfer among middle and senior executives indicates that problems for the individual relocating vary according to life stage (Marshall and Cooper, 1979). For example, young, single employees have the pressures of starting a new job and being alone in a strange town or city. They need to build a completely new life structure, without the support of a partner, family or friends while trying to maintain former contacts. The young marrieds usually have the least constraints but the dual career couple faces additional problems when one partner is forced to relocate. Children find relocation stressful; infants experience insecurity when their routines are disrupted. Older children must become familiar with new schools and learn to make new friends. The partner left at home does not have the organization and related structure of work to help in the building of a new social network and so might be more lonely and unhappy initially. Guest and Williams (1973) found that satisfaction with overseas relocation among executives was strongly influenced by the wives' adjustment to the move. Actual relocation is, therefore, a stressful event; but the decision not to move or accept a transfer may also be a source of pressure, if the individual feels that job security and career aspirations are threatened by their actions. This is likely to be a significant source of stress for married women, with both career and family commitments. However, for many individuals the stress of relocation is preferable to unemployment.

Unemployment

Fear of redundancy or forced early retirement creates obvious insecurities in the workplace. Anxiety levels increase and interpersonal relationships at work deteriorate, if the individual perceives a competitive atmosphere associated with retaining a job. Having been made redundant, the individual may suffer a variety of possible negative consequences: loss of status which accompanied the job, a sense of failure, loneliness and isolation, low life satisfaction, lowered self esteem and depression, etc. (Fryer and Payne, 1986). Jahoda (1979) reports that high blood pressure, feelings of irritation, depression and low self-esteem were associated with unemployment but those who found new employment experienced a rapid reduction in elevated blood pressure. Kasl and Cobb (1970) confirmed these findings and report similar patterns in levels of serum cholesterol and uric acid associated with unemployment/employment patterns. In addition to the acknowledged psychological and behavioural impact of being unemployed, a growing literature suggests a strong link between physical illness and unemployment. For example, the unemployed reported significantly more symptoms of bronchitis, ear, nose and throat problems, allergies, obstructive lung disease, increased blood pressure and heart disease than the employed. Although the relationship between unemployment and mortality is still debated, some evidence also indicates a positive association between long-term unemployment and reduced longevity (by as much as two to three years depending on when the person had been made redundant).

Surveys have shown that negative feelings and states associated with redundancy and unemployment change over time (Swinburne, 1981), and will vary as a function of age and career-stage of the person. All of these factors need to be considered in the understanding of the response to stress associated with redundancy and/or unemployment.

Marital status

Potential stressors exist for a person by virtue of his or her marital status. Young singles are less likely to be constrained in their choice of employment and career moves but are often faced with the decision of whether to marry before establishing a career, or to delay marriage and family in order to concentrate on work. However, the older, single adult may feel that career moves are limited because the organization prefers to promote the individual with a supportive family network (i.e. the manager with a 'company' wife is seen as an additional asset in certain occupational groups and where social interaction is an important part of the job). Obviously, gender differences will exist here. Research evidence suggests that female managers, for example, are less likely to be married than male managers and are less likely to have child dependents (Davidson, 1987). As Cooper *et al.* (1988a) suggest, married males tend to be viewed as an asset in the organization, whereas the married female a liability.

If the option to marry is taken, new challenges, satisfactions and strains will be encountered. Compatibility of the marriage roles adopted by the couple is one factor to consider in the understanding of the potential stressors and strains in the relationship and of the home/work interface. Handy (1978) suggests that husbands and wives may differ in their needs for achievement, dominance, affiliation and nurturance. Combinations of these needs produce various marriage patterns, some potentially more stressful than others. For example, where both the husband and the wife have high needs for achievement and dominance, problems may arise when children arrive on the scene. The husband will expect his wife to adopt the traditional sex-role stereotype and give up her job. However, this view of marriage assumes that choice is possible and does not take account of the fact that in many marriages, both partners need to work because of economic pressures and are not following any career structure in a professional sense. As Hall (1976) suggests: 'the traditional family model of the husband as breadwinner and wife as homemaker, together 'till death do us part', is becoming a vestige of past society'. Many potential stressors exist for dual-career families.

Dual-career families

Over the past 25 years significant changes in female work patterns have been observed. By 1985 over 38% of the UK labour force were women and 66% of women were in paid employment (Social Trends, 1987). Although a significant proportion of women are in part-time, low status, low-skilled jobs; opportunities for job sharing have increased, so that more and more family units may be described as dual-career couples or families. Economic pressures, and the social and psychological need to develop one's self identity, are the motivators for women to pursue a more active role outside the home in full-time careers or education. These changes in the patterns of employment for married women are, in part, blamed for the increase in the divorce rate. Many studies have indicated that marital adjustment is more of a problem for dual-career wives than non-working wives, and dual-career families experience higher levels of stress. Problems of role-conflict and identity crises are cited (Pahl and Pahl, 1971) and stress may result when one partner's career conflicts with the other's (e.g. as in promotion or transfer). The dual-career couple also need to make joint decisions about career planning and the future; this is an issue that many organizations still fail to understand or appreciate. For example, a manager in a service sector organization reports that he was offered a promotion and transfer from the North to the South of England. It was agreed that he would discuss the situation with his wife and then announce a decision. When he told the boss that he had decided not to take-up the offer (one of the reasons being in consideration of his working wife) he was told: 'Oh, we will probably be able to find some clerical work, or something for your wife to do!' At the time, his wife was the higher wage-earner, and Principal of a large college of further education, and was very successfully mapping-out her own career in higher-education management!

Some of the barriers to womens' advancement in the workplace are slowly being eroded. Organizations are aware that talent should not be wasted. Skill shortages predicted for the 1990s will result in a need to utilize all manpower as fully as possible. Perhaps economic factors will also help to change social attitudes towards dual-career families and reduce the burdens (often self-imposed) of role constraints (the products of socialization and sex stereotyping). Unless the problems that arise can be successfully resolved, many individuals find that they face the stressful experience of divorce and perhaps single parenthood. As Fisher (1988) suggests: 'domestic problems, sometimes work created, occupy a significant proportion of total problems reported at work'.

Divorce and single parenthood

As in the response to unemployment, people involved in a divorce usually go through a series of stages, including shock, despair, depression, loneliness, lowered self-esteem and, finally, recovery. The new roles that emerge put strains and pressures on the individual, especially if it involves single parenthood. Stressors associated with family life cycles and child rearing are burdens more acutely felt by the single parent, for example, finding good child caretaking facilities is vital; school holidays and child illness are difficult problems that must be overcome. Since these issues affect an increasingly larger percentage of the workforce, it would seem that organizations might be more realistic about the spill-over problems that exist. Some more progressive companies are prepared to offer counselling services, flexible work schedules and career breaks to help employees cope positively with potentially distressful life-events and personal circumstances which may occur. It is often difficult to convince an organization of the merits of understanding work-stress, and so they are even more reluctant to spend valuable resources on this holistic life-style approach. To encourage this it is necessary to view the approach to stress as a preventative strategy — to be aware of potential dangers and to take action as necessary — and not in negative, defensive terms. This also embraces the view that response to stress is not invariant; individual differences are observed because many characteristics of the person moderate or mediate the response to a stress agent. These are discussed in chapter four.

4

Stress Response Moderators and Individual Differences

The review of potential stressors presented in the previous chapter suggests that pressure and strain in the environment is all pervasive. This is misleading. Indeed, our contemporary conceptualization of the stress process acknowledges that situations are not inherently stressful or damaging. An event is only stressful if it is perceived as such by the individual. Shakespeare's Hamlet decrees; 'there is nothing either good or bad, but thinking makes it so'. This is an extreme view but it does illustrate the importance of interpretation of events, and explains why response to stress is not invariant. An imbalance in perceived threat and the ability to meet demands defines an experience as distress or strain. Thus, stress is in the eye of the beholder. It is not advantageous to discuss the issue of individual susceptibility, unless there is an understanding of why some individuals in an environment become ill and adversely suffer the consequences of stress exposure, while others survive and thrive under the same conditions. Therefore, response to stress is the product of the situation and the individual, taking into account all the factors which influence resistance and/or increase vulnerability (i.e. factors that protect or predispose). Thus, it is necessary to understand potential individual moderators and mediators of the response to stress. Included in this 'person-factor' are the many personality traits, characteristics and behaviour patterns, based on attitudes, needs, values, past experience, life circumstances, life stages and ability (which includes intelligence, education and training).

This approach to the understanding of stress is termed the interactive model; 'researchers assess how the characteristics of the individual (the employee) and those of the situation (work or job) work simultaneously and in interaction to produce stress and physiological, psychological, and organizational consequences' (Sarason and Sarason, 1981).

The complexity of understanding stress in terms of individual differences is illustrated by Table 4.1. Beehr and Newman (1978) conceptualize job stress and employee health in terms of a facet analysis model intended; 'to delimit and make explicit the phenomena one wishes to investigate'.

This includes environment, personal, and process facets; human and organizational consequence facets; adaptive responses facet and a time facet. Table 4.1 lists only the elements included in the person facet that according to Beehr and Newman ought to be

Table 4.1 Facets of the job stress–employee health research domain — the personal facet

---

1. Psychological condition (personality traits and behavioural characteristics)

— Type A	— impatience
— ego needs	— intrapersonal conflicts
— need for clarity/ intolerance for ambiguity	— self-esteem
— introversion/extraversion	— motives/goals/aspirations
— internality/externality	— typical anxiety level
— approval seeking	— perceptual style
— defensiveness	— values (human, religious etc.)
— intelligence	— personal work standards
— abilities	— need for perfection
— previous experience with stress.	— satisfaction with job and other major aspects of life.

---

2. Physical condition
    — physical fitness/health
    — diet and eating habits
    — exercise, work, sleep and relaxation patterns.

---

3. Life stage characteristics
    — human development stages
    — family stages
    — career stages.

---

4. Demographics
    — age
    — education (amount and type)
    — sex
    — race
    — socio-economic status
    — occupation, avocation.

Source: Beehr and Newman (1978).

studied in order to understand the job stress and employee health domain. Other reviews describes this person-facet as personal conditioning variables (McMichael, 1978); Innes (1981) describes mediating factors of a set of learned responses, which may be construed as fairly stable personality dispositions. These stable, individual differences in coping skills, and the ability to learn them, are acknowledged as making a person more or less susceptible to stress. Internal qualities of the individual are discussed by Schuler (1980) under the categories of needs and values, abilities and experience and personality characteristics of the person. All are seen as important to the individual's perception of the work environment.

The personal factors reviewed in this chapter will be examined under two main headings, 1. personality characteristics; and 2. personal conditioning variables (e.g. age, experience and social support).

PERSONALITY CHARACTERISTICS AS MODERATORS OF THE STRESS RESPONSE

Within this domain, stress researchers are confronted with three main problems:

1. It is necessary to make the assumption that individuals know their true needs, motives and desires; can express them to another person; and are also willing to express honestly these personal characteristics. There are many reasons why a person in the organization might withhold the truth, especially if career aspirations might be affected by the response.

2. The second problem refers to construct validity i.e. is the characteristic being operationalized and measured? This is an important issue in the study of personality 'type' and the stress prone individual (e.g. Type A coronary prone behaviour).

3. Are personal characteristics relatively stable, enduring traits or styles of behaviour, or are transitory, dynamic states and/or moods being measured? This is a controversial area which debates the extent to which personality exists and develops, or whether behaviour is socially learned through

information processing (Mischel, 1976). Within this argument there are important implications for stress intervention programmes and the change or modification of deleterious behaviour styles.

Despite these problems, some attempts have been made to understand certain dimensions of personality as moderators of the response to stress. These include: extraversion – introversion, neuroticism, Type A behaviour, locus of control, and the 'Hardy' personality. Each will be reviewed in turn. Research into personality characteristics as modifiers of the response to stress focuses mainly on differentiating individual characteristics between high- and low-stressed individuals. Typically, this may examine the relationship between psychometric measures (e.g. Minnesota Multiphasic Personality Inventory (MMPI); Cattell's 16 Personality Factors scale (16 PF); Eysenck and Eysenck Personality Inventory (EPI/EPQ)) and response to stress and/or stress-related illness. Some attempt has also been made to investigate personality characteristics as modifiers of accident vulnerability. The personality dimensions, extraversion and neuroticism have received considerable research attention as mediators in stress/health outcomes, and the stress/accident relationship.

Extraversion – introversion

Although there is still a need for consensus on the structure of personality, the extraversion – introversion dimension consistently emerges as an enduring personality characteristic of the individual (McCrae and Costa, 1985; Kline, 1983, 1987). Research evidence suggests that this dimension mediates the response to a potential stressor and thus influences vulnerability. Eysenck (1967) describes personality in terms of type — or second, higher order factors — where type is defined as a group of correlated traits. Traits are simply described as groups of correlated behavioural acts or action tendencies. The extravert is seen as sociable, cheerful, talkative, lively and outgoing, whereas the introvert is quieter, shy, more withdrawn and unsociable. The majority of the population are at the mid-point of the E–I dimension. A high heritability ratio is claimed for the extraversion dimension and at least half the total variance in personality traits is due to genetic causes (Eysenck and Eysenck, 1985). Consistency in behaviour is

67

explained by this assumption. It is further suggested that physiological, neurological and hormonal factors will be the mediators of genetic determinants of behaviour and thus investigation of causal factors of personality should examine the individual from these perspectives.

Physiologically, differences in the E–I dimension are determined by the level of activity in the corticoreticular loop (Eysenck, 1967). Higher levels of cortical activity are observed in introverts, so they are in a significantly higher state of arousal than extraverts. This observation has implications in the prediction of performance. Physiological arousal progressively increases during the daytime, so extraverts are suboptimally aroused in the morning and introverts are supraoptimally aroused in the afternoon (Eysenck, 1982). Research indicates that the body temperature of introverts is higher than that of extraverts early in the day, but is lower in the evening (Eysenck and Eysenck, 1985). Self-reported ratings of subjective alertness supports these observations. Individuals will confidently discuss their best or preferred time of day for working and show preference for being an 'owl' or a 'lark'. Studies of differences in circadian rhythms show that morning people show a steeper rate of increase in body temperature during the morning and reach their peak temperature earlier in the day, compared with evening people. A longitudinal study conducted by Larsen (1985) supports these findings and the observation that introverts reach their arousal peak earlier in the day than extraverts. In addition, the sociability component of extraversion accounted for the 'time-of-day effect' much more strongly than did the impulsivity component.

Two interrelated arousal mechanisms are believed to exist (Broadbent, 1971; Eysenck, 1982); a lower and an upper mechanism. The lower-mechanism controls well established decision processes, and is directly affected by sleeplessness, noise, amphetamines and chlorpromazine (a drug effective in suppressing nausea and vomiting). An upper mechanism is believed to monitor and change the parameters of the lower mechanism in order to maintain level of performance. It is this system that is affected by extraversion, time of day, alcohol and task duration (Broadbent, 1971). Eysenck (1982) called the lower mechanism a passive arousal state, and the upper mechanism an active, effortful reaction.

The higher level of cortical arousal observed among introverts is also the basis for the postulate that introverts are more sensitive to stimulation than extraverts. Optimal or preferred levels of stimulation are higher in extraverts than in introverts; as Eysenck (1967) suggests, extraverts are characterized by stimulus hunger, whereas the behaviour of introverts is suggestive of stimulus aversion. It is also believed that introverts have less tolerance to intense or painful stimuli. Typically, experiments show that extraverts select and tolerate higher levels of light and sound that introverts and have a greater ability to tolerate pain or an aversive stimulus (i.e. introverts consistently have a lower sensory threshold than extraverts). The effects of extraversion on vigilance performance is also partially explained in terms of arousal theory. Vigilance tasks are performed best in states of high arousal and it has been observed that vigilance performance is better in the evening than in the morning. This time-of-day effect is eliminated by the introduction of an arousing stimulus (e.g. intense white noise). Since these observations (Eysenck and Eysenck, 1985) are based on laboratory studies; they provide a theoretical basis for understanding and predicting behaviour but the results must be treated with some qualification. Results are not consistently produced and the problem of generalizability remains a cause for concern. It is also observed that performance is curvilinearly related to arousal (i.e. the inverted U hypothesis) so under and over arousal can adversely affect performance. The complexity is deepened further by the suggestion that arousal levels do not determine behaviour in a direct way because behaviour is also mediated through cognitive control mechanisms. Thus, feedback about performance will take into account a state of arousal. For example, an 'owl' forced into an early morning drive, recognizes that it is not a 'good' time of day, and is likely to be extra careful and vigilant to compensate for known dispositional weaknesses. Moreover, the study of behaviour in social situations and/or occupational settings is much more difficult, because the observations are the product of the situation and the personality of the individual. Despite this, field studies do indicate that personality characteristics mediate in response to the environment, and have an effect on behaviour.

Extraversion–introversion and behavioural response

Arousal theory explains the differences in preference for social contact between introverts and extraverts. Social interaction and interpersonal intimacy increases arousal level, thus, the stimulus-seeking extravert will be positively influenced by social contact. Observations of interview and group-discussion situations indicate that extraverts engage in more gaze behaviour, maintain less interpersonal distance and show a higher rate of verbal interaction than introverts. Bendig (1963) found that desire for social contact also influences occupational choice, with extraverts expressing more interest in work demanding a high level of interpersonal contact (e.g. selling and social work). In a work setting, described as light, machine-paced work, Cooper and Payne (1967) found that extraverts (females) were more likely to show less adjustment to the job, have more non-permitted absenteeism and shorter length of service on average than more introverted workers. The follow-up study twelve months later confirmed this prediction by showing that extraverts had a higher labour turnover rate than introverts. These findings are explained in terms of arousal theory; extraverts, with low arousal levels or high arousal threshold will require and seek more stimulation and be less tolerant to monotonous, routine conditions.

The degree of extraversion is also suggested as a modifier of response to stress (Eysenck, 1967; Brebner and Cooper, 1979). The extravert is seen as geared to respond and will attempt a response when given the opportunity. Kahn et al. (1964) found that reaction to role conflict was mediated by personality. Introverts reacted more negatively and suffered greater tension than extraverts. However, extraverts are more likely to participate in behaviours that may both exacerbate the response to stress and constitute an additional source of stress: extraverts drink more alcohol than introverts, are more likely to seek the stimulation afforded by cigarette smoking and consume spicy foods (Eysenck, 1965). As Eysenck suggests; '... the problems of lung cancer and CHD are medical, (but) ... the epidemiological aspects of these problems are related to constitutional differences in personality'.

Although environmental pressures initiate the smoking habit, genetic predisposition is responsible for maintenance of the behaviour, which is motivated by boredom and emotional strain (Eysenck, 1980). Low scores on the Lie scale (L) originally designed to establish the individuals who attempt to 'fake-good' or give socially-desirable responses, are now also associated with smoking behaviour. Recent research suggests that low L scores are indicative of non-conforming rebellious behaviour (Eysenck, 1980) while individuals who score high on the L scale are seen as agreeable, conscientious, responsible and well-disposed towards others (McCrae and Costa, 1985). Golding *et al.* (1983) found that smokers were characterized by low L and higher psychoticism (P) scores than non-smokers, but no differences in extraversion levels were observed. Smokers in this study were more likely to use cannabis and other drugs and also consumed significantly more tea and coffee.

Alcohol consumption is related to diseases of the heart and liver, it also renders the individual more vulnerable to accident involvement. The extravert is at risk because he is more likely to consume alcohol and is also less tolerant of the effects of it than the introvert (depending on habituation levels). According to Eysenck, alcohol is a depressant drug which has extraverting effects; thus the extravert drinker is directed to the point of no return more quickly by the effects of alcohol consumption. Personality disposition, therefore, has an impact on behaviour and may ultimately and indirectly increase accident risk.

Fine (1963) found that extraverts have more driving accidents and traffic violations than introverts and intermediates. However, although introverts had significantly fewer incidents and violations, a considerable number of incidents were recorded among this group. Similar findings are reported by Craske (1968); a relationship between accidents and extraversion was observed, independent of severity of the incident. Craske observes that the predisposition for extraverts to report to hospital with accidents might explain the association, it is thus part of the complainer syndrome observed in heart disease health checks. Although no association was observed between accident involvement and neuroticism, an item analysis showed that neuroticism items associated with guilt or depression, and extraversion items related to impulsiveness were significantly related to accident repetition. Accident rates among pilots in South Africa were also associated with neuroticism and extraversion (Feldman, 1971). Shaw and Sichel (1971) found that safe bus drivers were predominantly stable introverts, whereas most of the accident-prone drivers were neurotic extraverts. Over a ten year study period it was observed that after an initial induction period, most drivers displayed a stable, predictable pattern of accident behaviour, and in most other incidents, explainable circumstances were very apparent.

However, for a very small percentage, no particular interval pattern emerged. These 'erratic' individuals also tended to be heavy drinkers and were involved in reckless and dangerous driving accidents. The results also showed that the introversion-extraversion dimension held the strongest association in the personality–accident relationship ($r = 0.61$), whereas the stability-accident criterion association correlated at moderate levels ($r = 0.47$).

General emotionality: stability — neuroticism

Eysenck (1967) identifies the factor of neuroticism in the structure of personality, which predisposes a person to respond to stress with neurotic symptoms. Although it is agreed that neuroticism is a major factor in the structure of personality (Kline, 1983, 1987) some debate exists on whether anxiety and the neuroticism dimension may or may not be the same disposition and if the distinction is correctly being made between trait and state conditions of neuroticism/anxiety. In this discussion, the terms neuroticism and anxiety are used with the same meaning and trait anxiety refers to the individual's susceptibility to anxiety. Thus, the differences in state anxiety between groups high and low in trait anxiety should be enhanced as the degree of situational stress increases (e.g. as in threat to self-esteem) (Eysenck and Eysenck, 1985).

Physiologically, individual differences in neuroticism are associated with activity in the visceral brain, especially hypothalamic activity and responsiveness of the sympathetic nervous system; high activity is identified with high neuroticism (Eysenck, 1967). Again, the majority of the population score on the mid-point range but the typical, high scoring individual is described as a worrier who tends to feel depressed, has considerable mood swings, sweats easily and feels anxious before important events.

Neuroticism and behavioural response

Furnham (1981) found that neurotic individuals tend to avoid stimulating, active and unusual situations more than stable individuals. In intimate, interpersonal situations, attempts are made to reduce the level of intimacy by gaze avoidance. Although shyness is associated with anxious behaviour, Eysenck and Eysenck (1969) postulate two distinct forms of social shyness. Introverted shyness stems from the preference to be alone, although the introvert is capable of functioning effectively in company. However, the neurotic individual may desire the company of others but is also fearful of it because of worries of inadequacy. In the work environment, neurotics and neurotic-introverts are the most susceptible to stressful situations. High emotionality is likely to affect performance, but can both hinder or facilitate performance (Kline, 1983). Cooper and Payne (1967) found that neuroticism was related to poor job adjustment and frequency of non-permitted absence in routine, monotonous work. Studies utilizing personality measures, such as the MMPI and the 16PF, indicate that neuroticism/ emotional instability and introversion are related to fatal heart disease (Jenkins, 1971) and angina pectoris (Baaker, 1967; Lebovits et al., 1967; Finn et al., 1969). However, these studies are mainly retrospective and thus the observed emotional instability, anxiety and introversion may be a reaction to heart disease and not a precursor. One investigation does implicate personality as a significant predictor of fatal CHD: high anxiety and neuroticism scores among students were predictive of fatal CHD, the cause of death indicated on death certificates years later (Paffenbarger et al., 1966).

Although no relationship has been observed between neuroticism and cigarette smoking, alcohol is the most commonly used drug to alleviate stress and anxiety and it would therefore seem that neurotics might be more likely to consume alcohol. However, the behavioural outcome here also depends on the neuroticism–introversion or neuroticism–extraversion structure of personality. The incidence of peptic ulcer disease is linked to psychological factors but the causal relationships between personality and the disease remain unclear. Langeluddecke et al. (1987) found that gastric ulcer patients had higher trait anxiety and psychoticism levels than community controls. This finding is consistent with previous results. However, it is not known whether these traits are directly or indirectly related to ulcer incidence because high levels of anxiety and/or neuroticism may also be associated with higher alcohol consumption, heavy analgesic usage or other factors which may predispose the individual to gastric ulcers (Richardson, 1983). Overall, relatively little research is available on the real-life behaviour of stable introverts, or stable extraverts but according to

Eysenck (1967) neurotic introversion is associated with phobias, obsessive-compulsive rituals, anxiety states and neurotic depression (i.e. dysthymia). Neurotic extraverts are most susceptible to hysteria.

Although the introversion–extraversion and neuroticism–stability dimensions are postulated to mediate in the response to stress and, thus, determine vulnerability to disease and illness, the concept of Type A coronary prone behaviour has recently received significantly more research attention, presumably because of the hypothesized links between this style of behaviour and increased risk of CHD. This moderator of behaviour in the response to stress will be reviewed next.

Type A coronary-prone behaviour

Type A behaviour pattern is also a style of behaviour which acts as a modifier of response to stress (McMichael, 1978). Interest in this concept is fuelled by the reported links between Type A behaviour (TAB) and increased risk of heart disease. Although these links are not consistently observed, the concept continues to generate serious interest, especially among researchers investigating the issues of person–environment (or employee–job) fit. It seems that the Type A behaviour style might be deleterious to both the well-being of the individual and to the organization in some situations. Therefore, an understanding of this behavioural moderator in the response to stress is important. The TAB concept, originally described by Dunbar (1943) characterizes the coronary patient as compulsively striving, self disciplined, with an urge to get to the top, and with mastery of others. Despite this, the link between this stereotyped behaviour and increased risk for heart disease is usually attributed to cardiologists, Friedman and Rosenman (1974). Observation and interview data suggests that the individual labelled Type A pattern (TAP) may be described as highly competitive, unrelenting, hard driving and achievement oriented; has a strong sense of time urgency, hurried and explosive speech patterns, quick motor movements, a guilt or unease when relaxing or not working, is aggressive, hostile, restless and impatient, especially when unable to rapidly overcome obstacles to their own satisfaction.

In a work setting, Type As,

1. Work long hours constantly under deadlines and conditions of overload;
2. Take work home on evenings and at weekends; they are unable to relax;
3. Often cut holidays short to get back to work, or may not even take a holiday;
4. Constantly compete with themselves and others; also drive themselves to meet high, often unrealistic standards;
5. Feel frustrated in the work situation;
6. Are irritable with work efforts of their subordinates;
7. Feel misunderstood by their superiors.

(Brief *et al.*, 1983).

The Type B person is characterized by an absence of these characteristics.

Two major prospective studies, the Western Collaborative Group Study (Rosenman *et al.*, 1964, 1966, 1975) and the Framingham Heart Study (Haynes *et al.*, 1978a, 1978b, 1980, 1981) support the proposed relationship between TAB and increased risk for CHD independent of traditional biomedical risk. However, the relationship between TAB and CHD among blue-collar workers is not established by these studies. In addition, recent UK research does not support the original findings. Over a six year period, TAB (measured using the Bortner scale) did not predict major ischaemic heart disease events among a random sample of 6000 British males in the 40–59 years age group (Johnston *et al.*, 1987). Mann and Brennan (1987) also used the Bortner scale to measure TAB among 7426 participants taking part in mild hypertension trials. Controlling for age, social class, smoking habit and hypertension factors; no relationship between Bortner scores and cardiovascular disease events (death, stroke, or myocardial infarction) over the five year period was observed. However, as the authors suggest, their respondents were unrepresentative in two respects; they were volunteers and all had mildly elevated blood pressure. In addition, use of the Bortner, self-assessment questionnaire might not be as satisfactory as the structured interview technique to classify TAB, even though validity and reliability is claimed. Similarly, Bass and Akhras (1987) studied TAB among British males awaiting coronary artery bypass graft surgery. One month before surgery, no associations were observed between Bortner scores and angiographic indices of CHD. They did find that an inability to suppress fear strongly correlated with angiographic readings (i.e. inability to control emotions). Although they acknowledge that the disease could be causing the fear, rather than the reverse, high correlations between spouse and patient ratings suggested that it was a reflection of trait and not state measures.

These studies have all used the Bortner scale and the samples include all socioeconomic groups. Although some control was made for the social class variable, this, together with the type of measure used, might explain some of the differences between the UK findings and the original studies. However, they do highlight a need to consider social class differences. All studies found that non-manual working males scored higher than manual workers and in one study it was observed that Type A scores declined with age. Yet as Mann and Brennan report; 'this association is the reverse of that for overt CHD where older age and lower social class have the greatest incidence rate' (Rose and Marmot, 1981) Caplan *et al.* (1975) agree: in the study of a wide range of occupations in the USA, the highest Type A scores were recorded for family physicians and administrative professors, although the indices of ill-health were greater for the blue-collar groups observed. Tool and die makers scored the highest and assemblers on machine-paced lines and continuous flow monitoring, the lowest.

Perhaps the search for an independent risk factor for heart disease is a simplistic notion. It is widely accepted that psychological factors do play a part in the epidemiology of heart disease. Type A behaviour, hostility, neuroticism, anxiety and proneness to phobias have been implicated and of course cigarette smoking, which is not just a behaviour but a behaviour with a psychological purpose. The search for single, or independent risk factors may be futile in that risk factors are not additive but multiplicative. The whole may be greater than the sum of its parts (Johnston, 1989).

Type A behaviour in the work environment

Although certain inconsistencies on health outcomes are reported, empirical evidence supporting the behavioural predisposition of Type As is available. Brief *et al.* (1983) found that Type As perceive exposure to greater levels of job stress in work overload conditions than Type B individuals and a strong, positive relationship was observed between subjective workload and dissatisfaction. The causal chain posited was:

$$\text{Type A} \rightarrow \frac{\text{subjective}}{\text{workload}} \rightarrow \frac{\text{workload}}{\text{dissatisfaction}} \rightarrow \text{depression}$$

Thus, Type A behaviour may be associated with the onset of other disorders, for example depression (although the reverse of this chain should also be considered). Observations also indicate that Type As are more likely to engage in active coping in threat situations; this produces activity and is linked to greater levels of physiological arousal. Constantly recurring sympathetic activity is associated with the process of atherosclerosis (Evans and Fearn, 1985). This study, which used the Framingham Type A Scale, also reports criterion validity for the time-urgency component of Type A: the Type A subjects completed computer based questionnaires significantly quicker than their Type B counterparts.

Type As appear to react adversely to highly-structured work settings which place strict controls on their activity. They tend to suppress subjective states, deny the physical effects of fatigue and strain and have an overdeveloped concern to gain and maintain control over potentially threatening situations. This may explain the lack of expected correlations reported in some studies. For example, no significant correlations were found between TAB in a managerial population and various stressor outcome variables, including job dissatisfaction, anxiety, depression, irritation and sleeping disorders (Howard et al., 1976). Smith and his colleagues (Smith et al., 1984) report similar denial by college students. In a study of the anger process and Type A pattern, they found Type As low in irritability had greater cardiovascular reactivity than did Type Bs low in irritability. They suggest that reduced reporting of irritation by Type As may reflect suppression or denial and might be related to enhanced cardiovascular response. Ivancevich et al. (1982) compared studies of groups of nurses and groups of managers; in one a self-report scale was used and in the other the structured interview. Both investigations provide support for the Type A construct. Type A was a significant stressor–outcome moderator, which made an impact on the perception of stressors, satisfaction levels and indicators of physical well-being (blood pressure measures among the managers, and blood pressure and cholesterol levels of nurses). However, these authors question the extent to which Type As create their own stress (i.e. quantitative work overload) by their style of behaviour. Thus, it may be self-imposed, rather than due to the requirements of the job. Sorensen *et al.* (1987) suggest that Type A scores may be, in part, a function of job experience and that the environment elicits and reinforces TAB. Jobs may also be chosen in keeping with a style of behaviour. They found that TAB was related to long work hours, high occupational mobility and non-supportive job related inter-actions with co-workers. Other studies have also found that social support level is inversely related to TAB among males. It is suggested that the TAB and the job experience relationship may be reciprocal. Job experiences may cause inception of the behavioural style and over time this is enhanced and reinforced.

Ward and Eisler (1987) have tried to explain the deleterious work behaviour of Type As. In an experimental situation they found that the achievement striving is characterized by a tendency to set personal goals in excess of performance potential and is associated with a low probability of achieving those goals. This chronic and frequent failure experience leads to dissatisfaction and negative psychological states. Type As were also consistently less satisfied with their performance and tended to evaluate it less favourably than Type B individuals. In addition to the active coping style preference already mentioned, other characteristics of the Type A person are proposed to explain their plight. Dembroski *et al.* (1985) suggest that potential for hostility and anger-in (with-holding of anger and irritation with others) are related to heart disease severity. This struggle with interpersonal relationships may also explain why Type As report lower levels of social support than Type Bs. Hostility as a behavioural style, implicated in increased risk for CHD, is also the subject of disagreement. The concept of hostility as measured by the MMPI is reflective of a generalized dislike and distrust of other people. There are some indications that it is predictive of heart disease and CHD deaths but other studies refute this assumption. However, it would seem that this predisposition, together with the characteristics of competitive drive and impatience, might result in poorer interpersonal relationships for the Type A individual, at work and at home; the consequences being in terms of reduced physical and psychological well-being.

Folsom's (1985) findings that Type A males relax less easily and therefore drink more frequently (but not more in amount per occasion) may explain the increased hostility and social aggression observed. As Folsom suggests, drinking may promote TAB rather than TAB leading to drinking and is, therefore, a concommitant of the Type A pattern. This study of males at risk ($n = 12866$) aged 35–57, found that Type As drank 30% more alcohol than Type Bs, independent of age, income, smoking and marital status. This is surprising in that Type A scores are positively associated with socioeconomic status, but that heavy alcohol consumption is associated more with non-manual occupational groups. A high percentage of cigarette smokers are found among the extreme Type A scorers (Howard *et al.*, 1976); and Caplan *et al.* (1975b) found that Type As are less likely to give-up smoking than are Type Bs.

The active behaviour style of Type As might also explain the higher physiological reactivity observed (or vice versa). Studies have shown that Type As respond with higher increases in heart rate, catecholamine levels and blood pressure than Type Bs, when challenged to perform well, or in choice-reaction tasks. After exposure to a stressor situation Type As also show greater platelet aggregation and raised serum cholesterol levels. Howard *et al.* (1986) show that extreme Type As (A1) have significantly higher baseline levels on all the coronary risk variables (except uric acid) associated with CHD (blood pressure, cholesterol, triglycerides and cigarette smoking). With increasing job ambiguity Type As (A1 + A2) showed an increase in blood pressure and triglycerides, although the degree of reported intrinsic job satisfaction moderated these outcomes. Very little sympathetic ANS arousal was observed among Type Bs exposed to an increase in ambiguity levels.

Type A in relationship to other personality dimensions

Howard *et al.* (1986) suggest that the TAP pattern is not considered to be a trait but a set of overt behaviours that are elicited from susceptible individuals. Despite this reflection, TAB is seen as a fairly stable and deeply ingrained predisposition to respond. Therefore, to understand this phenomena, researchers have investigated relationships between TAB and other personality characteristics. Flores and Valdés (1986) reported very strong correlations between Type A (Jenkins Activity Survey, form N) and extraversion (EPQ), impulsiveness (identified as a component

79

of extraversion) and susceptibility to reward. In a factor analysis, extraversion emerged as a well defined component of Type A behaviour, and in regression analysis, the predictors of Type A behaviour among medical students included extraversion, sincerity and impulsiveness. The extraverted temperament of Type As is supported by numerous other studies. Laboratory investigations indicate that Type As show optimum levels of performance under conditions of high level stimulation, whereas Type Bs achieve optimum results under lower level stimulation conditions. This is consistent with an arousal theory explanation of extraversion–introversion. Therefore, it follows that Type As would also be more extravert. The Type A individual, more susceptible to stress than Type Bs would also be expected to show higher levels of neuroticism. However, the relationship between neuroticism and TAB is not so consistently observed. Some studies found that Type As score high on N, others found low scoring relationships. But as Suinn (1976) suggests, given that TAB and anxiety are not related, it is surprising that the major impetus of intervention programmes is anxiety management. Unequivocal findings are not surprising in that a variety of measures and sub-scales are used to assess TAB (and its components) and various instruments are used to measure trait anxiety and neuroticism (Llorente, 1986). Since there is no real agreement that the various Type A assessment methods are valid, such inconsistencies are inevitable.

Eysenck and Fulker (1983) declare that Type A behaviour is not unitary; some aspects are related to E and some to N. From their own measure of TAB, they identified factors which were labelled tenseness (loading high on N) ambition, activity, and unrepressed emotion (loading high on E) but these two groups were 'almostly' unrelated. However, the heritability of these factors exceeds 50%, which is similar to the personality factors P, E and N. Although it may be accepted that TAB is a multi-dimensional construct, this should not deter this line of research. It is unlikely that any one factor of TAB or any one personality dimension will explain the incidence of heart disease. Many factors and variables are involved and so the search should continue for groups or patterns of behaviours that may in total have adverse consequences. The interactive quality of the factors involved must seriously be considered. Therefore, usage of a set of measures may help answer some of the complexities that exist. Bass and Wade (1982) used both the Bortner and the EPQ to investigate the CHD and personality relationships. One group of individuals had complained of angina but had no cardiac damage; the second group had slight cardiac disease; and the third group were seriously affected by cardiac impairment and required surgery. Although this was a very small scale study and they found:

1. Group one — no heart disease, had the highest psychiatric morbidity, high scores on N and E, highest scores on TAB;
2. Group two — slight heart disease, had the next highest psychiatric morbidity, the highest E of all groups and medium A Type scores (Type A score correlated with E);
3. Group three — serious heart disease; scored lowest on psychiatric morbidity, and lowest E, N and Type A scores (Type A score correlated with N score).

As Eysenck and Fulker suggest, high E and N scorers have been linked to a complainer syndrome, and this may also apply to Type As, who complain of chest pains which may be due to psycho-somatic disorders (especially hyperventilation). Thus, under-standing the complexity and interactive qualities of individual differences, as moderators of response to stress, is a formidable task. A similar situation exists in attempting to understand person-ality as causal in accident vulnerability.

Type A behaviour and accidents at work

Type A behaviour pattern, although identified with extraversion has received little attention by researchers investigating the accident process. Concern is mainly focused on white-collar professional groups and heart disease outcomes; occupational accidents are of minor concern among these populations. Although TAB may not be predictive of CHD risk among blue-collar workers (Haynes *et al.*, 1980), evidence suggests that TAB could be a predictor of accident involvement (Sutherland and Cooper, 1986). A study of offshore rig workers showed that 36% of individuals identified as Type A reported accident-involvement leading to injury, whereas only 13% of Type B individuals report being involved in such an incident. This difference may reflect only an individual's predisposition to report an occurrence (i.e. the complainer syndrome). However, it was also observed that Type As were significantly more dissatisfied with their job, demon-strated a greatly reduced level of mental well-being and were more anxious and depressed than their Type B counterparts. Thus, the blue-collar worker differs from managerial groups, or perhaps the motivation to deny psychological and physical states is lower among this group, or there is less pressure to provide a social desirable response. Increased risk of accident involvement may be a direct consequence of the style of behaviour (i.e. haste, time urgency, aggression and hostility). Thus, the relevance and importance of understanding TAB among blue-collar workers may be in relation to accident vulnerability, rather than risk of heart disease. This, however, should not be ignored, bearing in mind the general concern about increasing morbidity and mortality due to heart disease and circulatory disorders.

Although the CHD risk-factor situation is still not clear for blue-collar occupational groups (Kasl, 1978) it is necessary to consider ill-health as causal in accident occurrence. This is not a new idea; Newbold (1926) identified poor health as a factor in accident occurrence across a variety of industrial settings in the early 1920s. In fact, Hertz and Emmett (1986) found that after adjusting for potential confounding variables, including age, the presence of cardiovascular disease and the tendency to sleep nine or more hours a night, were identified as risk factors in occupational hand injury occurrence. Hypersomnia has been linked to psychological variables which may increase risk of injury (e.g. indices of anxiety or nervousness and mood depression)(Beutler *et al.*, 1978; reported by Hertz and Emmett). Medical conditions, medications and alcohol consumption also affect sleep patterns. Links between chronic medical conditions, including cardiovascular disease and motor vehicles crashes, have also been reported (Waller, 1965; 1967, cited by Hertz and Emmett).

A study by Evans *et al.* (1987) also investigated TAB, occupational stress and accidents among blue-collar workers in a cross-cultural study of bus drivers (matched samples) in the USA and in India. In self-report data, Type As reported greater job stress; official data indicated that Type As had more accidents, more recorded sick-day absenteeism and more official reprimands than Type B individuals but there was only little support for the reactivity hypothesis. For both samples, Type As and Type Bs; systolic blood pressure increased at work. However, as the authors suggest, the stressor, bus driving, is multifaceted and continuous, whereas most reactivity studies have used discrete, acute stressors. However, more sighing behaviour was observed among Type A drivers and this supports the clinical description of Type As in the structured interview situation.

Locus of control

Another personality characteristic which might be an important moderator of response to a stressful situation is described as locus of control. This construct, attributed to Rotter (1966) is based on a social learning theory interactionist view of the person. The individual learns from the environment through modelling and past experience and reinforcement of certain behaviours has an effect on expectancy. Eventually expectancy leads to behaviour. Locus of control refers to the extent to which the individual perceives that he/she has control over a given situation. Someone with an internal locus of control believes that he/she has control over what happens, and that decisions made and actions taken influence personal outcomes. The belief that he/she plays a role in determining the events that impinge upon him/her is viewed as a factor in the expectation of coping with a stressful situation and affecting change, thus he/she suffers less threat and fewer adverse consequences than the externally oriented individual who tends to believe in luck or fate. The external believes that he/she has little influence upon situations and outcomes.

Locus of control theory has received considerable attention in recent years. Internality is associated with academic success and motivation to achieve (Rotter, 1966). The external appears to be less able to deal with frustration, tends to be more anxious and is less concerned with achievement; thus, psychological adjustment and coping ability are poorer. Externals are likely to be compliant and conforming individuals, prone to persuasion and ready to accept information, whereas internals prefer to be in control and resist efforts aimed at manipulating their behaviour (McKenna, 1987). Phares (1984) suggests that the most basic difference between internals and externals is in the way that they seek knowledge about their environment. Internals put more effort into obtaining information because they feel in control of the reinforcement or reward that results from their subsequent behaviour. For example, Arndt et al. (1983) found that secretarial staff, classified as externals, were more reluctant to use word processing equipment than internals, who displayed a natural curiosity about the potential of the equipment. Thus, the internal–external dimension of locus control may be an important moderator in the stress associated with the introduction of new technology.

It is also likely that self-selection into occupations, on the basis of this dimension, is taking place. Internals, with a strong belief in his/her ability to control the environment may actually select-out of highly controlled jobs. For example, in the offshore environment of a UK gas-production platform, the living environment is artificially created and highly controlled; work schedules are routine and provide little opportunity for autonomy. This would be a stressful situation for the internal, thus, it was not surprising to find a relatively high proportion of true externals (25% with a score of 16 or more) compared to only 11% true internals (a score of 7 or less)(Sutherland and Cooper, 1986). This is significant, given the criticism of the validity of the I–E Scale (Rotter, 1966) on the grounds that it is socially desirable to be portrayed as an internal (Joe, 1971) and so individuals may fake-good. However, Rotter (1966) also suggests that both extreme externals and internals are more maladjusted psychologically than individuals scoring in the mid-range of the dimension.

The 'Hardy' personality

It has already been suggested that research efforts need to consider combination styles of personality as mediators of response to stress e.g. the introverted–neurotic compared to the extraverted–neurotic. One such approach which incorporates three basic traits is described as the 'hardy personality' (Kobasa, 1979). Hardiness is considered to keep a person healthy despite the experience of stressful life events. Stress resistance is expressed as commitment versus alienation, control versus powerlessness and challenge versus threat. Commitment means the tendency to fully involve oneself in whatever one is doing rather than disengaging. Challenge involves the expectation that it is normal for life to change and that change stimulates personal growth. Thus, the individual tends to look for stimulation and opportunities with an openness of mind and willingness to experiment. Control is defined as the tendency to believe and act, as if one can influence the course of events (the same description as applied to the internal oriented person in locus of control theory). As Kobasa (1982) suggests, hardiness facilitates a form of coping that includes the ability to keep specific stressors in perspective, knowing that one has the resources with which to respond, and seeing stressor situations as potential opportunities for change (even undesirable events are viewed in terms of possibility rather than threat).

Although the hardiness model is supported by prospective research findings, the sampling is limited to male, middle and upper-level executives and professional groups (e.g. lawyers). Being hardy is important for one's health especially when one is undergoing an intensely stressful time (Kobasa, 1982) but application of the theory to other occupational and social groups has yet to be demonstrated. This is a pity, since statistics indicate that mental and physical well-being in the general population decreases as a function of socio-economic status. Informed, progressive organizations realize the benefits of a stress-audit across all levels of the organization but many others still are only willing to commit resources to their management group, where it is perhaps least needed. With the pace of change and the increasing pressures on all employees, more should be done to understand the plight of shopfloor workers as well as managers.

Other personality characteristics

Various other personality characteristics have been suggested as stressor moderators. Mueller (1965) implicates low self-esteem with the tendency to perceive greater job overload. Self-esteem may also act as a buffer in the stress outcome process, for example, CHD risk factors rise as self-esteem declines (Kasl and Cobb, 1970). Tolerance for ambiguity (Ivancevich and Matteson, 1980), anxiety (Chan, 1977) flexibility versus rigidity and dogmatism (Brief *et al.*, 1981), need for power and affiliation (McClelland *et al.*, 1982), dispositional optimism (Scheier and Carver, 1985) and 'John Henryism' (i.e. active coping with environmental stressors through hard work and determination)(James *et al.*, 1983) are all independent variables that have been brought into stress research in the search to find the stress-resistant personality. Not surprisingly, some construct overlap occurs and unequivocal findings are due to inconsistencies in the way that a construct is defined, operationalized and measured. In addition, there is still a need for in-depth prospective research which investigates the interactive qualities of personality factors, while taking into account other personal and environmental-conditioning variables. Some of these will be considered in the next section of this chapter.

PERSONAL CONDITIONING VARIABLES AS MODERATORS OF THE STRESS RESPONSE

Within this category, Beehr and Newman (1978) include demographics, physical condition and life-stage characteristics of the individual, as moderators of the stress response (Table 4.1). Thus, some are internal (e.g. age, sex, race and education) and some are external conditioning factors (e.g. diet, social setting, climate). Extensive study of the stress response shows that certain characteristics are indicators of vulnerability. Although some of the factors are reviewed separately in the following discussion, the interactive quality must not be overlooked. For example, age, race and career-stage may be inexorably linked.

Gender

The changing role of women in contemporary society has produced a significant amount of research interest and this extends into the area of the stress–strain relationship. In terms of risk for stress-related illness, women have been at less risk than men but increasingly it is acknowledged that if women work like men, they die like men. For example, Davidson and Cooper (1983) found that certain stressors in society have a more adverse impact on women than men; these include male attitudes towards working women, lack of resource support for working mothers and expectations in child rearing practices etc. Behavioural response to stress includes a substantial increase in the proportion of women alcoholics in the early 1960s and late 1970s (Cooper and Davidson, 1982); female managers tend to smoke more than women in other occupational groups and more than their male counterparts (Jacobson, 1981); and female executives take significantly more tranquillizers, sleeping pills and antidepressants than male executives (Cooper and Melhuish, 1980). In a Swedish study of 8700 members of a white-collar union, Karasek et al. (1987) report higher levels of exhaustion, depression, headaches, respiratory problems, aches in the extremities and dizziness among working women than the men. The overall pattern of stressor and outcome associations were quite similar for men and women, although both job/outcome and family burden/outcome associations were stronger for women than for men. In addition, for full-time working women the associations are stronger with work than they are for family. As Karasek *et al.* suggest, this shows that it is mainly job-related problems and not family ones that are the cause of employees' psychological trouble (one exception being the strong significance of family problems for the heart disease measure).

Studies of women in the blue-collar environment are more rare and sex-difference comparisons are usually impossible because the nature of the work varies as a function of gender. However, a series of studies commissioned by the DOE (Shimmen *et al.*, 1981) among women engaged in factory work, does indicate the extent to which mental strain and ill-health are caused by the nature of production line work. All three studies indicated the pressures associated with a constant, unremitting round of activity throughout waking hours: a day which tends to start for women around 5 or 6 am and finishes about 9 or 10 pm, with little time for rest or relaxation. Assistance with housework was rare and the need to meet family commitments in relation to the job was a constant source of concern. Levels of mental well-being were significantly poorer among women who worked full-time rather than part-time, but it was suggested that this was attributed to their negative feelings about the work and the financial pressures they were under, rather than the longer hours that they worked (Shimmen *et al.*, 1981).

Although it appears that certain risk factors, related to response behaviours may be increasing among working women, there is evidence to suggest that catecholamine excretion in response to a stressor does vary as function of gender. Originally it was assumed that when catecholamine excretion is expressed in relation to body weight, no sex differences are observed. However, Frankenhaeuser (1975) and Johansson (1972) report differences between males and females when compared under conditions of stress rather than in the passive state. Excretion rates among twelve-year old boys and girls were investigated in both active and passive conditions. In the group of boys, there was a significant increase in adrenalin excretion in the active compared to the passive state but among the girls, excretion was only slightly higher in the active condition.

Similar findings are reported among adults when comparing routine activity and intelligence testing situations. Thus, it is suggested that women may be hypoactive in terms of their sympathetic-adrenomedullary response to stress (Cox, 1985).

Education, ability and experience

These variables are viewed as important moderators in the response to stress, because they influence the perception of demand and threat, and affect the needs and values systems of the individual. Coping mechanisms are dependent on the moderating effects of ability and experience and these are related to one's level of educational attainment. For example, an understanding of role or work overload as sources of stress must include the concepts of ability and experience. An individual with greater ability can accomplish more work in less time than an employee with less ability for the job. Thus, Sales (1970) has shown that objective, quantitative overload is negatively related to self-esteem and positively to tension and heart rate. French and Caplan (1973) support this finding with reported subjective measures of work overload. Qualitative work overload also relates to this moderator variable of ability, in that some employees could not complete the work successfully, regardless of the time allowed because they do not have the skill required to perform the task. Experience as a moderator is the essence of training, especially in coping with crises situations, where rote behaviour is necessary to override fear and panic. Familiarity with a situation acts as a moderator to impact on behavioural outcomes in the workplace (McGrath, 1970). Therefore, role play is experience and so is more likely to be effective in changing attitudes and behaviour than passive discussion sessions, lectures or propaganda messages.

Ethnicity

Membership of a particular racial and/or minority group can affect an individual's response to stress, in addition to being a source of stress itself. Shostak (1980) states that stress is experienced when: 'the common need to be part of the community at work is thwarted by sharp-edged divisiveness'. Racial prejudice may promote feelings of inadequacy, inferiority and/or low self-esteem and these will indirectly act as modifiers of response to stress. Low morale and poor motivation will also reduce tolerance to other stressors. Lack of role models in life generally or in the workplace can create a stress situation, and exacerbate response to other stressors, which leads to role conflict and role ambiguity for the racially different or distinct individuals, for example, occupying a job for the first time, without the support of a sympathetic peer group. However, expectations and aspirations (products of the socialization process which are potent conditioners in the formation and maintenance of culture and custom) also mediate the response to stress. The perception of stress associated with opportunity, constraint and/or demands may be moderated in accordance with the norms and values of a particular ethnic group.

Age, life stage and physical condition

Age is a significant moderator of response to stress and is considered here with the physical condition of the individual. Each life stage has its own particular vulnerability and coping mechanism (McLean, 1979) and so response to stress is an ever changing, dynamic process. The response of older individuals to experimental stressors indicates a stronger activation of the sympathetic nervous system, but in real-life working conditions, individual coping strategies may counter-balance this effect (ILO, 1986). Certain stressors, for example, related to career development (i.e. over- and under-promotion) can only be understood in relation to the stage of life of the individual concerned. As Levinson (1978a) states; 'regardless of occupation and individual differences, there are seasons of a man's life which when documented will point to likely periods of stress and why they occur'. In a study of middle-aged construction workers Theorell (1976) found the measure of discord among employees to be much higher in the 41–56 age group than in the 56–65 year olds. This suggests that age may perform a moderator role in the perception of job stress, linked to the factors of expectation and aspiration. McLean (1979) suggests that mid-life crisis increases one's sensitivity to stress, regardless of occupation and is, therefore, a period of particular vulnerability. Buchholz found that job discontent in the USA was related to age and was more prominent among younger blue-collar workers.

Their expectation and idealistic notions about work soon disappeared and they felt exploited and disillusioned (Buchholz, 1978).

The impact of stress may be influenced by the age of an individual in two ways. First, the biological condition of the person will mediate the response. For example, complaints about the physical strain of work, such as difficulties in adapting to shift work increases with age; and age, in relation to past experiences, will affect the way stress is perceived. Second, one's physical condition is likely to be related to the age of the individual. Intuitively it seems that an unfit or ill (physically or mentally) employee may be less tolerant and more vulnerable to other stressors at work. Hennigan and Wortham (1975) demonstrated that individuals in good physical condition and who were non-smokers, were able to maintain a low heart rate during the normal stress of the work day, whereas stress is more likely to increase the heart rate of others less physically fit. Low capacity to respond to a situation due to ill-health or disease can exacerbate a stress reaction. Research has also shown that, in addition to a reduction of the physiological consequences of stressful situations, regular exercise reduces symptoms of depression and enhances psychological well-being. Long-term participation in physical exercise has been found to change personality traits (i.e. trait anxiety and depression), whereas short-term participation affects mood states. Unfortunately, evaluation programmes are often poorly designed and restricted to clinical populations, and the results are not conclusive or consistent (i.e. type of exercise, duration, and measures used)(Falkenberg, 1987). However, introduction of employee fitness programmes seems to produce positive consequences for the individual and the organization. Individuals tend to report an improved well-being, which reduces absenteeism and turnover, which in turn can have positive effects on productivity and performance.

Diet

As Quick and Quick (1984) suggest; 'there are a small number of points at which diet and stress interact.' However, it becomes less clear when the response to stress becomes the source of stress itself. Overeating and the resulting obesity may be the response to a stressor situation but ultimately obesity will become the stressor which increases the likelihood of cardiac and respiratory illnesses or diabetes. An individual under pressure may respond by eating spicy foods, high in salt content and therefore will exacerbate a hypertension condition. As Quick and Quick indicate, use of certain palliatives such as caffeine, alcohol and tobacco will result in the development of arrhythmias (heartbeat irregularities), ulcers and gastritis among individuals predisposed to these responses.

Next in this section, social support is considered as a mediator in the response to stress. This is usually viewed as an environmental variable. However, it is argued that Innes' (1981) description of mediating factors as a set of learned responses which influence coping skills, might embrace this factor as a person-variable. Situations are assessed and judged in the knowledge and awareness of social support available. Thus, it will directly impact on the way a potential source of stress is perceived, the coping strategy used and therefore may also buffer the consequences of highly stressful situations.

Social support

The value of supportive relationships in one's social network, as a protection against adverse environmental forces or negative life events, has intuitive common-sense appeal. Conceptually, social support theory owes its origins to the discipline of sociology. Social identity and evaluation of self-esteem are based on social interaction (Mead, 1934) and 'anomie' theory (Durkheim, 1951) which states that psychological well-being is associated with social integration. In an attempt to understand why some individuals suffer adverse consequences from exposure to stressful situations and others remain apparently unaffected, the concept of social support is cited as an intervening or conditioning variable in the stress perception process. This apparently simple concept has generated an enormous body of research and argument over the past twenty years. Research efforts have attempted to understand:

1. Where social support comes from, and in what circumstances different sources of support may be beneficial, i.e. the role of social support;
2. Types of social support, i.e. emotional, instrumental and informational (House, 1981);

3. How the social support network reduces, moderates or buffers the impact of negative life events or stressors, i.e. is it a main effect or a buffering (interaction) process?

Much of the debate seems to be fuelled by variation in the conceptual definition of social support; differences in methodology (operationalization of the concept); the confounding of variables in cross-sectional designs (i.e. life events change may also alter the amount of support available to the individual), and the varying statistical analysis utilized (Thoits, 1982). However, the consensus is, that the deleterious effects of psychosocial stress may be lessened or eliminated in the presence of social support.

Figure 4.1 provides a conceptual framework for the proposed impact of social support on job stress and outcomes, with social support defined as that subset of persons in the individual's total social network upon whom he/she relies for socioemotional aid,

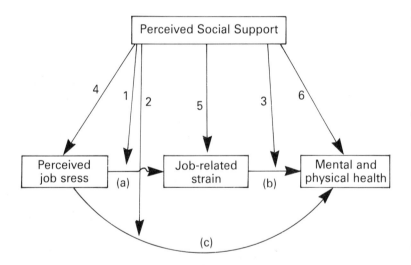

Figure 4.1 Social support. A model of potential relationships among perceived stress, social support and health.

Arrows 1 and 2: hypothesized buffering effects of social suport;
Arrow 3: support ameliorates the effects of job related strain on health;
Arrows 4, 5 and 6: main effects of perceived social support;
Arrows a, b and c: hypothesized effects from stress job-related strain and health.
Source: LaRocco, House and French (1980).

instrumental aid, or both (Thoits, 1982). It must also be acknowledged that it is not adequate to assess social support only in terms
of quantity (i.e. how many significant others) but also in terms of
the quality of these relations. Instrumental aid is incorporated in the
definition because it has socioemotional overtones, i.e. practical
help from others assures the individual that he/she is cared about
(Thoits, 1982). Perceived job stress (e.g. nightworking, role
conflict) may affect job related strain variables (e.g. job satisfaction
and self-esteem); this is represented by arrow a (Figure 4.1).
Arrows b and c also indicate that perceived-job stress and job-
related strain may have impact on an individual's psychological
and physical health (and perhaps accident vulnerability). It is
proposed that social support acts as a conditioning variable in
relationships between job stress, job strain and stress outcomes
(illness and accidents) (Caplan *et al.*, 1975; House, 1981; Dooley
et al., 1987). The impact may be in the form of a buffer or intervention process and:

1. Lessen the effect of job stress on job strain (arrow 1);
2. Moderate job stress/mental and physical health relationships (arrow 2);
3. Moderate job related strain/mental and physical health
   linkages (arrow 3);

or, that social support works by having a main effect, that is by:

4. Having impact on each primary variable directly; a simple
   additive effect (arrows 4, 5 and 6).

Numerous studies are offered to support the main effect model of
social support. It would appear that class, gender, the actual source
of support, the type of stress and the outcome observed will determine whether a main effect and/or buffering impact will operate.
Evidence presented for the buffering hypothesis does not clarify
this concept but suggests that it might be more beneficial to
consider social support as a coping mechanism. Overall, the evidence for social support impact seems to posit a main or direct
effect, with moderating effects having modest, highly selective
impact, both in terms of the type of support and the outcome
variable affected (Chisholm *et al.*, 1986). Therefore, this main
effect mechanism might be explained by re-conceptualizing social
support as a coping mechanism. For example, Lin *et al.*, (1979)
believe that social support is a coping mechanism that individuals

use under stressful conditions. Similarities between social support and coping are described by Thoits (1986). Three ways of coping with stressors are proposed:

1. Problem focused — this is direct action on the environment or self, to remove or alter circumstances perceived as a threat.
2. Emotion focused — this is action or thoughts to control the undesirable feelings that result from a stressful situation.
3. Perception focused — consists of cognitive attempts to alter the meaning of a situation, so it is perceived as less threatening.

Thoits identifies these strategies with the various forms of social support proposed by House (1981):

- Instrumental support with problem focused coping;
- Emotional support with emotion focused coping;
- Informational support with perception focused coping.

Therefore, both support and coping act to change the situation, change the emotional reaction to the situation and/or change the meaning of the situation. Although it is suggested that this provides a conceptual framework for understanding how others provide support, Kessler (1982) suggests that knowing help is available but coping with one's problems without using outside assistance leads to the best outcome.

Ben-Sira (1985) develops this idea further. It is believed that ultimately it is the individual who must meet the demand made, or restore the imbalance that exists. The mobilization and reliance on environmental resources (i.e. social support) is not the most satisfactory in the long-term, considering the costs of dependency, reduced self-esteem and the consequences of feeling inferior. Although the research is both cross-sectional and correlational, support is viewed in the proposed model of stress–disease relationships as part of a feeling of potency. This consists of feelings of confidence in one's own capabilities (self confidence and a sense of mastery) and in society (confidence in the reliability, predictability and meaningfulness of social environments, especially primary relationships). In fact, Wethington and Kessler (1986) argue that the perceptions of support availability are more important than actual support transactions and that; 'the latter promote psychological adjustment through the former'

(p. 85). Knowledge that social support is available affects the way a stressor is perceived and the coping strategy adopted; it is, therefore, a socially learned response and predisposition to respond in a certain way. In a longitudinal study of male business executives, Kobasa *et al.* (1985) found that social support was a modest buffer (together with hardiness and exercise) against illness likelihood. However, an observed correlation between hardiness and support suggests some construct overlap. Kobasa *et al.* believe that after controlling for the effects of hardiness, the more passive implications of social support remain (i.e. the reassurance about self and the distraction from troubles provided by sympathetic others). This interpretation is consistent with Cobb's view (1976), that social support consists entirely of information. Information leading the individual to believe, that she/he:

1. Is cared for and loved;
2. Is esteemed and valued;
3. Belongs to a network of communication and mutual obligation in which others can be counted on, should the need arise.

Although Dunkel-Schetter *et al.* (1987) acknowledge that coping style is not a stable predisposition but a process, it is suggested that both person predisposition and situational requirements will determine the support that a person receives. It was observed that person factors (i.e. attitudes towards help, self-esteem, religiosity and values) accounted for most of the variance in predicting receipt of emotional support. However, style of coping was a strong correlate of support received (i.e. problem solving, seeking support, and positive reappraisal). Therefore, coping style may provide clues to associates, indicating needs and desires for support. However, the interpretation most generally accepted is that social support influences the way a person copes (Cohen and Syme, 1985; Thoits, 1986).

Studies have consistently shown that individuals who lack social support from family, friends and the community have more symptoms of physical and psychological ill-health than those with support. Gore (1978) reports higher serum cholesterol levels, depression and illness among the unemployed who lack social support compared to those with supportive relationships. Lack of support from a spouse or partner was also related to poor mental well-being, anxiety and depression among construction site managers (Sutherland and Davidson, 1989). Bamberg *et al.* (1986) support this finding among a blue-collar group; lack of wife support was associated with somatic complaints and life dissatisfaction. In the work environment, the benefits of social support from a boss and/or co-workers, formally and informally, is well documented (LaRocco and Jones, 1978; House, 1981). Work-related sources of support can reduce work stress, indirectly improve health and buffer against the effects of stress on health outcomes (e.g. ulcers and neurosis). As House suggests; 'many different types of workers in many different situations are better off if they perceive others as willing and able to help (especially in an emotional sense) with work-related problems.'

Coping strategies

Lazarus (1966) suggests that one's appraisal of an event or situation determines the response. It is acknowledged that coping is not a stable individual trait or disposition but a transactional process, which is continually modified by experience. However, the way in which an individual copes may become an integral part of the vulnerability profile, in that an inappropriate strategy may add to the stress experienced. In addition, coping is not only a reaction to stress; it may be viewed as a preventive strategy, if a potential stressful situation is anticipated. (This is the most effective strategy for reducing the experience of work stress (Murphy, 1985)). Research shows that people use different methods of coping for different stress agents. Folkman *et al.* (1986) have provided a Ways of Coping Scale to help identify the coping process and consistency of style across repeat occasions. Ways of coping are varied and include, confrontive strategies, distancing, seeking social support, escape-avoidance, etc. Thus, coping is viewed as the cognitive, behavioural or somatic response which is intended to 1. eliminate or reduce the source of discomfort; 2. alter one's appraisal of the stressor; or 3. managing or reducing the feelings of discomfort (Murphy, 1985). Some research findings highlight the negative consequences of maladaptive coping. For example, in a study of more than 2100 women attending breast-screening clinics, it was found that those with a tendency to keep emotional material buried are significantly more at risk from breast cancer than women who express their feelings, seek help and acknowledge the underlying stress-related event (Cooper *et al.*, 1986). In the work environment, individuals attempt to cope with stressors by activating both emotion-focused and problem-focused strategies. But as Murphy (1985) indicates, the relative ineffectiveness of individual strategies are perhaps due to the lack of worker control over organizational attributes and the design of work.

Conclusion

A review of just some of the personal factors implicated as moderators in the response to a stressor situation explains the diversity of individual differences in outcomes and symptoms observed. Individual vulnerability to stress is dependent on a large number of complex factors including personality, personal history, needs, wants and coping strategies adopted. Therefore, dealing with stress in the environment is a two-fold process involving an understanding of potential sources of stress that might exist, and acknowledging the attributes of the individual that will mediate the cognitive appraisal and subsequent response to that situation. This approach is the basis of the person-environment fit model of stress described in Chapter Two. In the next chapters, symptoms of stress and behavioural response to stress will be considered in more detail.

5

The Consequences of Stress

Implicit in our contemporary approach to understanding the manifestations of stress are the assumptions that stress is a subjective experience and that the outcomes or symptoms of distress may be physical, psychological and/or behavioural. In this chapter the effects of stress will be considered in terms of costs to the individual, the work environment and society. The first section presents a review of disorders identified with occupational and psychosocial stress. These include cardiovascular and respiratory disorders, metabolism malfunction, cancer, mental illness and psychosomatic disease. This is followed by a discussion of the behavioural response to stress, including smoking, alcohol consumption and accident involvement. And finally, organizational costs including absenteeism, poor industrial relations, and labour turnover are considered. However, this method of classification is not meant to imply that the effects and costs of stress are discrete entities. Indeed, a significant problem for research persists: when does 'an effect' become the source of stress?, and so one of the main issues in health psychology is the identification of causal pathways and the mechanisms of internal function. The situation is complex because little is known about the temporal sequencing of the effects of stress and the relationships that exist between the variables involved. Figure 5.1 shows the complexity of this issue, and how exposure to stress might exert negative consequences indirectly, in addition to their direct impact.

Figure 5.2 illustrates a possible situation that might exist, which suggests that the impact of stress might also be cumulative. These areas of concern are referred to again in the discussion that follows.

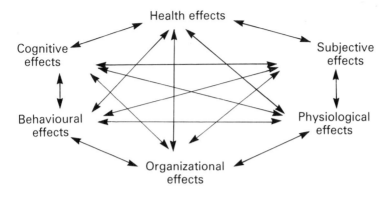

Figure 5.1 The interactive nature of the symptoms of stress.

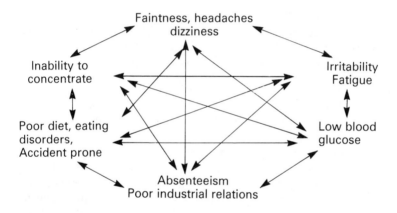

Figure 5.2 The interactive nature of stress symptoms – an example.

STRESS AND HEALTH OUTCOMES

The role of stress in health remains a contentious issue, because it is contingent on 1. the way that stress is defined; and 2. how the concept of health should be viewed. For example, medical and biological scientists can accept that heat, cold or ingestion of toxic substances can act as sources of stress causal in illness, disease or death, because they are concrete and observable (Hinkle, 1987). However, when health is defined as absence of disease and the

99

presence of physical and psychological well-being (WHO, 1977) and it is acknowledged that cognitive appraisal is central to human behaviour in the stress situation (Lazarus, 1966) then the stress–ill-health debate becomes more heated. Indeed, the social and behavioural sciences are concerned with the role that psychological factors play in the development of disease. In its purest form, this relates to the way that information arising from outside of the person, mediated by the higher centres of the central nervous systems, is causal in illness and disease (Hinkle, 1987). In addition, if one accepts Selye's (1956) view that impairment of function and structural change, are wholly or in part an adaptation to a source of stress, then all illness and disease are caused by stress (Cox, 1987; Hinkle, 1987). To embrace these ideas in total is to accept that stress agents exist which cannot be seen, or measured, and manifest in psychosomatic disorders equally ill-defined or unquantifiable. These views will only be accepted if the mechanisms that link stress with disease can be identified, and how such disorders are specifically affected by stress. Possible pathways and mechanisms are suggested by Krantz *et al.* (1985):

1. Stress may have direct psychophysiological effects which affect health. It is suggested here that psychosocial stimuli cause changes in bodily functioning and result in diverse pathological manifestations. Hormonal and chemical defence mechanisms are activated in the response to stress, as part of the 'fight or flight' mechanism described by Cannon (1935). Effector organs of the sympathetic division of the autonomic nervous system mobilizes the body for action. Sympathetic activity causes constriction of the cutaneous blood vessels, dilation of muscle blood vessels and the secretion of sweat. The hypothalamus, in the brain, responds by triggering the pituitary gland to release hormones which cause increased secretion of catecholamines (adrenalin and noradrenalin) from the adrenal medulla. Exposure to stress increases the production of cortisol from the adrenal cortex. Cortisol, the most active steroid of the glucocorticoid group, influences carbohydrate and protein metabolism. The synthesis of glycogen in the liver is promoted and gluconeogenesis from protein is encouraged (protein catabolism) by the glucocorticoids, thus the level of glucose rises in the blood. Cortisol also has

anti-inflammatory and anti-allergic properties. Overall, the process enhances one's level of arousal because cognitive, neurological, cardiovascular and muscular systems are stimulated. Therefore, in sudden shock the rate and strength of the heart beat is increased, glucose stored as glycogen in the liver is released for energy, gut movements are slowed, blood supplies are redirected from the skin and viscera to the brain and skeletal muscles, the bronchioles become dilated and so breathing is deeper, pupils dilate, contraction of the bladder and anal sphincters occur (but also the relaxation of the bladder), erector pili muscles contract (hair stands on end) and the secretion of sweat increases. Thus the body is prepared for an emergency.

It is suggested that modern man is denied the natural dissipation of these physiological changes — rarely can we fight, rarely do we run and so our natural response to stress may ultimately cause harm. Table 5.1 shows some of the long-term effects of those pressures on bodily functions (Melhuish, 1978). In addition, Albrecht (1979) believes that; 'people who have spent much of their time in an over-anxious or tense state have difficulty bringing into action the parasympathetic branch' (of the autonomic nervous system). Parasympathetic nerve fibres work antagonistically with the sympathetic nervous activity (i.e. if the sympathetic system causes a muscle to contract, then parasympathetic action relaxes it). Acetylcholine, the transmitter substance produced, stimulates the parasympathetic nervous system with a muscarinic effect (i.e. it acts peripherally with a slower, longer-lasting action and thereby slows the heart, produces contraction of the pupils, increases the secretions of the salivary and lacrimal glands and of the intestine). It has been shown that by training, voluntary control can be imposed on the autonomic nervous system. This is the rationale that underlies the art of yoga and meditation. Presumably Albrecht is suggesting that the opposite can also apply and one is ultimately conditioned to override the activation of parasympathetic activity by repeated exposure to stress. In terms of health outcomes, response to stress which leads to changes in hormonal functioning and the immune response are potential causes in the onset of disease.

Table 5.1 Effects of pressure on bodily functions

	Normal–relaxed	Under pressure	Acute pressure	Chronic pressure (stress)
Brain	Blood supply normal	Blood supply increases	Thinks more clearly	Headaches and migraines, tremor and nervous tics
Mood	Happy	Serious	Increased concentration	Anxious and loses sense of humour
Saliva	Normal	Reduced	Reduced	Dry mouth, lump in throat
Muscles	Blood supply normal	Blood supply increases	Improved performance	Muscular tension and pain
Heart	Normal heart rate and blood pressure	Output rate and blood pressure increases	Improved performance	Hypertension and chest pain
Lungs	Normal respiration	Respiration rate increases	Improved performance	Coughs and asthma
Stomach	Normal blood supply and acid secretion	Blood supply decreases acid secretion increases	Reduced blood supply reduces digestion	Heartburn and indigestion giving ulcers
Bowels	Normal blood supply and bowel activity	Blood supply decreases motility increases	Reduced blood supply reduces digestion	Abdominal pain and diarrhoea
Bladder	Normal function	Frequent micturition	Increased nervous stimulation gives frequency	Frequency and prostatic symptoms

Sexual organs	(M) Normal sex (F) Normal periods, etc.	(M) Impotence (blood supply decreases) (F) Irregular periods	Decreased blood supply	(M) Impotence (F) Menstrual disorders
Skin	Healthy	Dry skin, blood supply decreases	Decreased blood supply	Dryness and rashes
Biochemistry	Normal, oxygen consumed, glucose and fats liberated	Oxygen consumption increases, glucose and fat consumption increases	More energy immediately available	Rapid tiredness

Source: A. Melhuish; *Executive Health* (London: Business Books), 1978.

2. Stress may lead to health impairing habits or behaviours. If it is not possible to remove the source of stress or escape from the experience of threat, the individual may resort to the use of palliatives. The negative impact of stress may therefore be reduced by escapist eating, drinking alcohol or the use of other drugs such as tobacco, tranquillizers, sleeping pills or analgesics. Involuntary reactions may be equally damaging in the long-term; for example, disturbed sleep patterns or poor appetite ultimately evolve into habits or life styles that are risk-factors for certain kinds of disease (Maes *et al.*, 1987).

3. The stress of illness may cause illness behaviour which influences the course of a disease. Therefore, the way in which a patient perceives and copes with the stress of illness is the mechanism that influences the disease. For example, Maes and Sclösser (reported by Maes *et al.*, 1987) have shown coping variables (reacting emotionally in asthma attack situations, focusing on asthma in everyday life and maintaining a restrictive life-style) explained a considerable part of the variance in the well-being of asthmatic patients (measured as the number of hospital admissions, or the number of days absent from work because of asthma). This topic of perception and coping style will be reviewed in chapter seven. As Hinkle (1987) indicates; 'it is clear that 'psychological stress' can lead to alterations of internal functions down to the biomedical level, and that they are potential 'causes' of disease, but they do not usually act independently of other mechanisms.' This is discussed further in relation to certain stress-related diseases and illness.

Cardiovascular disease

Death due to cardiovascular disease is the most prominent killer among industrialized nations. Ischaemic heart diseases, acute myocardial infarction and cerebrovascular disease all feature significantly in the top causes of death in the mid-eighties in England, Wales and Scotland, among men and women. (Table 5.2). Heart disease is responsible for 38% of male, and 17% of female deaths among 35–64 year olds in England and Wales. The

Table 5.2 Top causes of death, England and Wales (1985) and Scotland (1986), by gender, ages — all number of deaths and death rate per 100 000 population

	England and Wales				Scotland			
	Males		Females		Males		Females	
	No.	Rate/100000	No.	Rate/100000	No.	Rate/100000	No.	Rate/100000
Disease of the circulatory system	139903	575	147151	575	15206	614	16218	613
Acute myocardial infarction	61099	251	45227	177	7761	313	6194	234
Other ischaemic heart diseases	30527	126	26251	103	2258	91	1925	73
Cerebrovascular disease	27590	113	45629	178	3243	131	5347	202
Cancer of trachea, bronchus and lung	25994	107	9798	38	2865	116	1284	49
Malignant neoplasms of female breast			13513	53			1313	50
Disease of respiratory system	12311	51	6501	25	1343	54	886	34
Bronchitis, emphysema and asthma	10709	44	5518	22	590	24	353	13
Pneumonia	10403	43	17528	69	1691	68	2422	92
Disease of pulmonary circulation and other heart disease	8392	34	14443	56	942	38	1395	53
Cancer of prostrate	6628	27			538	22		
Embolism, thrombosis and other diseases of arteries, artioles and capilliaries	6416	26	4586	18	420	17	353	13

Table 5.2 continued

	England and Wales				Scotland			
	Males		Females		Males		Females	
	No.	Rate/100000	No.	Rate/100000	No.	Rate/100000	No.	Rate/100000
Cancer of stomach	5922	24	4049	16	519	21	442	17
Cancer of colon	4923	25	6364	20	513	21	652	25
Diseases of the nervous system	4570	19	4802	19	317	13	322	12
Mental disorders	4158	17	7853	31	325	13	624	24
Motor vehicle traffic accidents	3379	14	1453	6	442	18	164	6
Cancer of rectum	3289	14	2751	11	305	12	319	12
Cancer of bladder	3251	13	1418	6	311	13	155	6
Other diseases of digestive system	3168	13	5389	21	376	15	636	24
Diabetes mellitus	3156	13	4296	17	232	10	286	11
Suicide	2949	12	1470	6	410	17	158	6
Atherosklerosis	2179	9	4395	17	211	8	403	15
Hypertensive disease	1978	8	2603	10	170	7	202	8
Chronic liver disease and cirrhosis	1388	6	1194	5	216	9	164	6

Source: World Health Annual Statistics, 1987.

Department of Health and Social Security indicate that in excess of 43 million days were lost from work due to ischaemic heart diseases and cerebrovascular disease during 1984–85 (Table 5.3: Employment Gazette, August, 1986).

However, this is not a problem confined to mainland UK. An awareness of the magnitude of the issue has assumed interest at supranational level, and the WHO has monitored the situation over the past 10–15 years. Table 5.4 shows the extent of the problem, by country and gender. In the cardiovascular disease 'death league' table for 1980 among men aged 40–69; Northern Ireland rates second to Hungary, Scotland is fourth and England and Wales are ninth. All have death rates per 100 000 population more than twice the levels recorded in Japan and France (bottom of the table for the 27 countries listed). Many countries have made significant efforts to reduce these alarming statistics. Table 5.5 shows the percentage change in cardiovascular mortality over a 10 year period (approximately 1972–1982) and the decreasing trends are encouraging; most pronounced is in Japan (a 36% decrease among males, and 42% among females). In England and Wales the percentage decrease is nearly 17% for men, and 20% for women. Scotland report similar decreases. However, countries showing large increases include Bulgaria, Hungary and Poland. Although the percentage decrease for US is 45% for men and 42% for women, Table 5.6 shows that the numbers of deaths and death rates in 1984 are still sobering statistics. Acute myocardial infarction alone killed 279 122 people. The situation assumes particular significance because heart disease often kills when individuals are in their peak years of economic activity. Therefore, it is costly in terms of unrealized human potential and for industry, when an organization fails to capitalize on many years of investment in development and training. Cardiovascular diseases may also exist for many years before they are clinically manifest and so it is important but a difficult task to identify the risk factors involved.

Stress as a risk factor for cardiovascular disease

Epidemiological studies have identified several risk factors for coronary heart disease; these include genetic influences, high blood pressure, high serum cholesterol levels, high lipoproteins in blood, cigarette smoking, obesity, glucose intolerance, physical

Table 5.3 Days lost from work for stress-related illness in Great Britain, 1982/3 and 1984/5

Cause	Male/Female	1982/3	1984/5	% Change over two years
Psychoses	M	7098538	8138000	+16.04
	F	3253344	3275080	+ 0.66
Neuroses	M	17432981	17938743	+ 2.90
	F	9951749	10162450	+ 2.18
Personality	M	160100	162200	+ 1.31
disorders	F	153600	131600	−14.32
Mental	M	1312400	1310286	− 0.17
retardation	F	786000	823000	+ 4.74
Migraine	M	158529	136300	−14.02
	F	177683	62800	−64.65
Hypertensive	M	9477164	9890527	+ 4.36
diseases	F	1997336	2060400	+ 3.16
Ulcers	M	2216132	2088828	− 1.75
	F	294295	312659	+ 6.24
Depressive	M	6439698	6134613	− 4.47
disorder	F	4276919	4201100	− 1.77
Alcohol	M	896600	895401	− 0.13
dependence	F	79600	38800	−51.26
Ischaemic	M	29092909	32912455	+13.13
heart disease	F	1908911	2389044	+25.25
Cerebrovascular	M	6222500	7011600	+12.68
disease	F	529800	920700	+73.78
Total days lost in	M	80417551	86618953	+ 7.71
above causes	F	23409237	24377933	+ 4.14
Total number of	M	271715438	253562397	− 6.68
days lost	F	89229711	74546812	−16.52

Source: Department of Health and Social Security (DHSS) tables, S/IV, *Employment Gazette*, August 1988.

Table 5.4 Age-standardized mortality from cardiovascular diseases in 1980 (rates per 100 000 population aged 40–69 years, by gender)

	Male	Female	
Hungary	840	424	Romania
United Kingdom (Northern Ireland)		399	Hungary
	830		
Finland	793	362	Bulgaria
United Kingdom (Scotland)	792	356	United Kingdom (Scotland)
		346	United Kingdom (Northern Ireland)
Czechoslovakia	775		
Poland	734	331	Czechoslovakia
Ireland	690	328	Yugoslavia
Romania	652	304	Poland
United Kingdom (England and Wales)	650	302	Ireland
Bulgaria	643	300	New Zealand
New Zealand	632	283	Israel
		253	United Kingdom (England and Wales)
United States of America	596		
Australia	584	244	United States of America
Austria	555	230	Australia
Yugoslavia	550	226	Austria
Germany, Federal Republic of	535	221	Finland
Canada	520	195	Canada
		194	Germany, Federal Republic of
Norway	520		
Denmark	517	191	Belgium
Sweden	497	190	Denmark
Belgium	488	185	Italy
Israel	487	166	Japan
Netherlands	465	155	Norway
Italy	433	155	Sweden
Switzerland	385	155	Netherlands
France	323	134	Switzerland
Japan	316	112	France

Source: *World Health Statistics Quarterly*, **38** (1985) p. 151.

inactivity and certain sociocultural and psychosocial factors. Both independent and interactive effects have been observed between these factors. For example, in a study of several thousand men in the US, high blood pressure, high serum-cholesterol levels and cigarette smoking were identified as CHD risk factors. However, only 14% of the men with all three risk factors developed CHD

Table 5.5 Percentage change in age-standardized death rates from cardiovascular diseases

Country	Period	% Change
Canada	1972–1982	−25.8
United States of America	1970–1980	−28.4
Japan	1972–1982	−36.4
Austria	1972–1982	− 7.4
Belgium	1971–1981	−24.7
Bulgaria	1972–1982	34.1
Czechoslovakia	1972–1982	12.0
Denmark	1972–1982	− 8.2
Finland	1970–1980	−19.6
France	1971–1981	−22.7
Germany, Federal Republic of	1972–1982	−11.2
Hungary	1972–1982	33.0
Ireland	1970–1980	− 2.5
Italy	1970–1980	− 8.9
Netherlands	1972–1982	−16.1
Norway	1972–1982	−10.1
Poland	1970–1980	31.3
Romania	1972–1982	15.7
Sweden	1972–1982	− 2.5
Switzerland	1971–1981	−11.2
United Kingdom:		
England and Wales	1972–1982	−16.7
Northern Ireland	1971–1981	− 7.3
Scotland	1973–1983	−16.2
Yugoslavia	1971–1981	23.5
Australia	1971–1981	−32.1
New Zealand	1971–1981	−22.8

Source: *World Health Statistics Quarterly.* **38** (1985), p. 151.

over the ten year observation period. In addition of all the men who developed the disease over a ten year follow-up, only 17% had all three risk factors and only 58% had two or more risk factors. As Herd (1988) reports, other factors are also important in the aetiology and pathogenesis of arteriosclerosis. Various studies indicate that other factors may be attributable to occupational and psychosocial stressors. Jenkins (1983) suggests that biobehavioural research on the development of cardiovascular disease has been stimulated because standard biologic risk factors have limited ability to identify many new cases of ischaemic heart disease.

Table 5.6 United States of America, 1984. No. of deaths and death rate per 100 000 population

	Males		Females	
	No.	Rate	No.	Rate
Diseases of the circulatory system	487 461	423	490 710	404
Acute myocardial infarction	159 934	139	119 188	98
Other ischaemic heart diseases	129 527	113	132 639	109
Diseases of pulmonary circulation and other heart disease	95 314	83	98 033	81
Cerebrovascular disease	61 697	54	92 630	76
Diabetes mellitus	14 859	13	20 928	17
Hypertensive disease	13 478	12	17 863	15
Atherosclerosis	9 240	8	15 222	12

For example, in 1910, Sir William Osler noted that angina pectoris was especially common among the Jewish members of the business community and he attributed this, in part, to their hectic pace of life. In addition, Russeck and Zohman (1958) compared young coronary patients between 25 and 40 years of age (some with confirmed myocardial infarctions, others with only angina pectoris) with healthy controls and found that 91% of the coronary patients reported prolonged stress related to work responsibility, compared to only 20% of the controls. 25% were previously coping with two jobs, an additional 46% had been working 60 hours or more per week, and 20% reported frustration, discontent, insecurity or inadequacies associated with their job. These observations, linking negative affective states with heart disease are not new. Jean Nichols Corvisart des Marets (1755–1821) an eminent cardiologist who was said to have founded cardiac symptomatology and described the mechanics of heart failure (1806), observed that heart disease had two principle causes, 'from the action of the organ and from the passions of man' and this included 'anger, madness, fear, jealousy, despair, joy, avarice, cupidity, ambition, ... revenge!'. Wolf (1971) found similar reports of dissatisfaction and dejection among myocardial infarction patients compared to a matched control group. He also observed an association between emotional state and fluctuations in physiological state. A marked variability in blood pressure (both systolic and diastolic) was observed among those with coronary heart

111

disease and this was most marked among those who subsequently died from CHD. This psychophysiological responsiveness to emotional stress is referred to as reactivity. Evidence from other studies tend to support these observations but the retrospective design generally used does not permit us to state whether the observed differences are causal in the development of heart disease or the effect. It is therefore necessary to consider evidence from prospective studies. Generally, these results seem to show that temperament and behavioural patterns are risk factors for coronary disease (Byrne, 1986; Wolf, 1988).

Most notable in this field of study of psychological character-istics as risk factors for heart disease, is the Type A coronary-prone behaviour pattern. Links between TAB and increased risk for CHD were established by the Framingham Study (Haynes *et al.*, 1978, 1980) and the Western Collaborative Group Study (Rosenman *et al.*, 1964). More recent evidence has not always supported the original findings; for example, in the Multiple Risk Factor Intervention Trial (MRFIT, 1979, 1982). However, a recent study of 2289 male and female patients undergoing diag-nostic coronary angiography, Williams *et al.*, (1988) found a relationship between TAB and coronary atherosclerosis (CAD) severity after age, sex, hyperlipidemia, smoking, hypertension and their various interactions were controlled for. This association was dependent on age: Type As (assessed by structured interview, SI), aged 45 or younger, had more severe CAD than did Type Bs; among patients aged 46–54, CAD severity was similar between Type As and Bs; and for patients of 55 years of age or more, there was a trend towards more severe CAD among Type Bs. These authors suggest that the reversal of the Type A–CAD relationship among older patients may be due to survival effects (i.e. surviving Type As may be biologically hardier than their Type B counter-parts) and so failure to consider Type A by age interaction and use of small sample sizes could account for the failure to observe similar relationships in other recent studies. In addition, this relationship was only present when Type A was assessed by SI; no effect was noted between CAD severity and TAB classified with the Jenkins Activity Survey.

Current research now tends to focus more on the components of TAB and the debate on how they should be measured (i.e. structured interview versus self-report questionnaires). But as Herd (1988) suggests, the interview situation does not provide information concerning the frequency of exposure to challenging situations and presumably an individual with a higher frequency of challenging situations would be at higher risk for any damaging effect of Type A behaviour. This is an important point because it is also believed that the true Type A might actually create stress by their style of behaviour. Therefore it would seem that the situation is still far from resolved.

Williams *et al.*, (1985) have attempted to identify the psychological aspects of TAB which might be the most deleterious and, subsequently, receptive to modification. They found that the hostility/anger dimension was positively associated with coronary occulsion. In a re-evaluation of the data from the Western Collaborative Study, Hecker *et al.* (1988) have found that of the twelve operationally defined terms, only hostility remained a significant risk for CHD incidence. Type A structured interviews administered at intake were re-assessed for 250 CHD cases and 500 matched controls at the 8.5 year follow-up. Among the components of TAB, hostility played the leading role in predicting incidence of CHD and remained a significant predictor when controlling for the global Type A rating and for standard CHD risk factors (i.e. serum cholesterol, diastolic pressure and number of cigarettes smoked). Hostility is thus viewed as a predisposition to express, both directly and indirectly, various types and degrees of anger and related mood states, including irritation, annoyance, disgust, resentment and frustration. It also seems that hostility emerges as a significant predictor of heart disease and mortality rates in general. Shekelle *et al.* (1983) report that the mortality rate among males with low hostility (Ho scale from MMPI) measured 25 years earlier was 18% compared to a 30% rate among those with high Ho scores. These findings are supported by Barefoot *et al.* (1983) in a study of physicians, originally measured for levels of hostility while in medical school. They also noted that high Ho scores were associated with a high mortality rate in general — a six-fold relative risk of dying in the 25-year period, compared to those with low Ho scores. A more recently reported investigation (Siegman *et al.*, 1987) indicated that the same age dependent effect existed as in the Williams *et al.* (1988) survey: non-neurotic hostility was associated with CAD severity only among younger patients in the study sample.

Currently, research efforts seek to identify the biological mechanisms that link TAB to disease outcomes, and the hyper-

113

responsivity (both neuroendocrinal and physiological) of Type As is considered to be the biological precursor to atherogenesis (production of fatty degeneration in arteries) (Ivancevich and Matteson, 1988). Numerous studies demonstrate that Type As respond to challenge, high demands and loss of personal control with a greater elevation in systolic blood pressure, heart rate, cortisol, adrenalin, noradrenalin, and skeletal muscle vasodilation than Type Bs.

The circulation of catecholamines plays a role in cholesterol mobilization which leads to the formation of plaque, and a series of elevations in blood pressure and heart rate are thought to damage the inner layer of coronary arteries and to contribute to atherosclerosis and consequently CHD. Lipid metabolism is affected by neuroendocrine function and under ideal conditions the free fatty acids released provide energy. However, if mobilized fatty acids are not metabolized, the subsequent paths of the lipids may enhance the risk of cardiovascular disease (Herd, 1988). Thus, the sedentary Type A individual, primed for 'fight or flight' action does not engage in the physical activity necessary to burn-up the fat freed, intended to fuel muscle action. Figure 5.3 Flight Path to a Heart Attack (Carruthers, 1976) shows the combination of factors that might result in a life-threatening crisis.

Many of these studies have focused on laboratory experiments and others have concentrated on white-collar, professional groups within the organization. However, there is statistical evidence to show that cardiovascular disease increases as socioeconomic status decreases (Table 5.7)

Table 5.8 verifies this observation and shows that reported decreasing national trends in deaths due to cardiovascular disorders are among the higher socioeconomic groups. In fact, the death rate per 100 000 among the unskilled has increased over a ten year period (1972–1983) by 30% for ischaemic heart disease and 32% for cerebrovascular disease. Marmot's (1983) prospective study of civil servants in London showed a two-to three-fold inverse gradient in ischaemic heart disease (IHD) mortality by socio-economic level. This observation could not be explained by differential use of medical care services. Although it is acknowledged that other risk factors tend to be higher among individuals in the lower socioeconomic groups (e.g. smoking, diet, blood pressure) this does not completely explain IHD mortality.

Some studies show that social support resources are implicated

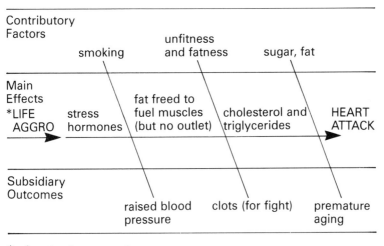

Contributory
Factors

Main
Effects
*LIFE
AGGRO

Subsidiary
Outcomes

*refers to stress agents

Figure 5.3 Flight path to a heart attack. Source: Carruthers (1976).

in the development of IHD (Ruberman, 1984) and angina pectoris (Medalie *et al.*, 1973). It is hypothesized that certain religious groups (e.g. Mormons or Seventh Day Adventists) and/or cultural groups (e.g. in Japan) have a low incidence of heart disease because strong support networks exist within cohesive communities. Whereas, in contemporary society the highly mobile, nuclear family would be at higher risk because social support systems are less evident. However, findings are not consistent and often studies are confounded. For example, dietary differences could explain the observations and in cross-sectional surveys an association between low social support and MI might exist because of a change in the level of support (i.e. as in the death of a partner or divorce). Thus, a hypothesized stressor buffer or moderator is actually the source of stress because life events change and alters the amount of support available to the individual (Thoits, 1982). Some large scale prospective studies have been conducted (Ganster and Victor, 1988) but none have established causal links between levels of social support and heart disease risk. Although studies identifying the physiological mechanism between social support and health outcomes are rare, Knox *et al.* (1985) reported inverse associations between the number of contacts with acquaintances and plasma

115

Table 5.7 Deaths by major causes and types of occupations, 1979–1980, 1982–1983 (Standardized mortality rates = 100)

Causes of deaths, persons aged 20–64 (Males)	Professional and similar	Intermediate	Skilled non-manual	Skilled manual	Partly skilled	Unskilled
Malignant neoplasms						
Trachea, bronchus, and lung cancer	43	63	80	120	126	178
Prostrate cancer	77	104	103	112	97	109
Ischaemic heart disease	70	82	104	109	112	144
Disease of circulatory system	69	80	102	108	113	151
Cerebrovascular disease	62	72	89	109	117	179
Pneumonia	33	50	79	90	105	211
Bronchitis, emphysema, and asthma	34	48	85	110	115	211
External causes: injury/poisoning	67	70	78	93	121	226
Mental disorder	35	48	55	84	97	342
Chronic liver disease and cirrhosis	79	103	95	88	106	182
Ulcer of stomach and duodenum	39	55	80	94	124	261
All causes	66	76	94	106	116	165

Source: UK Office of Population Censuses and Surveys: HMSO (1986).

Table 5.8 Socioeconomic differences in frequencies of death and acute illness 1970–1983; Males aged 16–74, Great Britain

	Professional and similar		Unskilled	
	2-year-period ending:		2-year-period ending:	
	1972	1983	1972	1983
*Deaths due to:				
Ischaemic heart disease	88	70	111	144
Cerebrovascular disease	80	62	136	179
Malignant neoplasms — trachea, bronchus and lung cancer	53	43	143	178
Acute illness				
Restricted activity: days per year	12	16	28	44

*standardized mortality rates = 100
Source: Office of Population Census and Surveys: HMSO (1986).

adrenalin and heart rate of young, hypertensive males. However, it will be difficult to identify causal relationships and physiological mechanisms because heart disease may be present many years before it becomes clinically manifest and levels of social support and need for social support also vary with time. In fact, an alternative view suggests that social support acts as a psychological mediator in health outcomes — supportive relationships and the perception that others will provide aid leads to positive affect and a stable psychological state. Consequently, this leads to better physical and mental health (Cohen and Syme, 1985) because social support reduces the impact of stress by increasing one's self-esteem and sense of personal control. This is discussed further in relation to the stress and cancer outcome relationship. Perceived degree of control features significantly as a variable in the work environment, which might influence the incidence of heart disease.

For example, Alfredsson *et al.* (1982) demonstrated in a case-controlled study, that increased risk of myocardial infarction was associated with work and occupations characterized by hectic work and low control over the degree of variety and work pace. One of these authors, Karasek (1979) has produced a two-dimensional job model which attempts to explain the increased risk of heart disease in terms of work stress — inadequate stimulation and low margin for decision making. (Figure 5.4).

117

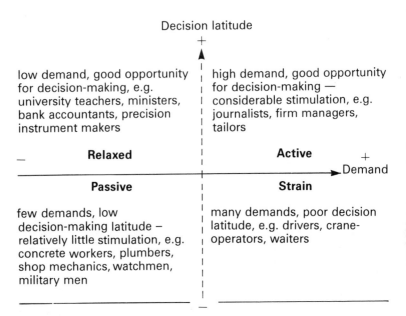

Figure 5.4 Two-dimensional job model. Examples of occupational groups by classification based on Swedish and American research in the 1980s.
NB 1. An individual's situation may diverge considerably from the pattern for the whole group.
  2. Work situations are dynamic, not static.
Source: Karasek (1979).

A strain job is characterized by many demands, time urgency or role conflict, with poor opportunities for decision making. Physiologically, stress reactions are catabolic (i.e. hormonal secretions of adrenalin, noradrenalin and cortisol) and cardiovascular reactions include high blood pressure, increased pulse rate and heightened myocardial electrical excitability (i.e. sinus arrhythmia). Normally cortisol helps to maintain blood volume, but in higher concentrations inhibits response to inflammation and prevents the body from coping with disease. Secretion of cortisol is controlled by adrenocorticotrophic hormone (ACTH). The neuroendocrine system regulates ACTH secretion, which rapidly responds to stress (e.g. stress associated with noise, fear, pain, fever and hypoglycaemia). In an active job, characterized by the mental stimulation of choice and decision making, anabolic physiological reactions are observed, that is, increased secretion of hormones such as oestrogen, testosterone and insulin. As Selye and Bajusz (1959) suggest; 'These hormones stimulate the formation of new cells and enable the body more easily to withstand the catabolic processes which in a stressful situation may break down proteins or deprive the myocardium of 'useful' salts e.g. potassium and magnesium'. Research findings from retrospective and prospective studies generally support Karasek's model, that individuals in occupational groups doing strain work run the highest risk of myocardial infarction (Theorell, 1986). In a Swedish prospective study, hectic work pace, lack of control and lack of opportunity to learn new things were associated with a significant increase in relative risk of myocardial infarction. This relationship could not be accounted for by frequency of heavy lifting, level of education, or the percentage of smokers in a given occupation. However, for other demand variables (threat of unemployment, shift working, piece work and accident risk), there were no consistent trends (Alfredsson *et al.* 1982). It seems therefore that it is not simply strain *per se* (i.e. any demand and low decision latitude) that increases risk of myocardial infarction. LaCroix and Haynes (1986) also tested the demand-control model in the Framingham Heart Study. Around 900 middle-aged men and women were surveyed in the mid 1960s and then monitored over a 10-year period for the development of IHD. Based on job title classification alone, both men and women in high strain occupations had approximately one-and-a-half fold higher risk of developing IHD; but when self-ratings of perceived job demand and control were used, the heart disease risk associated with high job strain was three-fold for women in high strain jobs. This highlights the importance of individual perceptions of work circumstances.

To avoid the confounding effects of age and secondary structural change, Knox *et al.* (1985) examined a population of young males in a ten year follow-up study. The interaction of certain work environment factors, social support networks and medical variables were observed in a small group of male hypertensives. Use of path analysis showed that a significant amount of variation in blood pressure could be explained by psychosocial and occupational stressors. Figure 5.5 details these findings. The combination of high venous adrenalin level and heart rate, enhanced blood volume and low renin (a finding possibly complicated by the smoking factor) are indications of a strong neurogenic component

119

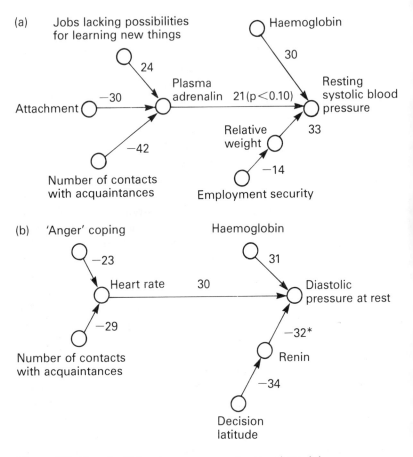

Figure 5.5 Elevated blood pressure: a structural model.
(a) Lisrel analysis of psychosocial and physiological factors in relation to SBP at rest; (b) Lisrel analysis of psychosocial and physiological factors in relation to DBP at rest. No significant correlation found when separate analysis on non-smokers was performed (decimal points omitted).
Source: Knox *et al.* (1985)

in young hypertensives and stressors at work and availability of social support are hypothesized to assert influence through increased sympathetic stimulation (Knox *et al.* 1985). From this type of investigation, our understanding of the influences of psychosocial and occupational stress on health outcomes and cardiovascular disease will be advanced.

Gastrointestinal disorders

Although deaths due to stomach and duodenum ulcers do not feature as major causes of death (Table 5.2); it appears that death from these conditions is also related to low socioeconomic status and is cause for concern within those groups. Incidence of peptic ulcers was originally associated with white-collar, professional occupations. Clearly this is no longer a correct assumption. Table 5.7 shows that deaths due to ulceration of the stomach and duodenum are many times more prevalent among unskilled occupational groups and across all socioeconomic groups, in fact, the rate increases as socioeconomic status decreases. It is suggested that the model proposed by Karasek (Figure 5.4) might also explain this observation, that in passive jobs a higher incidence of ulcers would be observed. Brady's work (1958) on animals shows that although very high demand and control is associated with severe ulceration of the stomach, for humans in less rigorous work schedules, the inability to control a work situation (i.e. passive jobs characterized by a low demand, low decision latitude environment) may be much more stressful and thus more likely to cause ulcers. Selye (1956) describes these organic diseases as disease of adaption. Response to a stressor is non-specific but individuals respond to stress with a preferred pattern of psychophysiological response. This is termed the Achilles heel or the organ inferiority hypothesis (Wolff, 1953). For example, studies indicate that individuals with stomach ulcers tend to respond to stress with gastric secretion and individuals with cardiovascular disease are characterized by greater variability in heart rate and respiration (Masuda *et al.*, 1972). Evidence of psychological mediation in health outcomes was observed in a large-scale study of male manufacturing plant workers. House *et al.* (1979) found that the effects of work stress can be buffered by a supportive supervisor and this had significant effects on health outcome measures. Low levels of reported support from the boss were related to the occurrence of ulcers, angina pectoris, itch and rash.

However, it is also necessary to consider work patterns as causal in gastrointestinal disorder. Irregular meals are related to digestive disorders, especially peptic ulceration (Sergean, 1971) and many blue-collar workers are required to work various shift patterns includng night working. Tasto and Colligan (1978) suggest that 20% of the working population in Europe and North America are

121

working some form of shift system, yet it is also believed that around 20% of the labour market is unsuited to this work arrangement. Although some self selection out of unsuitable work will occur, it is suggested that many individuals will stay in a job that is clearly detrimental to their health, when the labour market is poor and they perceive no real alternative employment. Dirken (1966) found that in general, shift workers suffered a decreased sense of well-being, and that this was explained, in part, by the home and housing conditions of the lower socioeconomic status occupations (i.e. cramped conditions, inability to get adequate day-time sleep etc.). The role of stressful events in peptic ulcer disease has been examined in several studies. Gilligan *et al.* (1987) suggest that the unequivocal results obtained are perhaps due to the use of insensitive life-events inventories, a focus on relatively acute or discrete life events and distorted recall by subjects with known disease — chronic and on-going life stressors tend to be overlooked. To overcome some of these problems, Gilligan *et al.* used a life events schedule to measure life events and chronic difficulties among duodenal ulcer patients and control subjects. This semi-structured face-to-face interview technique records events in detail and considers the social context, time of occurrence and duration. Events are also classified on a stress rating and assessed to the extent that they were independent/dependent on the effects of ulcer disease. The results supported earlier findings, that is, it is not acute life events which have a role in duodenal ulcer onset or relapse but chronic difficulties of long duration and those perceived as threatening, which are associated with this disease. As expected, duodenal ulcer was more common in divorced, separated or widowed subjects (i.e. those most likely to have chronic difficulties). These authors argue that chronic difficulties produce chronic emotional arousal (anxiety or depression) and this is associated with chronic autonomic and humoral changes that might be linked to duodenal ulcer disease in some way (Gilligan *et al.*, 1987).

Diabetes mellitus

The British Diabetic Association (1988) recognizes diabetes mellitus as an important health problem, which seems to becoming more common. Approximately 1.2% of the population have diabetes (Williams, 1985; reported by BDA, 1988) and this rises to more than 4% among those over the age of 65. Death may be due to diabetes, for example, from diabetic ketosis or diabetic kidney failure but in many instances death results from heart attacks or strokes (both are more common among the diabetic population). Fuller *et al.* (1983) estimate that about 40000 people with diabetes die each year. If analysed by age and gender, it would appear that approximately 20000 die prematurely each year as the result of having diabetes (reported by British Diabetic Association, 1988).

Diabetes is not a new disease; the earliest description dates back to the second Century AD in the writings of Arataeus of Cappadocia who coined the term from the Greek word meaning 'syphon'. This, presumably because untreated diabetes is characterized by an insatiable thirst and excessive urination of sweet urine (termed mellitus, meaning honeyed in the 17th Century). Diabetes is defined as the existence of abnormally high glucose in the bloodstream and is a disorder of carbohydrate metabolism due mainly to insulin deficiency. It is in this context that stress and the stress-related stimulation of blood sugar is implicated in the onset and cause of diabetes mellitus in those individuals predisposed to diabetes (Quick and Quick, 1984). Thus, stress may act as a 'trigger' for a dormant condition. In the 1950s, various studies demonstrated that carbohydrate metabolism and subsequent elevation of blood glucose was the result of exposure to a stressor agent in non-diabetic individuals and removal of the stress, facilitated return to normal (Cox, 1985). Woods and Porter (1974) observe that both uncontrolled diabetes and increased sympathetic nervous system activity are characterized by symptoms of elevated glucose levels, decreased glucose tolerance, increased lipolysis (decomposition of fat), glycogenolysis (conversion of glycogen into glucose) and ketosis. However, the relationship between stress and diabetes is still not acknowledged because research evidence remains equivocal. Criticism has been levied on the methodology used in terms of 1. use of unrepresentative samples; 2. the mixing of Type I and Type II diabetes patients; 3. the lack of certainty that an experimental stressor condition was actually stressful (i.e. the intensity and controllability of the stimulus might be important factors); 4. that blood glucose might not be the best measure of the impact of stress; and 5. not enough attention was paid to circadian rhythms and the high degree of individual variation that exists in patients and controls (Shillitoe, 1988; review).

Type I and Type II diabetes mellitus are the two main groups of this disorder, although the distinctions are not absolute (Bell *et al.*, 1980). Juvenile-onset diabetes (Type I) tends to occur with an abrupt onset in patients under 25 years of age. These individuals are deficient in insulin — there is little or no insulin in their plasma and no insulin response to glucose load (Insulin dependent diabetes). Maturity-onset diabetes (Type II) develops insidiously in middle age, often in obese patients. Type I diabetes generally requires insulin injections, whereas Type II is usually diet and/or oral hypoglycaemic controlled. Although it is acknowledged that the disease develops spontaneously, probably as a result of hereditary predisposition, the mode of inheritance is not understood. Twin studies show that the situation is complex and that other factors, such as injury to the pancreas, obesity, repeated pregnancy and the ageing process, are implicated (Danowski, 1963). Population surveys indicate that many apparently healthy people have a mild form of maturity-onset diabetes (Bell *et al.*, 1980). In these patients, fasting blood glucose levels may be normal but after a glucose load, the blood glucose level rises higher than in asymptomatic people and remains higher longer. The cause of this so called slow-response is still unknown.

In addition to the possibility that stress may have a direct impact on diabetes by producing glycaemic changes, it is also likely that the effects may also be exerted indirectly. Stress can influence eating behaviour and dietary habits in non-diabetics and diabetics (i.e. among depressed or anxious individuals escapist drinking or eating is a maladaptive response to a stressor agent). In both of the studies reported by Cox *et al.* (1984) and Hanson and Pichert (1986), the worry and harrassment of daily life were related to changes in eating patterns and dietary violations among patients. Therefore, lack of adherence to a regimen may exacerbate an established condition, ultimately resulting in coma or death, in the extreme.

The link between diabetes and psychosocial factors has been observed from early writings. It tends to be associated with affluent societies and was attributed to prolonged sorrow by Willis in 1679 (Shillitoe, 1988). In fact, one predisposing factor thought likely to have contributed to the increased rate of diabetes in contemporary society is the high incidence of obesity. As already mentioned, stress may therefore be implicated indirectly in the stress-strain-illness onset or development chain. Because of the potential problems that exist in laboratory experiments, some researchers have attempted to investigate the relationships between stress and diabetes outside the laboratory and to consider environmental stress agents in the form of major life events and/or the daily hassles of life. Again the problems associated with retrospective studies, the use of insensitive or invalid measures, have produced conflicting evidence. Some researchers have found an increase in life events in children and/or adults prior to diagnosis, others have not reported any significant effects (Shillitoe, 1988). Some investigations suggest that the study of daily-hassles might provide a more sensitive measure of common psychosocial events. The findings, to date, indicate that it is necessary to distinguish between positive and negative experiences, that is, stressors producing happiness tends to send blood-glucose down, whilst stressors that produce feelings of worry, sadness and frustration are associated with increased blood glucose (Cox et al., 1984; Hanson and Pichert, 1986). Both of these studies found that blood glucose level is associated with the number of reported negative hassles, even when controlled for the effects of diet, exercise, insulin and food intake, etc.

Another line of research has tried to identify what is known as the diabetic personality, a specific type of person more prone to develop the disorder. Since this research, originating in the 1930s/ 1940s, seems to confound susceptibility to disease and response to illness symptoms, it adds nothing to our understanding of the aetiology of the disorder. Although more recent studies have focused on the use of standardized personality measures, rather than psychoanalytic techniques, there is no evidence to support this notion of a diabetic personality. As Cox (1985) suggests, marked individual differences occur, thus the search for the global diabetic personality is futile. However, there is some suggestion that personality differences do seem to explain how an individual copes with the disease and in this respect, the research may be worthwhile, especially if personality is acknowledged in the widest sense, and not as a fixed, unchangeable entity.

Given the paucity of evidence in demonstrating the effects of stress on diabetes onset and development, it seems paradoxical that stress management techniques are used in the control of the disorder (i.e. stress control is associated with decreased adrenal cortical activity). Indeed, there is evidence to suggest that stress control in the form of relaxation techniques leads to increased glucose tolerance and decreased plasma cortisol in patients with Type II diabetes (Surwit and Feinglos, 1984). Various authors have indicated improvement in metabolic control due to relaxation training, counselling, exercise and/or biofeedback; these include lowered blood glucose levels, a decrease in the range of daily blood glucose levels and a reduction in the amount of insulin required. Unfortunately, the evaluation of stress management techniques also tends to be criticized because of the difficulty in controlling extraneous or secondary variables, the use of unrepresentative samples (i.e. often referrals or volunteers) and small sample sizes. It is also difficult to know if the effects are due to the treatment or the increased attention in general, which also helps the patient to reflect on related issues (e.g. diet, improved mood etc.) or simply due to the Hawthorne Effect (Roethlisberger and Dickson, 1939). Nevertheless, as Shillitoe (1988) states; 'these patients may have felt subjectively better, their adjustment may have been better in some way' and so '... any improvement must be regarded as worthwhile if the patient is willing to modify habits and behaviours in order to achieve it'.

Allergies and skin disease

Asthma

This commonly refers to allergic asthma, which is characterized by difficult and laboured breathing, mucus sputum, wheezing and sense of constriction in the chest. Bronchial asthma has long been considered to be associated with family conflicts, dependency states and heightened emotional arousal (Weiner, 1977). The symptoms of asthma in predisposed individuals may be precipated by emotional and/or psychosocial events and, as such it is classified as a psychosomatic illness (Groen, 1971). Asthmatic attacks in children might be triggered by both pleasant and unpleasant states (e.g. anxiety or anger and laughing or crying). And as Weiner suggests, the anticipation of an event contributes to the onset of an attack in up to 50% of patients.

Resistance to the notion of stress-induced asthma still exists, although some attempts to explain a possible mechanism have been made. As Irwin and Anisman (1984) declare ... 'allergy may result from an inhibition of suppressor T-cells, which under normal circumstances may act as dampners of antibody production. Stressors could therefore exacerbate allergic symptoms by depressing T-cell activity and consequently enhancing the IgE antibody response. Alternatively, non-immunologic processes such as neurotransmitter release may contribute to the observed effects in a direct influence on mast cells'. Adrenalin and noradrenalin both influence the release of histamine from mast cells and this causes the stimulation of mucous gland secretion. Thus, a beta-adrenergic defect may be responsible for symptoms of allergy in some individuals (Barnes *et al.*, 1983). Since DeAraujo *et al.* (1972) also believe that coping style affects the ability of individuals to control symptoms (reflected in the amount of medication required) it would seem that the investigation of psychosocial factors involved in the onset and cause of asthma does warrant further attention.

Hay fever; skin disease

Allergies due to a hypersensitivity reaction may result in symptoms of hay fever, urticaria (hives) and asthma. These allergies may also be triggered or exacerbated by stressful events. The role of psychological factors in dermatologic disorders was recognized by Wilson (1857). Emotional arousal, often stress induced (Chue, 1976; Schmidt *et al.*, 1985; reported by Gil *et al.*, 1987) is thought to be associated with many skin disorders such as neurodermatitis, acne and eczema. Laboratory studies of eczema have shown that emotional arousal in predisposed individuals leads to specific changes in skin cells (Quick and Quick, 1984). Subconscious conflicts and personality predispositions may also be important factors in skin diseases. Various studies have shown that stressful life events precede the symptoms of skin conditions. For example, Gil *et al.* (1987) have shown that measures of stress and family environment were important predictors of symptom severity in children having severe chronic atopic dermatitis (AD), even after controlling for demographic and medical status variables (age; and IgE, an immunoglobin which increases during allergic reactions). Children from families high on an independent/organized factor had fewer and less severe symptoms of AD (emphasis on planning, regular routine, self reliance, independent thinking, clearly designated responsibilities). However, the authors also suggest that such families may also be better with treatment or encouraging the children to be more responsible for their own medical care.

Although these disorders are not considered life threatening, they are most distressing. However, given financial constraints, the high costs of longitudinal, large-scale studies and the ethics involved in experimentation with human subjects, it is unlikely that our understanding of these issues will progress rapidly in the near future. Retrospective research into life stress and illness is likely to be unreliable because recall is not accurate and may be distorted by the illness or disability. However, continued emphasis on a multidisciplinary approach, especially from a psychobiological, and/or prospective approach must be encouraged.

Cancer

Speculation on the potential role of psychological factors in the aetiology and development of cancer has a long history. Claudius Galen, physician (AD 130–200) proposed an association between affective states (i.e. melancholia) and susceptibility to cancer, although the first English definition does not seem to appear until 1601 (Rosch, 1984). However, since Gendron (1701) (reported by Rosch, 1984) declared; 'disasters of life as occasion much trouble and grief' as causal in cancer, such references linking negative life events and cancer are found throughout the 19th and 20th centuries. These all suggest that certain personality predispositions, the loss of a near relative, disappointments and/or an uneasy mind, are in some way linked to the onset or development of cancer (Rosch, 1984; Cooper, 1988).

Life events and cancer

In 1926, Evans, a Jungian psychoanalyst observed that many cancer patients had lost a close personal, emotional relationship prior to illness onset. These early notions have generated a considerable amount of research into life events viewed as a form of social stressor, which is causal in the onset of illness (Paykel, 1982). The rationale is that a life event brings change to the individual's social or personal environment, which necessitates adaptation. LeShan's (1959) early review of 75 studies on psychological factors in the development of malignant disease, concluded that 'the most consistently reported, relevant psychological factor has been the loss of a major emotional relationship prior to the first-noted symptoms of neoplasm.' He later developed hypotheses about mortality rates and predicted that cancer mortality rates should be highest for widowed, next highest for divorced and lowest for married and then single persons, if the theory of loss of emotional relationships was valid. The analysis of epidemiological data from a number of studies showed that some of the data were consistent with this hypothesis. However, the results obtained over the past 10–15 years are far from unequivocal (Cooper, 1988), probably because of the methodological problems associated with data collection (Paykel and Rao, 1984). Most information is obtained retrospectively and so there are recall problems. Use of self-report questionnaires (e.g. the Holmes and Rahe Social Readjustment Rating Scale) are inadequate because they tend to ignore the qualitative nature of life events. As Cooper *et al.* (1985) indicate, events may have differential meanings for each subject and/or may also be culturally specific. For example, divorce or retirement from work may bring escape from a previously high stress situation. However, these situations are high-stress life-events on the Holmes-Rahe Social Readjustment Rating Scale (SRRS), whereas in-law troubles ranks much lower as a source of stress. However, a close knit, extended family environment would suffer more stress in this situation than an individual from a highly-mobile, nuclear family. This questions the validity of using standardized, weighted life-events scales because it is necessary to consider perceptions and reactions to events, not only events in isolation. Use of the interview would provide the depth of information needed. Nevertheless, this method has different, yet otherwise challenging problems to overcome (interview bias etc). It is also possible that the illness itself produces a life event change and so it is necessary to establish defined time periods which antedates the onset of illness. In both heart disease and cancer, this is difficult. Thus, it is necessary to date the appearance of first manifestation of the disease and identify independent events that could not have been brought about by the illness, if it were present and, of course, acknowledge that the aetiology and/or development of the various forms of cancer may be differentially affected by psychosocial factors.

Some studies have attempted to overcome these problems; one is reported by Cooper *et al.* (1986). It involved a large-scale, prospective study on 2163 patients attending breast screening

129

clinics. The Cooper, Cooper and Cheang Life Events Scale was used, which included 42 items (generated from a pilot sample of British females) and 10-point Likert-type scales on the degree of the stressfulness of the event. These women were subsequently diagnosed as having cancer, a cyst, benign breast disease or disease free breasts. A well-woman control was also used. It was found that the cancer group had experienced significantly more loss- or illness-related events, perceived life events generally as more stressful, used fewer and poorer coping skills and were significantly lower on Type A behaviour (e.g. less assertive, directed emotions inward).

Another study which explored traumatic life events and cancer, by utilizing an interview method, was carried out by Smith and Sebastian (1976). It examined the emotional history of 44 cancer patients and 44 patients with physical abnormalities which were non-cancerous. Structured interviews were carried out to try to identify the frequency, intensity and duration of emotional states in each person's life, which involved questions about family life, childhood, social and sexual life, career, religion, etc. Their approach was far more open-ended than traditional life events research, in that they relied on interview responses to the following: 'I am going to ask you to remember events that have occurred in your life which have made you feel very concerned, emotional, stressed and so forth. I will ask you to relate the kind of events that provoked emotional feelings in you, the date, the intensity and duration of the events and emotional conditions. We will begin with early childhood and end up with questions about your present life situation.' Critical incidents were then recorded and were rated as high, medium or low and the intensity and duration of the emotional events for each person were rated on a 15-point scale. It was found that there were significantly more frequent and intense emotional events prior to diagnosis among cancer patients than among the comparison groups. Similarly, Witzel (1970) interviewed 150 cancer patients and 150 patients with other serious diseases. He took personal histories of past illnesses and found that non-cancer patients had a significantly larger number of reported incidents of medical problems throughout their lives than cancer patients. They reported being out-patients three times more often than cancer patients, being in a hospital bed three times more often, having temperatures in excess of 38.5°C seven times more often and experiencing twice as many minor illnesses and operations. The authors contend that this does not necessarily contradict the other research on adverse life events because these critical medical incidents may signal the disease process itself. As Fox (1978) has suggested; 'developing cancer had mobilized the immune response, which is capable of fighting many diseases and which, because of its aroused status, could do so more successfully than that of non-cancer patients.'

Other research in this area is being undertaken which attempts to predict cancer from psychosocial factors. One such study was carried out by Horne and Picard (1980) among lung cancer patients, who were selected on the basis of the presence of an undiagnosed, subacute or chronic lung lesion visible on previous roentgenographic examination. The patients were then interviewed extensively on a variety of psychosocial factors: childhood stability, job stability, marriage stability, lack of plans for the future and recent significant loss. A composite score was devised for each patient on the basis of these five life areas. The patient's clinical pathology from 15–38 months after the psychosocial interview was determined, to see if predictions could be made from the life events to the diagnosis. The composite score was predictive in 80% of the patients with benign lung disease and in 61% of lung cancer patients. In fact, the predictive power of the psychosocial factors was as good as information on smoking history.

Studies by Greene and Swisher (1969) and Greene (1962) also show that psychological factors were implicated in the onset and development of leukaemia. In one twin-study, emotional trauma was evident in the twin who subsequently contracted and died of leukaemia, compared to the remaining healthy twin. Incidence of leukaemia and lymphoma over a 15-year study were associated with negative life events, such as emotional loss or separation. Again, these emotions of hopelessness, sadness and anxiety are typically described (Greene, 1962) and malignancies seem to be associated with what is termed general emotional inhibition, denial and repression. However, even in well-controlled, matched cases studies, it is difficult to establish cause and/or effect in the complexity of interactions that are observed in human behaviour. As Eysenck (1984) suggests; 'for example, the many sides of poverty are seen in the co-existence or co-occurrence of a large number of interrelated problems: physical illness, mental illness, low income, unemployment, social disorganization, racial discrimination, broken families, poor housing. Thus; 'a scientist who boldly steps in and imposes causal arrows on these variables had better have a strong research design to back him up.' This warning serves also in the study of the association between personality and cancer. Research findings indicate the importance of considering personality dispositions as a mediator in the response to stressful life events. However, it seems that personality may have an effect on the onset and development of cancer. For example, as Schmale and Iker (1971) found, both life events preceding the illness and personality disposition were associated with a high incidence of cervical cancer. If individuals with different personalities show differential incidence of disease, it becomes reasonable to ask what it is in the personality that causes the onset or development of an illness (Eysenck, 1984).

Personality predispositions and cancer

Early research attempts aimed to identify the cancer personality. Bacon *et al.* (1952) reported that women with cancer of the breast were unable to discharge or deal with anger, aggressiveness or hostility and covered over with a facade of pleasantness. Kissen (1963) also noted frequently occurring personality profiles among 355 male patients with lung cancer. These individuals were charac- terized by an inability to express emotions or to get 'things off their chest'. Although this behaviour was described as typical of both childhood experience and present adult condition, it might only have been response to the illness situation. Indeed, many studies of this nature tend to indicate differences between cancer and non- cancer patients after the disease is diagnosed. These studies, therefore, may suffer from problems of distorted or poor recall caused by present illness, use of inappropriate comparison groups, and non-representative sampling. As Craig and Abeloff (1974) indicate, an awareness of having cancer can alter various person- ality measures. Although not completely free of these confounding effects, the study reported by Schmale and Iker (1971) shows the potential impact of personality style and life events on cancer onset. They were able to predict the diagnosis of cancer of the cervix from personality questionnaires completed by asymptomatic women but with suspicious Pap smears (examination of stained cells from smear taken from uterus). The disease occurred most frequently among those with a helpless-prone personality or with a sense of hopeless frustration caused by exposure to irresolvable conflict during the preceding six months. However, their measure of hopelessness was based on the analysis of taped interviews and not objective, reliable, validated measures. Goodkin *et al.* (1986), using both interview and objective measures among cervical cancer and non-cancer controls (with uterine leiomyomas), investigated the role of stress in the promotion of cervical intraepithelial neoplasia (CIN) to invasive carcinoma. They found a modest stress-promotion correlation but this was greatly enhanced by significant interactions with low levels of co-operative coping style and for high levels of premorbid pessimism, future despair, somatic anxiety and life-threat reactivity. Although all data was collected prior to feedback of histological diagnosis and it is claimed that there was no evidence of a persisting suspicion of cancer among the groups, it is possible that these hospitalized groups may have preferred to repress or deny their true feelings. Other studies have looked at differences that exist between personality and the incidence of disease prior to diagnosis. Kissen and Eysenck (1962) used the Maudsley Personality Inventory (MPI) and found that, controlling for psychosomatic disorder and age, matched controls had much higher 'N' (neuroticism) scores than those subsequently diagnosed with lung cancer. Thus, lung cancer patients differ in that they either lack, or suppress, emotionality. Subsequent work by Kissen (1963) indicates that very low N scorers have approximately a six-fold possibility of developing lung cancer as compared to high N scores. Their findings are also supported among patients found to be suffering from breast cancer or bronchial carcinoma. Despite this consensus, the fact remains that all patients did actually have cancer when they completed these objective questionnaires and so one cannot be sure whether the illness affected the outcome in some way and that prognosis was not impossible, or suspected by the wary patient.

To avoid the methodological issues of time and cost problems inherent in prospective designs, some investigations have utilized a retro-prospective design. Thus, pre-existing records collected years before a disease develops are eventually used to investigate the relationship between psychosocial/psychological factors and the onset of disease. Shekelle *et al.* (1981) used this method in a study of 2020 men. Clinical depression was assessed with the MMPI and 17 years later it was observed that subsequent death due to cancer was twice as high among males scoring high on the depression continuum. The data indicate that the risk was prevalent during the whole 17-year period, but was most prominent between 12 and 17 years. Bieliauskas and Garron (1982) indicate that; 'because of the prospective nature, the long period, the use of quantitative measures, attention to their risk factors, and the large number of subjects, this study provides significant evidence of prospective increases in risk of cancer death with increased depression.' Nevertheless, there were a number of methodological weaknesses. First, the MMPI absolute depression scores for the cancer deaths were not in the pathological range, only linearly more depressive than for the non-cancer deaths. Second, we have only a 'one point of time' measurement of depression (i.e. 17 years ago) and do not have information about the change that may have taken place in the psychological state of the individuals assessed. Using the same design in a ten year follow-up prospective study in Yugoslavia (Eysenck, 1988), 1353 subjects were measured on various personality dimensions and behaviours related to cancer and heart disease risk, utilizing both questionnaire and interview methods. Ten years later, diagnoses of death were made and deaths due to cancer were significantly associated with high scoring individuals on the rationality and anti-emotionality dimension (i.e. the opposite of neuroticism-anxiety) and the hopelessness/helplessness score. An additional factor, harmonization (i.e. the tendency to shun quarrels and try to bring about harmony among and with people split on some issue) also correlated highly with the occurrence of cancer.

Dattore *et al.* (1980) carried out a very well-designed study of 200 patients (75 cancer and 125 non-cancer patients), on whom premorbid MMPI personality data were available through Veterans' Administration Hospital records. Extensive screening of records was involved to ensure comparable samples. They found that the two groups were significantly different on three scales: repression, depression and denial of hysteria. Their findings on repression were in the direction of earlier studies; that cancer patients showed significantly higher scores. Their results on depression were unexpected but understandable: they found that cancer patients had significantly lower depression scores than controls. They argued 'since depression represents such a threatening emotion to the cancer patient, one would expect to see relatively little acknowledgement of depression by subjects in the cancer group.' In addition, they found that cancer patients scored lower on the denial of hysteria measure, which they interpreted as indicating that they were more insightful and introspective than non-cancer patients, which is also consistent with earlier theoretical speculations.

In a long-term prospective study, medical students were closely observed during the four year medical training and subsequently followed during their work as physicians (Thomas, 1977). This data suggests that cancer tends to occur in individuals who are low-key, non-aggressive and unable to adequately express their emotions. Similar to Dattore's findings, this small group who developed cancer were also significantly lower on depression and anxiety scales than those who developed other illnesses (e.g. mental illness or hypertension) or who remained disease free (Thomas and Greenstreet, 1973). Temoshok and Heller (1984) suggest that discrepancies may be attributed to differences in the type of assessment used to measure depression i.e. self-rating versus independent rating by observers. And as Bahnson (1981) indicates, the interaction of variables may produce unequivocal results; 'it is not loss and depression alone that usher in cancer but the combination of depleting life events with a particular ego-defensive and coping style.'

Other research has shown that extraverts are more prone to cancer. Hagnell (1966) carried out an epidemiological survey of 2550 Swedish women over a 10-year period. It was found that a significantly higher proportion of women who had developed cancer, had originally been assessed as having a substable personality. This classification of personality types, developed by a Swede, Sjobring (1963), utilizes four dimensions: 1. a capacity factor; 2. a stability factor; 3. a solidity factor; and 4. a validity factor. The substable personality is described as; 'warm, hearty, concrete, heavy, industrious, interested in people, social, tending to personal interrelations and inhibition'. Hagnell's findings did not support earlier or subsequent research observations, as his results showed that cancer patients were substable more often than one might expect. Substability in Sjobring's system has traits in common with Eysenck's classification of extraversion, which refers to the outgoing, uninhibited social proclivities of a person. Prompted by Hagnell's findings, Cooper and Metcalfe (1963) carried out a survey on 47 women with cancer, using the MPI to assess extraversion. They concluded that women who develop breast cancer do have significantly higher extraversion scores and that this is a constitutionally determined characteristic of these patients rather than a temporary reaction to their illness. This finding confirms Hagnell's result but does not agree with Kissen's hypothesis that cancer is associated with individuals who have poor emotional outlets and repress their feelings.

In the review of 29 studies which focus on the endogenous psychosocial aetiology and exacerbation of human cancer (that is, arising from internal states stemming directly from influence on or by the psyche), Temoshok and Heller (1984) conclude:

1. One is struck by the paucity of positive findings, given the number of variables studied and the effort invested. Many of these negative findings, however, support one consistently appearing theme: that cancer patients have difficulty in expressing emotions, or even feeling them.

2. There is enough convergent evidence, from prospective, longitudinal and retrospective studies, to discern a constellation of factors that appears to predispose some individuals to develop cancer or to progress through its stages more quickly.

3. Recent controlled studies support many earlier hypotheses derived mainly from clinical impressions.

4. Evidence from prospective and retrospective studies converges, for the most part, suggesting that there is little substance to the argument that knowing one has cancer (or has knowledge without conscious awareness) results in psychological and physiological reactions that compromise the validity of retrospective findings.

5. In addition to the emotional expression patterns noted in 1, personality traits or long-standing characteristics of persons who develop cancer or have a less favourable course include niceness, industriousness, perfectionism, sociability, conventionality and more rigid controls of defensiveness.

6. Underlying attitudes or tendencies of helplessness/hopelessness and of giving up rather than fighting are characteristic of persons with a more unfavourable course of cancer.

7. The existence and number of past or recent life events appears to be less important than how these were cognitively, emotionally, or behaviourally dealt with.

Haney (1977) argues that personality predispositions may not be directly linked to cancer but will help to determine 'the psychic and somatic insults to which the individual will be exposed, and the meaning these exposures will have for the individual.' There is likely to be a psychocarcinogenic process in operation, which works in such a way that the stressor and bodily predispositions interact and co-vary in the direction of an ultimate carcinoma, one feeding the other. As Eysenck (1988) suggests, there is still much to be understood about personality, stress-strain and cancer inter-actions, but there is 'too much empirical material to doubt that stress-strain interacting with personality, plays a causal role in the genesis of cancer, probably in combination with such factors as smoking and drinking.' Various psychobiological mechanisms are proposed in these associations.

The relationship of psychological factors to cancer

There have been a number of explanations of just how stress may cause disease. Foque (1931), for example, believed that there was a multiplicity of secondary causes for cancer, such as X-rays, chemicals and viruses. However, in his view, the cells had to be in a receptive state before the cancerous process could start. He believed in 'the role of sad emotions as activators and secondary causes in the activation of human cancers'. These, he added; 'through the instrumentality of the nervous system's effect on metabolism, act on the endocrine balances of the body in such a way that the cell is put into a state where it is sensitive and recep-tive to the carcinogen.' Fox (1978) suggested that there are two primary cancer-causing mechanisms: 1. 'carcinogenesis, the production of cancer by an agent or mechanism overcoming existing resistance of the body'; and 2. 'lowered resistance to cancer, which permits a potential carcinogen normally insufficient to produce cancer to do so' (e.g. weakened emotional state). This latter mechanism involves the immunosuppression system of the body, with an immune deficient individual at risk of one form of cancer or another depending on the vulnerability of particular organs.

Selye (1979), on the other hand, suggested that all organisms go through a general adaptation syndrome, which passes through three stages:

1. Alarm reaction, (or shock phase: the initial and immediate reaction to a noxious agent) and a countershock phase (a mobilization of defences phase in which the adrenal cortex

becomes further enlarged and secretes more corticoid hormones).
2. Stage of resistance, which involves adapting to the stressor stimulus, but decreasing one's ability to cope with subsequent stimuli.
3. Stage of exhaustion, which follows a period of prolonged and severe adaption. (Figure 2.2, Chapter Two).

Thus, hormonal attack (particularly ACTH) on the body is the ultimate cancer-producing weapon, if it is activated at a frequent, continuous and high level. Selye (1979) believed that stress plays some role in the development of all diseases; 'these effects may be curative (as illustrated by various forms of externally-induced stress such as shock therapy, physical therapy and occupational therapy) or damaging, depending on whether the biochemical reactions characteristic of stress (e.g. stress hormones or nervous reactions to stress) combat or accentuate the trouble.' As Rosch (1984) reminds us, both hormonal factors and the immunologic competency of the individual influences malignant growth and the central nervous system plays a dominant role in the control of these determinants of malignant activity. The role of stress is emphasized because endocrine and immune function are sensitive to its influence and states of mind have long been suspected for having an effect on the immune system (Baker, 1987). Very basically, the immune system is primarily based on the white blood cells. T-lymphocytes, concerned with cellular immunity, consist of helper cells, which amplify the immune reaction, suppressor cells, which down-regulate it and natural killer (NK) cells: B-lymphocytes and plasma cells secrete antibodies, known as immunoglobulins which are specific for specific antigens (Baker, 1987). Evidence for emotional factors, acting via the immune system, in the onset or development of disease has a long history. For example, the occurrence of trench-mouth (ulcerative gingivitis) in World War I was associated with the stress of trench warfare and is believed to be due to the failure of the normal immune response. Similarly, diseases linked to immune deficiency and the stress of academic pressure, bereavement, shift work, and sleep deprivation are reported (Baker, 1987 for a full review).

It is hypothesized that malignant cells which develop in organs and tissues are recognized and destroyed by an efficient immune system, whereas in susceptible individuals, decreased immune defences lead to rapid growth of abnormal cells. This also applies to infectious diseases which spread rapidly, if the body does not respond by producing antibodies. Malignancy only develops if there is some dysfunction of the defence mechanism and it is in this aspect of the cancer process that may be vulnerable to the influence of psychological factors (Irwin and Anisman, 1984). The release of corticosteroids, in response to stress, which reduce inflammation in damaged or infected tissues, is one underlying biological mechanism which explains the link between psychological factors and the immune system. Cortisol, the principal corticosteroid, can decrease the number of antibodies produced and reduce the size of the lymph nodes (thus the number and responsiveness of lymphocytes circulating in the blood). Also, neuropeptides (e.g. B-endorphin and met-enkephalin) which seem to be released in response to uncontrollable stress, can alter the activity of lymphocytes and natural killer cells. The clinical appearance of two closely related viruses are linked with cancer (Rosch, 1984). Herpes zoster infection (shingles) is associated with diminished immunologic defences and patients also have a higher incidence of cancer. Herpes simplex II virus which is responsible for recurrent genital lesions is believed to predispose to cervical cancer. Studies carried out by The Ohio State University College of Medicine (Kennedy, Kiecolt-Glaser and Glaser, 1988, for a brief review) show changes in antibody levels to latent herpes viruses associated with examinations, suggesting virus reactivation, probably resulting from poorer cellular immune system competence. This finding is independent of changes in nutrition. On the day of the examination, the students' natural killer cells were significantly less active than they had been a month earlier. Psychological variables including loneliness, attachment (to an ex-spouse) and depression were also found to be associated with immune system changes. For example, separated and divorced males show a poorer cellular immune competency than married males (even when controlled for smoking, drinking and drug taking behaviour, ie. possible responses to change in marital status). Stress and a hopeless response to the situation are postulated in the promotion of cervical intraepithelial neoplasia (CIN) to invasive cervical carcinoma, through the immune system as the mediating mechanism. Various studies have shown that psychosocial stress and personality characteristics interact to induce immune system deficit and breast cancer disease onset

(Goodkin *et al.*, 1986). Thus, physiological predispositions to promotion may be described for hopelessness in that depressed people are known to have increased corticosteroid levels. Therefore, a woman with CIN and a high degree of premorbid pessimism and/or future despair, might suffer increased cortisol levels, resulting in decreased T-cell growth factor and promotion. In the Goodkin *et al.* study, cervical cancer patients were also observed to have an unco-operative coping style (forceful, social alienation and high somatic anxiety). Thus, they might show elevated adrenalin levels and stimulation of c-AMP, with a similar consequence of immunosuppression and promotion of CIN to invasive carcinoma of the cervix (Goodkin *et al.*, 1987). Potentiating variables, therefore, share a common endpoint of immunosuppression and promotion is possibly arrived at through distinct endocrine pathways. Note that this study also points to the importance of adequacy of coping skills in the development of cancer.

Although the immunosuppression model is widely accepted, it is criticized in that an increased incidence of malignancies have not been observed among patients with immunodeficiency disorders and the administration of immunosuppressant drugs in mice does not cause increased rates of neoplasia (Irwin and Anisman, 1984). In addition, it is suggested that the immune system might not respond uniformly to all types of cancer, and in some, may not be involved at all. However, as Irwin and Anisman suggest, many clinical investigations have demonstrated that psychosocial factors may influence the course of various immunologically mediated diseases; 'The extent to which stressors exert a significant influence may depend on the coping style of an individual and the resources or social support available'. They state evidence from animal studies to show that neuroendocrine and neurotransmitter activity is altered by exposure to stressor situations and these parallel the immunological changes associated with stress. However, factors of controllability, chronicity, severity and repeated exposure are moderators of the response to a stressor. In addition, hormones involved in the stress response have the capacity to alter directly and/or indirectly, humoural and cell-mediated immune processes; and conversely, it appears that the immune system may influence central nervous system activity (Irwin and Anisman, 1984).

Autoimmune diseases

An acknowledgement that the brain and the immune system may interact to influence susceptibility to disease has produced a new field of research known as psychoimmunology. The Links are thus proposed between stress and autoimmune disorders such as rheumatoid arthritis, pernicious anaemia, myasthenia gravis, systemic lupus erythematosus (SLE) and multiple sclerosis. By the production of autoantibodies and cell mediated processes, the body becomes intolerant of its own tissues and begins to attack its own cells. Some studies have reported associations between certain personality dispositions and/or negative life events and the onset and development of these disorders. Baker and Brewerton (1981) found that 12 of 22 female patients with rheumatoid arthritis had experienced a life event of moderate or consistent emotional stress, compared to three of the age-matched controls. The traumatic events had nearly all occurred less than three months before the onset of the disease and tended to be anxiety-provoking, rather than depressing. Many other studies report similar findings, however, the evidence mainly relies on retrospective investigations based on small sample populations and poor control group comparisons (Irwin and Anisman, 1984; Martin, 1987; Baker, 1987). It is believed that autoimmune diseases may be due to reduced activity or a dysfunction of suppressor T-cells and a consequent increase in B-lymphocyte activity, rather than a generalized hyperactivity of the immune system (Kohler and Vaughan, 1982).

As Baker (1987) indicates, the immune system consists of many subsystems and there are many ways of measuring function. Subsystems may not move in the same direction to any specific stress and even when the stress is specified, it is mediated by a high degree of individual variability to that stimulus (both inter and intra differences). However, there is sufficient evidence to say that the emotions have important effects on the immune system.

Mental well-being

Days lost each year due to psychological disorder, that is reduced mental well-being, nervous debility and tension headaches etc., continue to show an increase. Table 5.3 indicates the number of work days lost in Great Britain for certain mental and stress related causes; both psychoses and neuroses causes show increases among men and women over a two year period (1982/3–1984/5). Of the 328 million days lost in 1984–5, 53 million (16%) were due to mental health causes. A look at the reasons given by British men for days off due to stress-related illness (Table 5.9) indicates a high increase over a twenty-five year period in the category of 'nervousness, debility and headache'. This, of course may simply reflect changing attitudes toward psychosomatic illness, i.e., men are now prepared to admit that they suffer from these illnesses. However, as shown in Table 5.10, other evidence indicates that the problem is real.

In England, general practice consultation rates for mental disorders were 300 per 1000 population, exceeded only by coughs, colds and bronchitis (Table 5.10). 5% of men and 12% of women were on tranquillizers in 1976. By the mid 1970s, the number of prescriptions for tranquillizers dispensed by the National Health Service in England had grown significantly (Table 5.11) (Melhuish, 1978).

Health costs for mental illness are reported to exceed $36 billion each year in the US. A recent survey showed that 3.3% of all visits to US internists resulted in diagnosis of mental illness. For individuals between 25 and 44 years of age, the percentage was nearly double (Cypress, 1984). The relaxant Valium is the fourth most commonly prescribed drug for Americans. In 1984, psychotherapeutic drugs made up approximately 25% of all out-patient prescriptions (Baum *et al.* 1984).

A study of a large out-patient and hospital care organization in

Table 5.9 Percentage increase in absenteeism due to stress related illness; Males 1954/5–1978/9

Diagnosis	Increase %
Nervousness, debility, headache	528
Ill-defined symptoms	101
Psychoneuroses and psychoses	49
Heart disease	134
Other forms of heart disease	38
Hypertensive disease	123

Source: Hingley and Cooper, *Stress and the Nurse Manager* (1986).

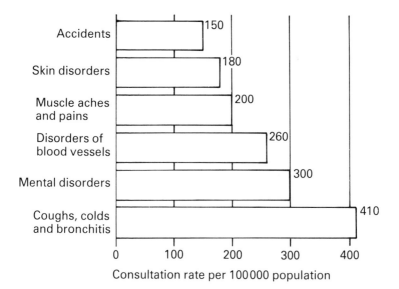

Table 5.10 General practice consultation rates for various illnesses and accidents

Source: Melhuish, *Executive Health* (1978).

the Washington DC area found that anxiety/stress was the topic most demanded by their patients in terms of health education and promotion (Nicholson *et al.*, 1983).

In the US, Shostak (1980) declares that 'blue-collarites' appear to share disproportionately in the nation's generally alarming mental health scene. One in four suffer from mild to moderate depression, anxiety or other emotional disorder at any given time.

The NIOSH report (1986) confirms these observations in that; 'mental disturbances, especially severe mental illnesses, are most heavily concentrated among workers with lower income, lower education, less skilled and less prestigious jobs'. Table 5.7, which lists death rates in the UK due to mental disorder, shows a similar pattern. The mortality rate among unskilled occupational groups is almost ten times higher than among professionals. The cause and/ or effect situation is complex. Studies of stress, emotional disorder and performance indicate that individuals who are emotionally disturbed, would be more frequently found in positions at lower occupational levels (Kornhauser, 1965). Relationships are also

143

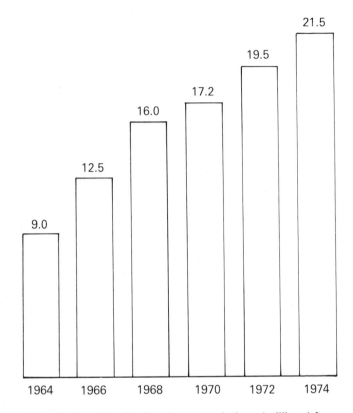

Table 5.11 National Health Service prescriptions (millions) for tranquillizers in England and Wales

Source: Melhuish, *Executive Health* (1978).

observed between emotional disorder and low educational attainment and intelligence (Miner and Anderson, 1958). Some evidence suggests that emotionally disturbed men gravitate to low-skill occupations but other evidence indicates that routine, boring work might cause emotional disturbance (Kornhauser, 1965). Poor mental well-being was directly related to unpleasant work conditions, the necessity to work fast, expenditure of physical effort and inconvenient hours. Since few would disagree that mental health is independent of physical health, the quality of mental well-being in the workplace is important. How an individual feels and thinks is dependent on the quality of physical health, and perhaps vice versa (Thorensen and Eagleston, 1984).

For example, Goldmeier *et al.* (1986) found that an association exists between psychiatric illness and the recurrence of genital herpes. Patients with high General Health Questionnaire (GHQ) scores have a sooner recurrence of the disorder but no other risk factor showed this relationship with time to recurrence. It is suggested that anxiety and depression can affect the recurrence rate of genital herpes via white cell dysfunction and so stress and emotional factors are implicated in the precipitation of a diagnosed condition.

Furthermore, a link between mental state and accident involvement has consistently been reported. In a review of the literature on shiftwork and accidents, Carter and Corlett (1981) found that; 'the mental state of the operator, whether he is fatigued or over-aroused, alert or distracted has been the most frequently suggested reason for accident-causation during shiftwork'. However, although extreme fatigue may have a detrimental effect on performance, moderate fatigue is not a significant factor in most occupational accidents. Carter and Corlett suggest that minor accidents are due to over-arousal or hyperalertness, which is associated with careless, and distracted behaviour. More serious accidents and errors of omission tend to be due to low levels of alertness and automatic cerebral functioning, for example, in monotonous, repetitive tasks, as described in Karasek's passive categorization (low demand, little decision making latitude, low level of stimulation). Studenski (1981) provides an illustration of stress in the work environment influencing emotional state. In a study of coalminers working in areas classified as low, medium and high accident rated mines, the occurrence of an incident produced a significant increase in anxiety among the men in the low and medium rated mines but not in the high accident rate mines. In this environment, anxiety levels actually fell following an incident. It is suggested that this is due to the (mistaken) implicit belief that a period of relative safety follows an accident. As the review presented by Miner and Brewer (1976) suggests, 'certain stresses in the occupational sphere can be a source of emotional disorder'. Therefore, stress is indirectly implicated in this stress-strain-accident outcome relationship because the individual is rendered more vulnerable, due to an impaired or reduced level of mental well-being. In fact, accident vulnerability also increases when the distressed individual engages in certain potentially harmful behaviours (e.g. the use of alcohol and other drugs).

Behavioural response to stress

Changes in behaviour that accompany exposure to stress include impulsive behaviour, excitability, restlessness, emotional outburst, excessive eating or loss of appetite, drug taking (including excessive drinking and smoking), absence from work and unstable employment history (Cox, 1985). Some of these behaviours might also have direct and indirect consequences for the health and well-being of the individual, and are likely to be causal in the accident process. In the following section, cigarette smoking, alcohol consumption and accidents will be discussed.

Smoking

People commonly turn to tobacco as a means of dealing with stressful situations. For example, one study of 35 000 nurses in the UK found that smoking was one of the most commonly reported ways of coping with stress (Hawkins *et al.*, 1983). The American Cancer Society suggests that the cost of smoking to the US economy has been estimated at $65 billion, due to lost productivity and medical treatment for smoking-related diseases. It contributes to an estimated 350 000 premature deaths each year (National Cancer Institute, 1985). The American Heart Association (1986) also notes; 'cigarette smoking is the biggest risk factor for sudden cardiac death: smokers have between two to four times the risk of non-smokers'. At least 25% of all deaths from CHD are caused by smoking; and in Great Britain, cancer of the trachea, bronchus and lung rate third as killer diseases of the 1980s among males in the 16–64 age group.

Approximately 30 major studies in ten countries have drawn an inescapable correlation between smoking and lung cancer: the heavy smoker is 20 times more likely to contract this disease than the non-smoker (Melhuish, 1978). High smoking levels are associated with neurosis and anxiety as well as physical illness (McCrae *et al.*, 1978). Thus, this behaviour is costly to society, industry and the individual. However, on a more positive note, smoking rates are declining. Between 1945 and 1972 smoking rates remained steady for men and increased in women. Smoking rates have fallen dramatically in Britain since 1972, leaving smokers as a minority. In 1972, 53% of all men were smokers, while only 38% of men smoked by 1982. Within the same decade, the percentage of women smoking fell from 41 to 33%. Table 5.12, the statistics available for Great Britain (1984) show that the percentage is now down to 36% overall for male cigarette smokers but both smoking and heavy drinking increases as socioeconomic status decreases. More men in the professional and managerial groups have given up cigarette smoking (current rate smoking 29–30%) and reduced their alcohol consumption (heavy drinkers 8–12%), whereas 45–49% of semi-skilled and unskilled workers are currently smoking and 24–26% are heavy drinkers (regularly 3–6 units of alcohol per day). The American Cancer Society (1986) have indicated that smokers in the US dropped from 42% of the population to 33%, while women smokers declined from 32 to 28%. The relatively smaller decrease in smoking among women may relate to an increased search for coping mechanisms among women juggling stressful home and work situations.

Higher occupational status is associated with better attitudes and access to health care and health screening and this could, in part, explain the differences between the various socioeconomic groups. However, personality and social influence also play roles in shaping behaviour. Cigarette smoking as a habit is acknowledged as socially acceptable within one environment but not another. Pressures to conform are strong. The role of personality (i.e. constitutional differences) also plays a part in individual differences in cigarette smoking behaviour (Chapter four). Therefore, smoking is a habit that may have a number of internal and

Table 5.12 Cigarette smoking and heavy alcohol consumption. British Males, by socio-economic status, 1984

Status	Current cigarette smokers %	Heavy drinkers %
Professional and similar	17	8
Employers and managers	29	12
Intermediate and junior non manual	30	15
Skilled manual and own account non-professional	40	25
Semi-skilled manual and personal service	45	24
Unskilled manual	49	26
All persons aged 18+	36	20

Source: Office of Population Census and Surveys, GHS 14. HMSO (1986).

external motives (Kalimo and Mejman, 1987). In addition to social pressure and personality disposition, the work environment and exposure to stress is also an important factor which influences smoking behaviour. Russek (1965) found that 46% of men in high stress occupations were smokers, compared to only 32% in low stress jobs. Caplan *et al.* (1975a) found that an inability to stop smoking was associated with high demand (i.e. quantitative workload; too much to do, time urgency etc.). Cigarette smoking is associated with tension and anxiety (McCrae *et al.*, 1978), and it appears that increased smoking under stress is proportional to the number of stressors within a given period of time (Lindenthal *et al.*, 1972). In a five-year retrospective study of accident involvement in a cotton textile plant, Metts (1982) found that smokers had a relatively greater risk of accident involvement. Only a very few employees actually smoked at the work station, so accidents were not simply the result of smoking activity (e.g. smoke in eyes or a preoccupation with handling smoking materials). However, the findings of this study were not unequivocal. Smoking and accident involvement was also due to the conflict resulting from certain types of tasks and not the behaviour of smoking alone; and individuals who had never smoked were more likely to have been involved in injury from the machines. Despite this observation, it is necessary to consider that a smoker may be involved in an accident or perform at a reduced capacity because concentration is impaired. This could be the direct effect of reduced nicotine levels and the desire to smoke in the addicted employee, who is unable to have a cigarette for extended periods of time at work; or because the chain of concentration is broken when the individual leaves a work station to have a cigarette. O'Connor (1985) indicates that perhaps it is more important to understand why an individual smokes. For example, under high stress it may be a secondary activity and a minor distraction from the task; in low activity, low stimulation situations, it might be associated with changing affective state to escape unpleasant situations, or to help overcome distraction and maintain a state of relaxation. However, this implies that individuals understand the reasons for their actions and/or are consciously aware. Difficulties would also be encountered because smoking behaviour is an addictive habit and expressed attitudes to smoking would be influenced by the process of cognitive dissonance.

Cigarette smoking contributes to death and illness in the form of

CHD and angina pectoris. Nicotine causes an increase in heart rate and blood pressure (indeed smoking a cigarette can raise systolic pressure by around 11 mm Hg and diastolic pressure by about 5 mm Hg in ambulatory and laboratory study conditions. These changes last for about fifteen minutes) (Pickering, 1988). In addition, carbon monoxide reduces the oxygen-carrying capacity of the blood and so forces the heart to work harder. In addition, inhaled substances cause damage to the lining of the blood vessels and enhance the likelihood that accumulations of cholesterol will occur in them (Hinkle, 1987). Smoking is linked to lung and bladder cancer, chronic bronchitis and emphysema. Research evidence shows that the consumption of nicotine and caffeine over long periods of time increases the probability of duodenal ulcers (Rowland *et al.*, 1988). In all instances, deaths due to these disorders are more prevalent among blue-collar workers. Although many cancer causes are job related, due to exposure to certain chemicals and substances (e.g. lung cancer among metal miners, prostate cancer in cadmium production workers; and leukaemia linked to low level radiation), Fink (1978) states that the major environmental cancer threat is cigarette smoking, perhaps followed by alcohol consumption.

Alcohol

As already mentioned, many more heavy drinkers are identified in the blue-collar occupational groups (Table 5.11). Alcohol is used to relieve stress and help the individual to manage a crisis, but in reality, alcohol renders the distressed person less able to cope. Table 5.3 shows that over 900 000 days were lost from work in Great Britain for 1984/5. This no doubt, considerably under represents the true picture of the extent of the problem, since people rarely admit to the amount of alcohol consumed and incapacity caused by this nefarious form of drug abuse. Indeed, the Health Education Authority (1987) estimates that over eight million working days is a better approximation of days lost each year due to alcohol consumption. Turning to drink is a coping mechanism adopted by all too many of us. The SAUS in Bristol (1985) suggest that between 1 and 5% of the British population are estimated to suffer from drinking problems and these problems can reflect themselves in the loss of jobs, cirrhosis of the liver, suicide, marriage breakdown, child abuse and accidents at home or work.

The cost of this in human terms is perhaps beyond meaningful calculation and so the real costs to industry and society are simply not known. The Capital Recovery Centre director, Jonathan Wallace (*The Times*, February 22; 1989) suggests that the real cost to industry is in excess of £2000 million when accidents, poor managerial judgement and judicial costs are included; whereas the Government currently estimates that alcohol abuse is costing industry £700 million per year. In the US, the National Institute on Alcohol Abuse and Alcoholism (1984/5) estimate costs to the US economy at $89.5 billion for 1980. Alcohol abuse is rated as America's third largest health problem after cancer and heart disease. Fleming (1986) suggests that costs may be as high as $120 billion annually. Studies of drinking problems in a number of occupational groups have shown the following:

1. Of 500 commercial airline pilots studied, 99% are at least occasional drinkers of alcohol. On days they are not flying, they admitted they consumed an average of five drinks a day. 13% indicated they used alcohol as a means of coping with stress. 52% said they drink more than two drinks everyday and 13% have been told they drink too much. More than a quarter of the pilots felt they needed to cut down on their drinking (Sloan and Cooper, 1986).

2. In another occupation involving serious safety risks, the offshore oil and gas industry, there seems to be a strong link between stress, alcohol consumption and accidents. As Burke (1985), editor of *Offshore*, suggests; 'one aspect of safety not discussed in polite places is the use and abuse of drugs and alcohol on a rig'. In fact, a study of about two hundred oil rig workers in the North Sea found that 61% often consumed alcohol during onshore leave as a method of relieving stress (Sutherland and Cooper, 1986).

3. Lachman (1983) estimates that alcoholic nurses in the US number over 40000 and Hawkins *et al.* (1983) found that alcohol, smoking and caffeine were the most common ways of dealing with stress among 35000 nurses in the UK. In addition, Hingley and Cooper (1986) report that 8% of nurse managers consume alcohol on a daily basis compared to 4.8% of the female population. In fact, the DHSS (1981)

indicate that alcohol abuse is becoming an increasingly severe problem for women generally. In 1980–81, 1 person in 2.4 requesting help to deal with alcoholism at local British councils was a woman, as compared to 1 in 4 applicants in 1974.

4. Shostak (1980) states that a high proportion of alcoholics in the USA are both employed and are blue-collar workers; '... as employees, they are often absent, accident prone and grievance prone. Most are believed to function at 60–70% of their potential and this in turn, is thought to demoralize many concerned co-workers and immediate supervisors' (Ray, 1973).

5. Figures available suggest that the average British manager is three-and-a-half times more likely to have an alcohol problem than the average Briton ... one in every 15 managers in this country is drinking alcohol at a level that will seriously detract from his efficiency at work and which will significantly affect all his work relationships (Melhuish, 1987).

Social influence and social pressure are strong influences in alcohol use and abuse (Plant, 1979), and Ojesjo (1980) suggests that occupation may be the most influential factor in determining drinking habits. In a study of hospitalization rates among US Navy enlisted personnel (Hoiberg, 1980), alcoholism rates increased considerably across pay grades within each occupational group, although it was possible to identify general, broad patterns of response to stress. Rates were consistently higher in occupations graded as non-traditional jobs (electrical, mechanical, maintenance specialist) compared to traditional jobs such as clerical, administrative and service specialists. Behavioural response to stress is, therefore, intricately linked to the culture of the organization. Margolis et al. (1974), Hurrell and Kroes (1975) and Selye (1976) have found that those individuals experiencing high job stress, drank more than those in low stress occupations, although it is not understood why some individuals under stress control their alcohol intake, whereas others become alcoholics. Robinson (1976) and Tsuang and Vandermey (1980) have suggested that genetic influence plays a significant part in severe alcoholism among males, although a distinction must be made between severe alcoholism and problem drinking. A genetic component could be the basis of certain personality characteristics, which are also likely to play a part in alcohol consumption and tolerance to alcohol (Chapter four).

Although some disagreement exists about the protective effects that alcohol in moderation gives to the heart, alcohol consumption has been associated with hypertension in a number of epidemiological studies (Larbi *et al.*, 1983); and it also contributes to obesity. Both high blood pressure and obesity increase the risk of CHD. However, the effects of alcohol on blood pressure show considerable individual variation (Pickering, 1988). Experimental studies are often difficult and/or confounded because the behavioural and physiological response to alcohol is affected by the person's gender, time of day, tolerance levels, previous use of the drug, the use of other drugs etc. Alcohol is used mainly for its mood altering effect (i.e. it is in the sedative-hypnotic class of drugs) but it is a toxic, habituating substance which directly or indirectly causes impairment of cellular function in every organ of the body (Fleming, 1986). It is absorbed quickly from the intestine, oxidized in the liver and the energy released there is adequate to meet most of its energy needs so that other nutrients are little used by the liver during oxidation (Bell *et al.*, 1980). Ethanol (i.e. beverage alcohol), diffuses rapidly into the brain where it has a depressant action. As Geller (1983) indicates, it depresses the nervous system when the drug level is up and causes a rebound excitement of the nervous system when the drug level falls. Alcoholic drink lowers the blood glucose level by inhibiting hepatic glucogenesis and by potentiating the insulin releasing properties of glucose and glucose-releasing foods. Thus, the consumption of large quantities of alcohol can cause hypoglycaemia.

Therefore, the effects of alcohol have immediate consequences in terms of behavioural change for the individual and those around him or her. Judgement and co-ordination are likely to be impaired and reactions are slowed; rendering the person more vulnerable to accident. The relationship between alcohol abuse and occupational accidents is a well documented and persistent problem in industry. The true extent of the problem is probably not known because of the conspiracy of silence that protects the worker. Individuals do not seem to realize that performance and judgement are impaired with intake of even relatively small amounts of alcohol but paradoxically, many people mistakenly believe that 'some' alcohol improves ability.

In the long term, liver damage and hypertension may lead to premature death, forced early retirement and incapacity from work and/or the social environment. Simple, linear relationships between alcohol consumption and outcomes may not be easily demonstrated, because as Gale (1987) suggests; 'causal relationships within complex systems are seen to be circular and not linear', that is, a person under stress may resort to escapist drinking, or the drinker may cope less well when confronted with a stress situation. In both instances, reduced physical and psychological well-being renders the individual susceptible to illness, disease and a further reduction in the ability to cope. This is termed the vicious, downward spiral of stress. This process is also prevalent in the study of accident causation, and the role of stress in increased vulnerability to accidents.

Accidents

Stress as causal in increased accident potential is a complex concept, not fully understood. In many instances, it is difficult to define the stressor and measure the effect. Often the issue of blame confuses an analysis. Accidents are not monocausal; the process is a complicated phenomenon consisting of three major factors; predisposing characteristics, situational characteristics and accident conditions (Suchman, 1961). Table 5.13 details the factors implicated. As host, there are many ways in which the individual is more or less susceptible to accidents. Cognitive appraisal of a situation affects response and reaction and so the person factor is a crucial variable in the accident process.

Before considering stress as causal in accident involvement, further comment on personal factors and accident potential is needed. This is a contentious issue with a long history, however, to state that approximately 90% of all accidents arise from some degree of human error or negligence (Bohemier, 1985) suggests that blame is set and that discussion serves no useful purpose. Yet, the statement is worthwhile if it is qualified further: since people design, build and install equipment; people use tools and equipment, ... by doing or neglecting to do, people create unsafe conditions and unsafe acts (James, 1983). Thus, an accident may be defined as an unplanned event, which could result in injury to persons, or in damage to plant, equipment, or both ... accidents

Table 5.13 Major factors in the accident phenomenon

Predisposing Characteristics	Situational Characteristics	Accident Conditions	Accident Effects
Susceptible host	Risk taking	Unexpected	Injury
Hazardous environment	Appraisal of hazard	Unavoidable	Damage
Injury producing agent	Margin of error	Unintentional	—

Source: Suchman (1961).

... are the consequences of unplanned (unsafe) acts or unplanned (unsafe) conditions performed or created by people (James, 1983). Acceptance of this concept and definition is a vital part of accident reduction as a proactive loss prevention strategy, that is, loss can be anticipated and measured, prevented or minimized. To simply accept that accidents are unpredictable, uncontrollable events caused by people and adopting a reactive approach (seeking cause and blame after the event to avoid further events) is unsatisfactory, inefficient and undesirable. More will be gained by understanding why people behave as they do, and how exposure to stress can affect behaviour. In fact, Warshaw (1979) states; 'of all the personal factors related to the causation of accidents only one emerged as a common denominator, a high level of stress at the time the accident occurred ... A person under stress is an accident about to happen'. There are several ways in which stress is implicated in the accident process, although these are not necessarily discrete, independent categories.

The physiological effects of stress include slowed reaction time, impaired concentration and poor physical co-ordination. Response to a stressor involves the activation of the sympathetic nervous system, which prepares the body for 'fight or flight' (Cannon, 1935). Glucose stored as glycogen in the liver is released; without an adequate intake of carbohydrate to maintain blood sugar levels, performance may be impaired, because the ability to concentrate is affected and vulnerability to accident-involvement enhanced. Poor environmental conditions (e.g. noise and temperature) are situational stressors described as external, performance shaping factors (Swain, 1967; cited by Miller and Swain, 1987). Direct physiological response is observable and the consequences are in terms of decreased level of motivation and effort, and increased rate of error. Noweir (1984) studied the effects of noise in the textile industry. The findings indicated that frequency and severity rates of accidents in high noise departments were greater than in low noise departments, even though the workers performed the same operations. Overall, in the three mills studied, employees in higher noise levels (above 90 dB(A)) were less productive, had more disciplinary actions, a higher rate of unauthorized absenteeism and absence due to illness, although differences were observed between workers from urban and rural communities.

It is also necessary to consider the stress/accident relationship in terms of load. Powell *et al.* (1971) found that the number of accidents appeared to be directly related to the amount of work that people did (load effect). Exposure to a stressor may cause over-arousal of physiological and/or psychological mechanisms and, thus, increase potential accident risk. Concentration is impaired if the individual has too many tasks to complete at the same time, or cannot cope with the task because skills are lacking (e.g. poor co-ordination). However, workload as a source of stress needs to be acknowledged as both overload and underload. Boredom and monotony on the assembly line, for example, may result in an accident, if the worker operates instinctively and thus fails to react to an emergency situation, or simply loses concentration. Fatigue due to work overload, unsatisfactory physical conditions in the work environment and poor relationships at work, all add to the stress chain (Kelly and Cooper, 1981) and, thereby, increase the likelihood of accident occurrence. Whitlock *et al.* (1977) have also shown that work-related stressful events may immediately precede automobile and domestic accidents in addition to industrial incidents. These spill-over consequences indicate the importance of considering the total lifestyle of the individual when assessing vulnerability to stress at work.

From a psychological perspective, insecurity, worry, fear and anxiety may impair the ability to concentrate (although this is also linked to physiological effects). Mental turmoil and distraction reduces efficiency and increases potential accident vulnerability. Mental and emotional factors play an important part in the thought process. What is often described as carelessness is more likely to be thoughtlessness because judgement of a situation is restricted or blocked. In addition, emotionally disturbing situations are often handled by misperception and distortion, so as to make them less threatening. Judgements are, therefore, likely to be unsound (Miner and Brewer, 1976). Hirschfeld and Behan (1963,

155

1966) also implicate psychological response in the stress/accident process. They have shown that stress is a prime contributor to the occurrence of an accident and that it is related to a slow recovery process and prolonged disability. Temperamental unsuitability to the situation or the task, personal and psychological problems are acknowledged as important individual factors that contribute to error in the offshore oil and gas exploration and development environment (Burgoyne Report on Offshore Safety, HMSO, 1981). Retrospective studies (Hellesøy *et al.*, 1985; Sutherland and Cooper, 1986) among offshore workers on drilling rigs and platforms in the North Sea, who regularly face dangerous and hazardous conditions, indicate that employees who have been involved in an accident at work, report less job satisfaction, demonstrate more depression and lower levels of mental well-being than their accident-free co-workers. However, it is not known if these observations are cause or effect. Prospective study may answer such questions.

Certain situations in the workplace elicit stress. Job and organizational structures that strictly control the workforce and impose constraint, do nothing to make the employee feel worthwhile. Change without consultation, unrealistic production expectations and a poor climate of interpersonal relations leads to reduced self-esteem. According to Opdyke and Thayer (1987), this leaves the worker feeling angry and powerless, thus; 'absenteeism, tardiness, sabotage, poor work quality, injury and illness, may be viewed as 'passive aggressive' employees' attempts to control work circumstances'. Research evidence indicates that organizational climate, measured as job satisfaction (Stagner *et al.*, 1952; Pestonjee *et al.*, 1977), is associated with accident rates. Although Pestonjee's study of workers in the mechanical section of a diesel locomotive plant found no difference in the job itself, satisfaction between accident and no-accident groups, significant differences in satisfaction with management, personal adjustment and social relations were observed. Smith *et al.* (1978) found that low accident-rated companies were significantly better than high-accident companies in terms of low absenteeism, labour turnover and the standard of selection procedures. In addition, the management commitment to safety training and use of experienced floor staff in employee training (rather than supervisors) were practices associated with low accident rates. These observations can be explained in terms of simple motivation theory, that is, that recognition and responsibility are important motivators which will promote job satis-faction (Herzberg, 1966). Satisfaction is a general indicator of all aspects of organization climate and safety climate (Sheehy and Chapman, 1987).

Exposure to increased risk is an obvious contributory factor in the occurrence of an accident; stress associated with dangerous and hazardous conditions and lack of training might increase accident potential (ILO, 1986). Constant fear of harm from exposure to toxic chemicals, explosives, radiation and/or other noxious agents are powerful sources of stress. Gertman and Haney (1985) studied the effects of stress on decision-making among test reactor site operators. Levels of workload, the detail of available procedures and personality (Type A and Locus of Control) were found to have an impact on performance. Previous studies (reported by Gertman and Haney) have also found that exposure to stress leads to increased error rate, narrowing of cognitive process, problem solving rigidity, preference for agreeable infor-mation, and easy information overload. Fault diagnosis and problem solving ability are also adversely affected by exposure to stress. In addition to actual objective risk, it is necessary to under-stand perceived risk as a contributory factor in accident involve-ment. Research evidence indicates that workers are likely to underestimate the risk of industrial accident, whereas the probability of occupational illness is correctly assessed (Sheehy and Chapman, 1987). Denial, or attempts to block out the reality of dangerous situations, may be a necessary coping mechanism, but discrepancies between subjective estimates of risk and their objective counterparts leave people poorly prepared to detect and cope with potential hazard (Sheehy and Chapman, 1987). However, some qualification of this assumption is needed. A distinction should be made between risk perception of the total environment as dangerous and risk associated with specific tasks that the individual must carry out in the course of duty. Raising the level of risk awareness in the environment (e.g. on an offshore gas platform, or in a nuclear power plant) might increase anxiety levels to an extent that the individual cannot function, with performance impaired and an accident more likely to occur. Raising the level of awareness regarding the risk associated with specific operations, allows the individual to reassess the risk in terms of error correc-tion potential and perceived degree of control in the situation.

In the US, compensation awards are made to individuals on the basis of psychiatric illness (i.e. functional disability). The cumulative effects of repeated and continuous exposure to stress over an entire career can be accepted as responsible for both physical and psychological ill health (Warshaw, 1979). Therefore, it is not inconceivable that awards will be made on similar grounds in accident involvement, that is, exposure to stress in the workplace will be recognized as the cumulative trauma which results in accident involvement. At the moment, the direct and indirect roles of psychosocial factors in the causation of accidents are still not clear and much needs to be done to clarify the situation (ILO; 1986). Accidents are not monocausal but are both a symptom and consequence of stress. Safety is more productive in the long run, when balanced against the cost of treatment of injuries, lost production time, compensation, replacement of workers and the cost of low morale in the workplace.

Costs of industrial accidents

Morgan and Davies (1981) state; 'there is no single basis for calculating the costs of occupational accidents. The basis depends on the purpose to which estimates are to be put'. In their analysis, the purpose was to indicate the scale of the problem to the community as a whole. The following statistics are presented with the same intention. In Great Britain alone, occupational accidents and disease in 1978 were calculated at an estimated cost of £2150 million. Losses due to alcoholism and vandalism in industry brought this figure in excess of £3000 million. This amount, according to Lord Kearton, former president of the Royal Society for the Prevention of Accidents, equalled the nation's income from North Sea Oil in 1978 (Chissick and Derricot, 1981). During 1980, there were 272 822 accidents at work, of which 565 were fatal (Health and Safety Executive (HSE), 1982). In an analysis of accidents occurring in 1981/2, and notified to HSE, Buck and Coleman (1985) estimated that incidents involving slipping, tripping and falling on the level (STFL) cost the nation in excess of £150 million annually. In the US, 1.9 million workers were injured in 1984, of these, 70 000 resulted in permanent disability and 11 500 were fatal. The overall cost to society of work-related accidents was $33 billion (Opdyke and Thayer, 1987).

However, this is only the tip of the iceberg (Heinrich, 1979; Morgan and Davies, 1981). It is believed that for every officially recorded injury (more than three days absence), there are one to three slight injuries (requiring one to three days absence), around 15–25 first-aid treatments (absence of less than one day) and 20–40 damage only incidents (Morgan and Davies, 1981). In addition to the direct cost of an accident, hidden variables should also be considered when assessing the true financial loss to an organization and the individual concerned. These include costs associated with:

1. Lost time of injured employee;
2. Time lost by other employees who stop work out of curiosity, sympathy, or to help;
3. Time lost by foremen, supervisors, safety officers;
   (a) to assist the injured,
   (b) to investigate the cause of the accident,
   (c) to arrange for production to be continued by some other employee,
   (d) selection, training or breaking-in of a new employee,
   (e) preparation of accident reports or to attend hearings, etc.;
4. Time spent on the case by a first-aid attendant/nurse;
5. Damage to machine tools and/or other property, or spoilage of material;
6. Incidental cost due to interference with production, failure to fulfil orders;
7. Employee welfare and benefit system;
8. Continuing wages of the injured employee;
9. Loss of profit on the injured employee's productivity, and on idle machines;
10. Consequences of the excitement or weakened morale due to the accident;
11. Overhead per injured employee which continues while the employee is a non-producer;
12. General administrative overheads; clerical and secretarial costs of processing reports and correspondence, stationery, etc.

(Heinrich, 1979; Bearham, 1976)

Accident statistics do indicate the enormity of the problem, but also assume that meaningful costs can be put on the price of a life prematurely ended. The true costs of an incident can have a significant, negative impact on the financial condition of an organization.

159

ORGANIZATIONAL COSTS OF STRESS

All of the stress-strain-health outcome relationships discussed so far in this chapter, have an obvious impact on the organization and industry. Both physical and mental illness renders the employee unfit for work, and combine both to lessen the satisfaction obtained from work and/or reduce job performance and productivity levels. Thus, there are various ways that stress symptoms or outcomes are reflected in the workplace.

Job satisfaction and dissatisfaction are psychological states which allow for numerous and varied action alternatives (Henne and Locke, 1985). [Refer to Locke (1976) for a review of the nature and causes of job satisfaction]. Although not fully supported or understood, links between job stress, dissatisfaction, reduced mental well-being and poor self-concept are suggested (Kornhauser, 1965; Lock, 1976).

For example, French and Caplan (1973) have shown that work overload, role ambiguity and role conflict contributes to several indicators of physiological and psychological strain, including job dissatisfaction, elevated cholesterol, elevated heart rate and blood pressure and smoking. Other studies have shown that opportunity for participation is positively associated with job satisfaction and higher productivity levels (Coch and French, 1948); and non-participation is significantly related to 1. overall poor physical health; 2. escapist drinking; 3. low self-esteem; 4. low job satisfaction; 5. intention to quit the job; and 6. low motivation to work (Margolis *et al.*, 1974). Studies by Sales and House (1971) in three different samples of occupations indicated that job satisfaction may be associated with CHD. These negative relationships were strongest among white-collar groups and particularly for intrinsinc job satisfaction rather than extrinsic satisfaction. Jenkins (1971) has also reported links between job dissatisfaction and CHD although these findings are based on retrospective studies and so no assumptions about cause and/or effect can be made. Therefore, it is acknowledged that job dissatisfaction may produce reactions which are detrimental to the organization's aims and objectives. However, the notion that a satisfied worker will be a productive worker remains a contentious debate. Henne and Locke (1985) provide an excellent review of this issue and conclude that low performance should be viewed as simply one action alternative that may be taken by some people under some circumstances in response to dissatisfaction. It is in this context that stress researchers have identified job dissatisfaction as one possible response to a stress agent in the work environment. The job situation becomes the stimulus, or stressor (i.e. the independent variable) and the measured degree of reported job dissatisfaction is the outcome, or strain response (i.e. dependent variable). Since all emotions entail automatic physical response which affect bodily functions, some reciprocal relationships between psychological stress, job dissatisfaction and ill health is assumed to exist.

Although Henne and Locke declare that a variety of action alternatives exist for the dissatisfied employee, organizations seem to be prepared to accept that protests and attempts to change a negative situation may manifest in the form of:

1. Poor industrial relations;
2. Poor productivity/performance;
3. Union activity, including strikes;
4. Sabotage, vandalism and stealing.

Empirical evidence supports these observations (Henne and Locke, 1985). Job satisfaction also assumes importance because several studies have shown that it is one of five domains of life that influence life satisfaction, an index of the quality of life (i.e. family, health, community, work and spare time activity, reported Brief and Hollenbeck, 1985).

Two further consequences of job dissatisfaction must be considered, in that the individual may withdraw from the organization to escape or avoid a negative situation through absenteeism or by quitting the job. Absenteeism may be due to many factors (family commitments, weather conditions, voluntary withdrawal and illness) but Miner and Brewer (1976) found that poor health, especially poor psychological well-being, is a major cause of absenteeism. Table 5.14, for 1984, shows that the average number of restricted activity days per year and the average number of physician consultations, increases as socioeconomic status of working males decreases, especially in the 45–64 age group. Certain differences in reporting requirements may confound these statistics, however, other sources also indicate that absenteeism among blue collar males is a serious problem for industry. The World Health Organization (1984) reports that absenteeism has increased in all industrialized nations over the last ten years. In the US, blue-collar absenteeism in many industries is as high as

161

Table 5.14 Acute sickness and consultations with general medical practitioners by age and socio-economic group, Great Britain, 1984

	Average number of restricted activity days per person per year (males)		Average number of consultations per person per year (males)	
	16–44	45–64	16–44	45–64
Professional	9	10	2	2
Employers and managers	10	18	2	3
Intermediate and junior nonmanual	14	25	2	4
Skilled manual and own account nonprofessional	18	30	2	4
Semiskilled manual and personal service	13	29	2	5
Unskilled, manual	14	44	2	8
All persons	14	26	2	4

Source: General Household Survey: HMSO (1986).

10–20% of the workforce (Lawler, 1971) and annually costs an estimated $26.4 billion (Steers and Rhodes, 1978).

There is a positive relationship between stress levels at work and frequency and duration of absenteeism; also a tendency for progression from absenteeism to labour turnover (Muchinsky, 1977). Job dissatisfaction is acknowledged as a major factor in blue-collar absenteeism from work, intention to quit, and labour turnover (Porter and Steers, 1973). Job satisfaction, job context, job content and personality factors have been shown to relate to labour turnover (Gruneberg and Oborne, 1982). Research evidence indicates that dissatisfaction with pay, failed expectations, inconsiderate leadership, lack of autonomy and poor social support from colleagues are all factors associated with high rates of labour turnover. In addition, certain person-variables are related to high turnover; together with age and tenure (i.e. the young and those identified as job-hoppers), high anxiety, ambition, aggression and emotional insecurity are characteristics of individuals who are more likely to leave the organization (Porter and Steers, 1973). Typically the negative correlations between satisfaction and turnover or absenteeism are not very large (about 30%); yet as Henne and Locke point out, a rational individual would not base such actions solely on feelings but also considers additional factors such as the cost of the action and the alternatives available (e.g. loss of earnings/bonus, the state of the labour market etc.). Clearly, labour turnover is a complex issue, but it is an important factor to consider when the high costs of training and induction of new personnel are assessed. It is also a critical consideration when the stability of the work group and/or the team is a prime factor in safe working practices. Constant change disrupts the work routine and the morale of the group. The Volvo experiment in Sweden, which reduced stress levels at work by changing highly repetitive, short-cycle work into jobs offering challenge, variety, and inter-personal contact through the introduction of autonomous work groups (a small group of assembly workers putting together a complete vehicle), showed that the workers generally responded with improved productivity, reduced levels of experienced occupational stress, and lower levels of absenteeism (Katz and Kahn, 1978).

One observation that might provide an alternative explanation for the job satisfaction and organizational outcome debate, is the argument that job satisfaction can be a dispositional source and is thus a determinant of job attitudes (Staw et al. 1986; Gerhart, 1987). This suggestion has obvious implications for the study of job satisfaction in the implementation of intervention strategies, such as job design, selection of personnel and the operationaliz-ation of job dissatisfaction as a stress outcome variable. Clearly this is an issue which will receive further attention. No doubt some differences in research findings may exist because of the variability in conceptualising job satisfaction, i.e. is it a global or multi-dimensional concept? The issue becomes more complicated by the findings reported by Howard et al. (1986). In a study of managers, classified as Type A or Type B individuals, it was observed that intrinsic job satisfaction appears to have both a direct and moderating effect on the stress associated with role ambiguity and changes in blood pressure. Therefore, they suggest that intrinsic job satisfaction is probably best considered as a moderating variable in the job stress model ... and that ... its relation to health may be more important than is generally recognized.

SUMMARY

In this chapter, the consequences and costs of mismanaged stress have been considered in terms of physical, psychological and behavioural outcomes. Unequivocal evidence to support these associations may not be available, because the temporal relationships between exposure to stress and the development of disease are not yet understood. In addition, such relationships may be circular, not linear, thus further complicating our understanding of cause and/or effect. However, it would seem that stress does play a role, either directly or indirectly in the health-ill health dimension, which is costly to the individual, industry and society. Many investigations have considered stress specifically among the medical professions; these studies are presented in the next chapter.

6

Stress and the Health Professions

Evidence from a growing body of research suggests that certain individuals, in a variety of occupations, are increasingly exposed to unacceptable levels of job-related stress. Our rationale for this book is the belief that individuals working as health professionals will perform more effectively, if they understand the role of stress in their own lives and the impact that it might have on others. In this chapter we are able to focus only on a few of these different groups; 1. dentists; 2. ambulance/paramedics; 3. nurses and; 4. doctors. Lack of space dictates this decision but does not imply that other occupational categories are less important. On the contrary, an understanding of stress is important for all health professionals because:

1. They play a major role in society, which is needed and valued. Stress can lead to burnout, illness, labour turnover, absenteeism, poor morale and reduced efficiency and performance. Thus, it is costly to the individual, the health providing bodies and society.
2. They have a profound impact on peoples' lives. In addition to the stressors that affect other professional groups, health professionals deal in face-to-face interactions with the client, in situations characterized by physical suffering, deformity and death. Additionally, they may inflict more pain or discomfort through treatment. As skilled employees, their competence is continually on trial and highly visible. The repercussions of mistakes are enormous in terms of the lives of others, the well-being of society and for the individual involved (i.e. self-esteem, fulfilment and satisfaction). Responsibility for others is an acknowledged

major source of stress (Caplan *et al.*, 1975b) and so the work of the health care professional would appear to be inherently stressful.

3. Exposure to increased risk of disease or injury may be an added source of pressure, which could be exacerbated because these individuals are not permitted to show symptoms of stress and are expected to remain controlled, calm and detached, whilst also expressing appropriate levels of emotional involvement and concern.

4. Many health care professionals work in boundary situations, i.e. at the interface between the stress of the patient, the family, other staff and the organization/ hospital. The organizational role which is at a boundary is by definition a potential high risk role conflict situation and is, thus, highly stressful (Kahn *et al.*, 1964).

In fact, these issues pose problems for researchers because it is necessary to understand that certain people might choose to be helpers, characterized by traits and predispositions not found in the population in general. In addition, standardized stressor and outcome measures may be confounded because defence mechanisms are activated against the situations which are encountered on a daily basis (Firth and Morrison, 1986). Although it is possible to identify categories of potential stressors, research efforts need to focus on different occupational health care groups because the valence of stressor factors will vary as a function of the job and outcomes will be mediated by a wide variety of personal factors. Despite this, similarities will exist and patterns emerge. In the discussion of each group that follows, the strains and pressures of the job are identified where available (i.e. the outcomes and symptoms of stress) and the major sources of stress described.

DENTISTS

From an early American study reported by Russek (1962), it was proposed that the high incidence of CHD among dentists might be due to the stressful nature of the job, rather than simply linked to diet and heredity alone. General dental practitioners and oral surgeons had the highest incidence of CHD compared to orthodontists and periodontists; but it is not possible to make any assumptions about cause or effect from findings such as these. It may be that a certain type of person with a predisposition to CHD is attracted to dentistry and to certain specialities in particular. Nevertheless, other more recent surveys and statistics have indicated that dentistry may be a stressful occupation because it is also associated with job dissatisfaction, high anxiety, perhaps linked with pain in the low part of the back and burnout, elevated rates of suicide, drug abuse, alcoholism, and divorce; in addition to an increased risk for cardiovascular disease (Howard *et al.*, 1976; Cooper, 1980; Edelwich and Brodsky, 1980). Bilodeau *et al.* (1983) found no evidence of a higher incidence of arrhythmias among dentists than in the general population (using ECG recording) and only rarely observed a change in ventricular rhythms when the dentist was confronted with a difficult patient — but it should be noted that this small sample of army dentists observed are not representative of dentists generally. Despite this, more studies of this type are needed to investigate the effects of a stressor on physiological change, in order to understand the mechanisms through which stress may exert a deleterious effect.

Given that an apparent stress condition seems to exist among this occupational group, many investigations have attempted to identify stressors associated with the dental profession. The stress experienced by dentists is, in many instances, typical of those individuals working in health care but the unique nature of the job highlights certain problems that are specific to this occupational group. In this review, the focus will be on investigations that have identified predictors of stressor outcomes (i.e. psychological or physical indicators of strain), rather than presenting the data on purely self-report surveys (see Cooper, 1980; Kent, 1987 for reviews). Although these descriptive studies provide vital information and are basic to more complex investigations in identifying potential stress agents, they do not permit us to distinguish between positive stress, which provides a challenge, motivation and the variety necessary for living and distress, which is destructive in its consequences. However, one study in this category should be mentioned because it identifies an important issue. Corah *et al.* (1982) asked dentists for information on both the frequency and the intensity of stress situations. They found that patients showing fear occurred usually more than twice a week for many of them but was rated the least stressful of the ten events identified. However, the most stressful situation seemed to occur when the patient grabbed the dentist's hand, yet this only happened very infrequently (i.e. once a week, or less for 94% of the sample). As Kent (1987) indicates in his review, the concerns tend to be more with the incidence of routine stressors in dentistry, (i.e. patients missing appointments and not paying bills), rather than major problems, such as the death of a patient.

One study reported in Canada (Howard *et al.*, 1976) and based on an in-depth examination of 33 dentists, aimed to identify the predictors of job satisfaction and to study the relationship between physical conditions and stress. They found that exercise versus non-exercise was related to physical working capacity (cardio-vascular fitness), and a lower average number of stress symptoms. These dentists were always or usually ahead of schedule and job satisfaction was predicted by the perceived degree that the job interfered with their personal life and the length of time spent in the same location. Times pressures, high caseload and falling behind schedule, were frequently reported stressors among dentists, which may be related to economic factors and financial worries associated with the need to build and maintain a practice. Howard *et al.* (1976) showed that dentists with the highest income of the sample (US\$36000 v. \$29800) tended to be behind schedule, worked longer hours per day, worked more evenings per week and took less time for lunch than the other respondents. In addition, higher stress symptom scores were associated with the higher income dentists; the need for a high income was related to a heavy work schedule and a stressful life-style. This high level of time spent in direct contact with patients may also render the dentist more vulnerable to burnout, especially since many dentists work in single practices and so have little opportunity to consult with peers about their problems.

In a larger study, dentists were screened while attending a California Dental Association scientific meeting. There were two objectives in this investigation. First, to find out what dentists themselves felt were the major sources of stress and second, to find out what job characteristics and personality factors are linked to physiological indicators of dentists at risk from CHD (Cooper *et al.*, 1978; Cooper, 1980). The results from 150 dentists indicated that coping with difficult patients, and trying to keep to a schedule were the most stressful aspects of the job. This was based on mean score ratings of the intensity of each stressor and the ranking position of the 15 stress variables identified in former interviews as potential stress agents. Also perceived as stressful, but to a much lesser degree, were the issues of too much work, unsatisfactory auxiliary help and administrative duties. It was expected that life stage and age (i.e. experience) of the individual would mediate in the perception of certain stressors. However, the age-related data indicated that coping with difficult patients and trying to keep to a schedule were considered to be the most stressful factors, regardless of age but attempting to sustain or build a practice was perceived as more stressful by the younger dentists. Multiple regression analysis was used to identify the predictors of physiological indices of CHD. Controlling for age effects, it was observed that four variables relating to the managerial and administrative aspects of dentistry, an anxiety predisposition (measured with the 16PF, factor QII), being perceived as an inflictor of pain and the job interfering with personal life, significantly contributed to 32% of the total variance on high diastolic blood pressure. However, the variable, coping with difficult patients correlated in the opposite direction from that one would have predicted. This suggests that either the dentist at risk does not face this difficulty, does not reveal it, has denied or repressed it or is truly unaware of the difficulty (Cooper, 1980) (Table 6.1). Nine variables significantly predicted high systolic blood pressure, contributing to 28% of the variance. Similar predictors again emerged as for raised diastolic blood pressure and it is interesting to note that for this group, too little work was predictive of raised blood pressure (i.e. an underload situation is thus a source of stress) (Table 6.2). It can be seen from Table 6.3 that there were also nine variables significantly predicting borderline or abnormal ECG readings (occurring among 17% of the sample) and together they contributed to 21% of the total variance. These were slightly different factors from those associated with raised blood pressure and included personality traits such as being emotionally less stable, controlled/socially precise and venturesome. Abnormal ECG was also predicted by routine and dull work, difficult physical conditions and low patient appreciation. No significant predictors of pulse rate were identified within the criteria probability ($p < 0.05$), presumably because pulse rate is less reliable than blood pressure or ECG. Overall, the only predictor variable to emerge across all health criteria measures was the pressure associated with the demands of sustaining and building a practice and this observation was supported by the findings of Howard *et al.* (1976). It is also important to note that

Table 6.1 Personality and job stressors as predictors of diastolic blood pressure

Personality and rated job pressures
Age
Dentist as inflictor of pain
Coping with difficult patients
Administrative duties
Too little work
16PF factor QII 'anxiety'
Sustaining and building a practice
Job interfering with personal life

$F = 6.88 \ p < 0.01$
$R = 0.32$
Source: Cooper (1980).

Table 6.2 Personality and job stressors as predictors of systolic blood pressure

Personality and rated job pressures
Age
Sustaining and building a practice
Too little work
Administrative duties
Coping with difficult patients
Unsatisfactory auxiliary help
Dentist as inflictor of pain
16PF factor QII 'anxiety'
16PF factor 0 'apprehensive'

$F = 4.70 \ p < 0.01$
$R = 0.28$
Source: Cooper (1980).

rated job pressures emerged as consistent predictors of health measures, whereas personality variables assumed only a minor role in the health outcome relationships. Although this study is limited in that it is restricted to a volunteer sample of almost exclusively male dentists attending a conference, it does provide an interesting insight into the combined use of self-report, subjective feelings and objective medical data in the identification of factors associated with increased risk of heart disease.

Table 6.3 Personality and job stressors as predictors of ECG

Personality and rated job pressures

Sustaining and building a practice
Low patient appreciation
Age
16PF factor Q3 'controlled, socially precise'
Interaction with patient
16PF factor H 'venturesome'
Routine and dull work
16PF factor C 'less emtionally stable'
Difficult physical working conditions

$F = 3.25\ p < 0.05$
$R = 0.21$
Source: Cooper (1980).

One final study will be presented in some detail in this section. It consists of an examination of job satisfaction, mental health and job stress among 484 general dental practitioners in the UK (Cooper *et al.*, 1987, 1988c). Using in-depth interview and a questionnaire survey with an 85% response rate, it was possible to explore the relationship between some of the possible causes of stress and stressor outcomes among a representative population of dental practitioners and to observe differences between male and female (18% of the sample) dentists. Table 6.4 presents the factor analysis solution of the potential stressor variables rated by respondents along a 5-point Likert-type scale and Table 6.5 shows the principle sources of stress (priority ranking) reported by male and female dentists. These findings support the work of Furnham (1983), that is, that stress factors are associated with 1. the needs of the dentist; 2. the needs of the patient; and 3. the needs of the practice. This third factor is linked to both of the other needs and focuses on the elements of scheduling pressures, income need pressures, staffing pressures and quality control pressures (Cooper *et al.*, 1987). On stressor outcomes, measured as reduced mental well-being and job dissatisfaction, male dentists showed significantly higher levels of free floating anxiety, depression and phobic anxiety than the normative population, while female dentists only showed higher levels on the anxiety dimension than the population in general; approximately one-third of the sample reported job dissatisfaction. However, this group had significantly lower scores

171

than the general population on the dimensions of depression, obsessionality and somatic anxiety, which indicates a better level of mental health on these dimensions (measured by the Crown Crisp Experiential Index, Crown and Crisp, 1979).

Using multiple regression analysis, it was observed that overall mental well-being was predicted by all the five job stressor factors identified (Table 6.4) and together these explained approximately 15% of the total variance of high mental ill health. When the regression statistics were run separately by sex, among female dentists, only three of the factors reached criterion (i.e. time and scheduling pressures, pay-related stressors and patients' unfavourable perception of dentists). For male dentists, the Type A coronary prone behaviour disposition and length of time since qualification (and all five job stressor factors) were identified as significant predictors of overall low mental well-being. Thus, the more one exhibits Type A behaviour and the greater work-induced stress is experienced, the more one tends towards a poor level of mental health. These effects also seem to persist regardless of work experience among the male dentists (Cooper *et al.*, 1988b). However, as more female dentists enter the profession, these effects might be seen over time among the women as well. The data were not as revealing for the precursors of job satisfaction among dentists and as the authors reflect, this may be a result of the ambivalent feelings dentists have. For example, previous research (Cooper *et al.*, 1978) shows that the activities dentists report liking most — human contact — were also a source of major problems. Thus, regression analysis revealed four factors (i.e. patients' unfavourable perception of dentists, time and scheduling pressures, staff and technical problems and marital status) predicting job dissatisfaction, but these explained only 10% of the total variance. When the analysis was run separately by sex, only factors one and three were identified as predictors of job dissatisfaction among the female dentists (11% variance); and for males, net pay and length of time since qualification entered the equation with the stressor factors to also explain 11% of the total variance. Status within the profession as indicated by whether employed full- or part-time and whether one owns one's practice, does not seem to influence either mental well-being or levels of job satisfaction. These results do contribute to a better understanding of mental ill-health among dentists but the observed relationship between work-induced stress and reduced well-being cannot be interpreted in any

Table 6.4 Factor analysis of work stressors for general dental practitioners

---

Stressor item

Factor 1 Time and scheduling pressures (22.6% of variance)
1. Working under constant time pressures;
2. Keeping to appointment schedules;
3. Too much work;
4. Maintaining high levels of concentration for long periods, and with few breaks;
5. Running behind schedule;
6. Working quickly to see as many patients as possible;
7. Seeing more patients than you want to, for income reasons;
8. Long working hours.

Factor 2 Pay-related stressors (8.1% of variance)
1. Conflicts between profit needs and professional ethics;
2. Earning enough money to meet your lifestyle needs;
3. Working constraints set by the NHS;
4. The piecework system of payment;
5. Inability to meet your own expectations and/or standards;
6. Quoting fees and collecting payments.

Factor 3 Patients' unfavourable perception of dentists (6.2% of variance)
1. Feeling underrated by patients;
2. Feeling isolated;
3. Lack of patient appreciation and awareness of the complex nature of the job;
4. Being perceived as an inflictor of pain;
5. Repetitive nature of work.

Factor 4 Staff and technical problems (4.9% of variance)
1. Staff-related problems, e.g. absenteeism, friction;
2. Unsatisfactory auxiliary help;
3. Equipment breakdowns and defective materials;
4. Unsatisfactory laboratory items and/or laboratory delays;
5. Interpersonal problems with work colleagues.

Factor 5 Problems dealing with patients (4% of variance)
1. The possibility of making mistakes, e.g. breaking a root tip;
2. Actually making mistakes;
3. Dissatisfied patients;
4. A patient having a medical emergency in the surgery;
5. Treating extremely nervous patients;
6. Coping with difficult, unco-operative patients.

Source: Cooper, Watts and Kelly (1987).

causal fashion. Clearly prospective, longitudinal research is needed. This would also help to determine the role of Type A behaviour as a mediator of the stress response, i.e. does TAB increase over time, especially among young female dentists as their numbers and length of time in the profession increases. It would

173

Table 6.5 Principal sources of stress—dental practitioners

Source/item	Male ranking (n = 399)		Female ranking (n = 85)	
	Rank	% giving 4–5 rating	Rank	% giving 4–5 rating
Medical emergency in surgery	1	54	1	72
Difficult, unco-operative patients	2	53	4	49
Running behind schedule	3	49	5	47
Constant time pressures	4	48	7	40
Very nervous patients	5	44	9	38
Dissatisfied patients	6=	41	2	54
Making mistakes	6=	41	(16)	
High concentration levels	8	39	(14)	
Earning enough money for lifestyle needs	9	38	(25)	
Patients querying your expertise	10=		6	44
Defects in equipment/materials	10=		8	39
Quoting fees and collecting payments	12		10	35

Source: Cooper, Watts and Kelly (1987).

seem that both UK and USA based dentists have the same major source of stress, i.e. keeping and maintaining a practice. Implicit in this is the need to work quickly under constant time pressures and to work long hours in order to see as many patients as possible for income generation. Clearly, this state of affairs seems to be detrimental to both the dentist, and to the public that they serve.

AMBULANCE AND PARAMEDICS

The rationale for presenting American studies of the relationship between work stress and burnout among paramedics, with data on the British ambulance service, is intended to pre-empt some of the problems that might be faced in the UK as personnel are expected to extend their training with paramedic instruction. Ambulance work offers variety, challenge, responsibility, service to the community and potential for the experience of stress (James, 1988). However, burnout, the negative consequences of exposure to stress, described as emotional exhaustion and cynicism towards one's work, might affect ambulance and paramedic personnel. Burnout is related to alcohol and drug abuse, poor physical health, family and work-related problems including increased absentee-ism, poor performance, loss of concern for patients, job dissatisfaction and labour turnover (Maslach and Jackson, 1981; Seamonds, 1983). Concern with the issue of burnout in ambulance personnel and paramedics is expressed for three main reasons; 1. at the scene of an incident these individuals must assume the full responsibility for dealing with any situation that arises (Hoiberg, 1982); 2. as emergency medical technicians they must often work under full public scrutiny, i.e. from the patient's family and other bystanders (Grigsby and McKnew, 1988); and 3. often in a potentially hazardous environment. They are also in a boundary role between the outside world of the public and the hospital system — an inherently stressful role (Margolis *et al.*, 1974). Thus, this group of individuals are subjected to the routine, work-related stressors common to all health care professionals but with additional pressures of trying to cope in emergency contexts. The work is also unpredictable and, therefore, potentially stressful. However, as James (1988) indicates, this might be a strong attraction of the job for some individuals, those wanting knife-edge, non-routine work.

Very little research to identify sources of stress has been carried out among this occupational group but recent attention has focused in this direction. James (1988) utilized interview and questionnaire methodology over a series of studies to identify and model the potential sources of stress as perceived by male, operational personnel within the British Ambulance Service in the South West of England. By using principal component analysis to identify orthogonal factors, a four-factor model of job stress was derived which accounted for 36% of the total variance. This included stressor variables associated with 1. organization and management; 2. new, unfamiliar and difficult duties (i.e. uncertainty); 3. work overload; and 4. interpersonal relations (Table 6.6).

Subsequent testing provided favourable reliability data for this model of stress (correlation coefficients in the order of .89–.97). By using multiple regression analysis, James observed that scores on the stressor factors were related to length of service and attributions of chance and powerful others, that is, where personnel perceive that chance and powerful others exert control over their life events and where length of service is short, the stronger is their perception of stress. Rank, type of work-shift and the personality

175

Table 6.6 Stress in British ambulance personnel. A four-factor model.

Factor 1 Organization and management aspects
Not being consulted by superiors;
Inadequate authority to carry out responsibilities;
Under-use of ability and potential;
Inadequate support from management;
No part in management decisions;
Poor or inadequate supervision;
Have to obtain information by indirect means;
Working with inadequate information;
Lack of recognition by superiors;
Not knowing what is expected of you;
Unable to have your own way;
Having to do things you disagree with;
Colleagues not doing the job the same way that you do;
Differences of opinion between control and operational staff;
Having to discipline colleagues;
Competition for promotion.

Factor 2 New, unfamiliar and difficult duties uncertainty
New or unfamiliar duties;
Crisis situations;
Effects of stress in others on you;
'Up-tight' between call-outs;
Critical/important decisions;
Relationship between stress and how you feel when you get to work;
Having to act in supervisory capacity;
Disagreeable duties;
Lack of control over situations;
Shiftwork;
Not knowing what is expected of you;
Working with inadequate information;
Dealing with anyone in pain;
Working with someone you do not like.

Factor 3 Work overload
Insufficient staff to cope with workload;
Too heavy a work load;
Tired or worn out at work;
Effects of work on health;
Inadequate pay for ambulance work;
Poor/inadequate facilities at work;
Relationship between stress and how you feel when you get to work;
Lack of recognition for good work;
Conflict of loyalty between home and work;
Ambulance Service more stressful than other jobs;
No part in management decisions.

Factor 4 Interpersonal relations
Dealing with injured children;
Death of patients;
Responsibility for work of others;

Working with someone you do not like;
Ambulance Service more stressful than other jobs;
Dealing with anyone in pain;
Colleagues not doing the job the same way as you;
Lack of recognition for good work;
Having to work with inadequate information;
Inappropriate or excessive discipline;
Differences of opinion between control and operational staff;
Having to obtain information by indirect means;
Competition for promotion

Source: James (1988).

variable of locus of control failed to predict any of the stress outcomes. Although this study begins to provide some insight on the potential stressors among ambulance personnel, it is necessary to extend this sample on a nationwide basis, if it is to be applied to the ambulance service in general. It would also be necessary to more extensively identify job predictors of stressor outcomes (i.e. physical, psychological and/or behavioural outcomes of symptoms of stress).

One study among paramedics in Maryland, USA, indicates that work-related stressors could be classified as administrative or clinical factors (Mitchell, 1984), with the former being the more significant. Administrative issues include long hours, excessive paperwork, lack of administrative support, the attitude of hospital personnel and low pay. Clinical stressors are associated with human tragedy, inherent physical dangers and the pressure to perform correctly in uncertain situations. Thus, there are some issues common to both UK and USA personnel. Such direct comparisons between James' study and the survey of work-stress burnout among paramedics in the USA (Grigsby and McKnew, 1988) cannot be made, because the aim of this investigation was to test a model of stress and burnout. These authors focused only on certain stressors, i.e. organizational characteristics and process, job demands and role characteristics and individual characteristics and expectations. However, a brief review of the results are informative because they provide some insight on potential problems of the ambulance service in the UK, as it continues to develop and change.

Using the Staff Burnout Scale for Health Professionals (Jones, 1980), the highest mean burnout score yet reported for any group of health professionals was obtained among 213 paramedics in the

177

State of South Carolina (85% male). Eighteen of the twenty-three independent measures significantly correlated with the burnout measure (Table 6.7). The strongest correlations were between job dissatisfaction and burnout ($r = 0.42$), and negative relations with co-workers and burnout ($r = 0.47$). Using stepwise multiple regression analysis, it was observed that eight variables contributed to explain 60% of the variance on burnout. The strongest predictor variable was 1. relationship with co-workers (almost

Table 6.7 Correlations of organizational, job and individual characteristics with the staff burnout scale

		Significance
1. Organizational characteristics and processes		
Work environment (negative)*;	0.36	<0.001
Social aspects (negative)*;	0.38	<0.001
Paperwork load;	0.27	<0.001
Pay inequality*;	0.21	<0.005
General job dissatisfaction.	0.42	<0.001
2. Job demands and role characteristics		
Number of 'runs' per month;	−0.16	<0.05
Weeks of vacation per year;	0.13	<0.05
Calls from home;	0.00	—
Physical threat on the job*;	0.23	<0.005
Certification requirements*;	0.36	<0.001
Negative relations with physicians;	0.23	<0.005
Negative relations with emergency department personnel;	0.33	<0.001
Negative relations with firefighters;	0.22	<0.005
Negative relations with law enforcement officers;	0.24	<0.001
Negative relations with co-workers;	0.47	<0.001
Negative relations with the public.	0.31	<0.001
3. Individual characteristics and expectations		
Age;	0.23	<0.005
Sex;	0.03	—
Marital status;	−0.06	—
Number of children;	0.19	<0.005
Year of EMT certification;	−0.01	—
Education level;	−0.06	—
Number of years expected to remain a paramedic.	0.31	<0.001

*two-item measure
$n = 206$
Source: Grigsby and McNew (1988).

22% of the variance), followed by; 2. job dissatisfaction (12%), and; 3. physical threat from job (13%). The remaining variables, negative work environment, certification requirements, age, paperwork load and negative relations with emergency department personnel all contributed to burnout in more minor, but still significant ways. As these authors suggest, burnout is a complex phenomenon which seems to be associated with organizational and job characteristics, rather than individual characteristics. Nevertheless it is not possible to make any assumptions about causality from these findings, and prospective research is still needed. The introduction of paramedic training into the UK might result in problems not yet anticipated, unless some of these issues are addressed. Ideally, any such investigations should start before changes are made and subsequent progress monitored carefully, to avoid the experience currently being reported in the USA.

NURSES

Within the National Health Service, nursing is the largest single professional group and constitutes over 50% of the total labour force. However, within this profession a wide variety of specialism is found, thus making any attempt to consider the relationship between stress and the occupation of nurse an impossible task unless certain qualifications are made, e.g. type of nursing, hospital and/or ward, etc. Since a review of the existing literature would also occupy a series of its own (and adequate reviews are available, see Marshall, 1980; Hingley and Cooper, 1986), this relatively brief section will be restricted to the discussion of studies that answer some of the research criticisms proposed by Marshall (1980) and aim to identify predictors of stress symptoms or outcomes among classified groups. This is consistent with our maxim that stress can have both positive and negative effects. However, the official statistics produced seem to indicate that there is a justified concern for the health and well-being of the nursing profession.

The Office of Population Surveys shows that nurses have a higher mortality ratio than might be expected in comparison to a professional group of workers (SMR for married women, aged 15–64 is 114 for nurses and 81 for professional women as a whole) and is also high compared to other traditionally female occupations (e.g. school teachers SMR = 80; typists, secretaries SMR = 68). Life expectancy is shorter among nurses than school teachers, typists, secretaries and social welfare workers (Hingley and Cooper, 1986). One study of 35 000 UK nurses indicates that smoking, alcohol and caffeine intake were commonly identified ways of coping with stress (Hawkins *et al.*, 1983). The links between these behaviours and the aetiology of heart disease and cancer have already been discussed. Although surveys show that the incidence of smoking among nurses compares favourably with the female general population, Hingley and Cooper (1986) found that nurse managers smoke more than other female professionals. These authors also found that around 8% of nurse managers admit to a daily intake of alcohol compared to 4.8% of the female population, and 52% of the sample identified alcohol consumption as a regular means of relaxation. Available information strongly suggests that women in the nursing profession are more likely to commit suicide than women in any other occupation. Gillespie and Gillespie (1986) also report that nurses top the list of all professionals in psychiatric out-patient referrals.

Although there are many reasons why an individual may be absent from work, Lunn (1975) points out that; it is not uncommon for hospitals to have to close some of their wards because of nurse shortages. These shortages are often attributed directly to sickness absence. Firth and Britton (1989) found that burnout variables were significant predictors of sickness absence and turnover among 106 qualified nurses working in long-stay settings in the UK. In a two-year follow-up study, it was observed that emotional exhaustion was associated with total time-off sick in the subsequent 12 months and was largely related to an increase in the number of episodes of absence lasting seven days or more. The role of social support as a moderator of stress was identified in this investigation, and absences of four or more days correlated with perceived impatience or defensiveness on the part of the immediate superior. Absenteeism is often a precursor for intention to quit and, in fact, Firth and Britton found that self-reported depersonalization towards the clients or others (a symptom of burnout) was a small, but significant predictor of turnover in the two year period. In a study of absenteeism among nurses, Clark (1975) found that:

1. Short term absence tends to increase as rank decreases and

pupil nurses take more frequent short spells of absence than all other grades of staff.

2. Differences observed between hospitals were not a function of size but may be explained in terms of the quality of interpersonal relationships. Wastage, however, does seem to be a function of hospital size and might be associated with communication problems characteristic of large bureaucracies.

3. Job satisfaction was not a significant predictor of absence behaviour. This conflicts with other findings that confirm a relationship between morale and absenteeism/intention to quit and may reflect differences in the way that the concept of job satisfaction is operationalized.

Without a standardized system of record keeping in the hospital services, it is not possible to produce accurate information on the costs of sickness, absenteeism and labour turnover among the nursing profession. However, scrutiny of the data available suggests that there is some cause for concern and this may be further exacerbated by the predicted demographic changes which could lead to staffing shortages in the nursing profession in the 1990s. Thus, there is a need to identify potential stressors and individual vulnerability to pressures in the workplace. Three broad categories of nursing will be considered; 1. qualified nurses; 2. student nurses and; 3. psychiatric nursing. It is acknowledged that such classification may be too broad and so the studies reported will also include a precise definition of the survey sample within each general category.

Qualified nurses

It was decided that another review of studies identifying sources of stress among nurses was not appropriate or necessary in this chapter. However, to provide a structure for the section, a summary of common stressors consistently identified is presented, together with the research criticisms put forward by Marshall (1980) in her extensive review. This is combined with a discussion of some recent studies that have attempted to take up these criticisms and challenges, to resolve the weaknesses of earlier research efforts. Having acknowledged that nursing seems to be a stressful occupation, it is thus more useful to consider research that does more than only identify stressor agents; nevertheless, some new surveys are included because they shed light on issues raised by Marshall (1980).

Stress among nurses

Table 6.8 shows the potential pressures that might exist in the nursing profession. Stressor agents intrinsic to the job of nursing include the necessity to engage in heavy physical work, in tasks that are highly unpleasant and which physically assail the senses. The nature of the work demands that shifts and unsocial hours are normally worked, and pay and/or benefits are not commensurate with the responsibility, task load or status of nurses. Work overload is the most commonly cited source of stress among nurses (Marshall, 1980). Overload may be of a quantitative nature because of staff shortages and this situation is exacerbated by absenteeism when the overworked employee becomes ill and/or unfit for duty (Jacobson, 1978). An emotional burden is also placed on absentee nurses because they also realize that they are adding to the problems of their already overworked colleagues. However, as Marshall (1980) suggests, it is necessary to probe this overload situation more deeply because as a respectable complaint, it might mask more serious issues. Overload might also be associated with qualitative load, that is the nurse experiences the stress of uncertainty in a situation because the work is too difficult

Table 6.8 Main stressor elements for the nurse

– nursing tasks
– workload
– death and dying
– uncertainty
– responsibility
– role conflicts
– relationships with: patients
relatives of patients
doctors
colleagues
– work:home conflict
– fulfilling others' expectations of the role of nurse

Source: Marshall (1980).

and/or training was inadequate. Underload is also potentially stressful, if the nurse believes that the opportunity to use his/her skills and abilities are denied. In some areas of nursing, workload and work situations may be unpredictable, for example, in the casualty or emergency wards and this creates uncertainties. It is also acknowledged that responsibility for people is more stressful than responsibility for things and is associated with increased risk for CHD (Wardwell *et al.*, 1964). The hierarchical nature of the workplace should provide clear guidelines related to the role of the nurse and the responsibility that is subsequently inherent to the job. However, in emergency situations and when staff shortages exist, these structures and demarcations breakdown, causing strains, conflicts, and pressures among the staff who must cope in a high-visibility environment and where they are denied the release of expressing felt tensions and stress.

Another significant stressor agent for the nursing profession is the issue of interpersonal relationships at work. Much has been written about the quality of relationships that exist between the nurse, patients, relatives, other work colleagues and superiors such as ward sisters or doctors. The nurse occupies an organizational role which is at a boundary, that is, acting between other departments or sectors of the health service and between the hospital/ health practice and the world of the public at large. Research has shown that these boundary roles are usually highly stressful and are subject to high role conflict (Kahn *et al.*, 1964). The nature of the nurse–patient relationship is of prime importance because it is a potential source of stress while at the same time providing a major source of job satisfaction (receiving positive feedback from patients and fulfilling a need to help). This serves to balance and attenuate stress and pressure (Marshall, 1980). Relationships at work with other colleagues and superiors can also act as a buffer against the strains and pressures of interaction with patients and relatives. Personnel who work with non-supportive, inconsiderate supervisors or colleagues are more likely to report negative feelings associated with job pressure (Buck, 1972; Lazarus, 1966). Poor quality relationships at work are associated with ineffective communication between individuals, job dissatisfaction and job-related threat to health (French and Caplan, 1973). As Marshall observes, the good ward sister provides support for subordinates and acts as an intermediary between them and the highly bureauc-ratized hierarchy ... bad sisters are an additional pressure for the nurse. The effective, supportive supervisor can ensure that potential nurse–doctor role conflict stress is also minimized (for example, by promoting an open organizational climate, adopting a considerate, rewarding style and using staff meetings to encourage participation in decision making).

Some of the pressures associated with relationships in the nursing profession are linked to the strains of fulfilling other people's expectations of the job. Conflicts are related to ethical issues, for example, the saving of life at any cost, the right to die with dignity, the morality of abortion, euthanasia, life support and brain-death, etc. The nurse is expected to cope without outwardly showing panic, tension, strain or symptoms of stress but at the same time is required to exhibit an acceptable balance between calm detachment and emotional involvement.

The importance of the quality of supportive relationships in nursing is again acknowledged as a buffer against the stress related to continual exposure to death and dying. It has been suggested that stress is directly and indirectly experienced through exposure to a dying patient. In order to cope, the nurse may adopt an impersonal attitude as a protective shield (Glaser and Strauss, 1968) and use avoidance tactics to reduce nurse–patient contact. These strategies may cause feelings of guilt and conflict related to the adequacy of medical and emotional caring thus provided. Research also shows that reaction to death is not invariant. It is a multi-faceted, complex concept which must take into account issues such as the age, status of the patient, perception of social loss, personal identification, degree of familiarity with the patient, and perceived responsibility for the patients death. Access to an adequate support network and training are viewed as coping mechanisms in these circumstances, however, it is likely that the pressures may spill over into home and social life and so the need for support will also extend into these areas of life for many nurses. Emotional involvement with patients, or reaction to a death at work, may spill over to home with detrimental consequences. In addition, as Marshall (1980) indicates, the tradition of the nurse as a single woman is fast disappearing, and many have family respon-sibilities which can have a negative spill over impact on work performance. Yet paradoxically, the family network can provide a source of emotional support which might be found lacking from work colleagues and superiors. An understanding of stress among nurses must, therefore, consider the home and work interface as a potential stressor and/or a mediator of the response to stress.

Observation 1

Most writers start by taking the existence of stress among nurses for granted (Marshall, 1980). Thus, is nursing stressful, what are the symptoms?

In the beginning of this section, concern was expressed for the health and well-being of nurses. Do recent studies reflect these concerns? One study reported by Nichols *et al.* (1981) is indicative of good morale and high levels of job satisfaction among nurses. This investigation was designed to assess nurses' reaction to intensive therapy work units (ITU) and make comparisons with nurses from renal units and medical and surgical wards. Consistently, in a sample of 119 nurses, ITUs were more likely to be described in positive rather than negative terms and 89% of the sample were basically happy with their job. One unit was predicted as problematic and confirmation of this was taken as validity of the questionnaire used in this survey. High fluctuation in workload, that is, it being too high or too low, was the most common source of discontent, and supports Marshall's review findings. In addition, 82% of nurses expressed dissatisfaction with feedback from the nurses in charge, or doctors. From these findings, the authors concluded that the claims of high levels of discontent and distress in ITU nurses did not stand up to empirical scrutiny. Furthermore, job satisfaction varied in relation to various psychosocial elements in the work setting, rather than the type of nursing involved. In fact, Hingley and Cooper (1986) reflect similar optimistic findings in their study of nurse managers (N = 515). Among this group, high levels of job satisfaction were reported and absence levels were low. However, labour turnover and loss to the profession was high (16%), so perhaps the dissatisfied nurse manager is quitting the job. This occupational group was also observed to be in good mental health, in contrast to the normative population on measures of anxiety, phobia and depression, although it was observed that some may be risking their health as a consequence of elevated smoking and drinking habits. However, this study was restricted to only nurse managers, who are often considered a source of stress among nurses in general.

Using a different approach, Pierce *et al.* (1987) investigated the

185

predictors of current stress states among Australian nurses ($n = 983$, a response rate of 67% from registered and student nurses). It was found that registered nurses in the high-stress group preferred slow change, and had poor self-esteem; those who felt poorly were also dissatisfied with their level of social support. Concern over the responsiveness of management in the hospital was the only important job-related stressor for this group. Student nurses who felt poorly or were dissatisfied with social support levels were ten times more likely to be in the high stress group. Job overload and unsatisfactory team status were the two most significant work-related stressors for the students.

The major weakness of these studies is their reliance on self-report data. However, it would seem that recent investigations have begun to overcome this problem by incorporating objective data into the research design. For example, Dončević et al. (1988) have combined physiological measurements with self-report data in a one-year longitudinal study of district nurses in Sweden. Although the groups studied were small ($n = 57$), they provided a representative sample and participation levels were high. The results clearly indicate that objective workload (measured in terms of size of district, number of patient consultations and home visits) was positively related to systolic blood pressure and morning plasma cortisol levels. These nurses also reported more sleep disturbances than the other nurses, and this may be a consequence or correlate of high arousal level (Akerstedt, 1987). Nevertheless, the general conclusion from the physiological data was that the district nurses in this study were in seemingly good health, with normal to good values for most measures taken.

As Marshall (1980) suggests, studies that actually measure symptoms of stress among qualified nurses are rare. It is simply assumed that a problem exists. Although it is acknowledged that it is unproductive to submit respondents to endless batteries of questionnaires without purpose, a requirement to evaluate stress management intervention demands that reliable pre and post outcome measures are obtained. Whenever possible, both objective and subjective dependent measures should be used. Also, we need more studies in the genre of Firth and Britton (1989) (i.e. a longitudinal survey, linking emotional exhaustion and role ambiguity with absenteeism), whereas, current research appears to be more preoccupied with the issue of differences in types of unit and types of nursing, etc. This introduces the second observation.

Observation 2

Is it useful, or meaningful, to generally discuss nurses and hospitals as homogenous categories? As Marshall (1980) points out, there are many distinctions which should perhaps be borne in mind when considering the pressures of nursing:

1. Specialization;
2. Level in the organization;
3. Experience;
4. Type of hospital;
5. Type of ward or unit.

Early researchers disagree about the extent to which stress in nursing varies as a function of the type of organization and/or type of patient, etc. or may be discussed in general terms (Marshall, 1980). However, it would seem that recent findings tend to support the view put forward by Weeks (1978), that a common set of factors is identifiable but these will assume differing priorities as a function of unit type and/or type of patient, etc. For example, in a study across five different types of nursing units, Gray-Toft and Anderson (1981) found that three major sources of stress were perhaps inherent to the job; that is, they were pervasive across patient-care units including medical, surgical, cardiovascular surgery, oncology and hospice nursing and were also experienced irrespective of the level of training received. They include stress related to:

1. Workload;
2. Death and Dying;
3. Inadequacy of preparation to meet the needs of patients and their families.

Other sources of stress identified as conflict with physicians and other nurses, lack of support and uncertainty concerning treatment, varied as a function of type of unit. Conflict with other nurses was significantly lower among hospice nurses than for all other groups, while nurses on the medical unit scored significantly higher on this factor. Uncertainty about treatment was also higher on the medical and oncology units but low in the hospice environment (i.e. palliative care for terminally ill patients). Unexpectedly, nurses on the medical unit had a total stress score which was significantly higher than hospice and surgical nurses and job satisfaction was also the lowest among this group. The level of stress among the hospice nurses was also unexpectedly low, given the exposure to death and dying. The authors suggest that the differences appeared to be related to the general work environment and the level of support received. The medical unit was older and included patients with a wide variety of medical conditions and communicable diseases that required isolation. Not surprisingly, levels of uncertainty were high. In contrast, the hospice was a new unit, with specially recruited and trained staff and a high staff–patient ratio. In this study, it was also observed that turnover was related to stress levels (NB path analysis shows that stress was a major determinant of the nurse's level of job satisfaction).

Some support for Gray-Toft and Anderson's findings is reported by Mitchell (1988) in a comparative study of hospice and hospital nurses (including coronary care, ITU and oncology). Greater levels of job dissatisfaction were reported by the hospital based nurses and more of these individuals had thoughts of changing their occupation within nursing or leaving the occupation altogether than for the hospice group. No differences were found between the two groups on self-report measures of anxiety, depression or somatic anxiety (using the Crown Crisp Experiential Index). However, predictors of strain and mental well-being varied as a function of type of unit, reflecting both work and life-style demands:

Predictors of overall mental well-being

Hospice
>Stress associated with staff support in decision making.

Hospital
>Home-work conflict stress (i.e. expected reaction of superiors).
>Dealing with relatives.

Predictors of Job Satisfaction

Hospital
>Home–work conflict
>Low status (i.e. EN v. staff nurse or sister).

Hospice
> Staff support and involvement
> Home–work conflict.

(Source: Mitchell, 1988)

The author suggests that the prominence of the home–work conflict issues among the hospital group might reflect the fact that these nurses tended to be younger and married and so were likely to have younger family/child commitments to cope with at home. That is, they continually needed to balance the demands of work and family life and feared the consequences of overspill from one into the other. Mitchell found that hospice nurses scored significantly lower on certain potential stressor items related to the death and dying of patients than the hospital nurses, although overall no significant differences were found between the groups on measures of occupational stress (Using The Nurse Stress Index, Hingley *et al.*, 1988; this measures 1. managing the workload; 2. organizational support and involvement; 3. dealing with patients and relatives; 4. home–work conflict and; 5. confidence and competence in role.) It would seem that, overall, their concerns are similar but there are variations in terms of anxiety or depression producing issues. These might be caused by the nature of the job or factors related to the home and work interface.

Additional studies are reported in this section, to show that it is both possible and useful to identify commonly-encountered stresses in the nursing profession, but other factors will dictate the success of stress management interventions. First, in a nationwide, semi-stratified survey of 1801 (78% response rate) general and obstetric nurses in New Zealand, Dewe (1987) identified five potential sources of stress by using interview and questionnaire methodologies:

1. Work overload;
2. Difficulties relating to other staff;
3. Difficulties nursing the critically ill;
4. Concerns over the treatment of patients;
5. Dealing with difficult or helplessly ill patients.

Using a three stage approach, this survey was concerned with obtaining information on both the causes of nurse's stress and the frequency of occurrence of stressful events. In Alberta, Canada, a study across 24 hospitals, representative of units in terms of size,

189

type and urban/rural locality, Leatt and Schneck (1985) identified five kinds of stress:

1. Emotional–traumatic experiences (death and dying, crises);
2. Psycho–geriatric workload;
3. Scheduling of work (i.e. unfinished work, staff shortages);
4. Physician–nurse relationship (poor communication, role conflict);
5. Personality role stress (ambiguity, conflicts within the nurse team).

Some variation existed as a function of unit type, for example, the stress of emotional – traumatic experiences was highest in ICUs, compared to surgical, medical, auxiliary (chronic), paediatric, psychiatric, obstetric and rural units, and psycho – geriatric workload stress was significantly higher in the auxiliary unit (elderly, chronically-ill patients). However, no other differences existed as a function of unit. Leatt and Schneck show that the management of stress at sub-unit level needs to take account of the size of the unit, the type of environment (degree of medical/ physician involvement), the structure (complex, centralized, etc.) and the technology (i.e. degree of stability, certainty and variability); and that some problems are modifiable through changes in organizational process and structural design but others will not be resolved by this type of intervention. Similarly, in a large-scale study ($n = 983$) within one large teaching hospital in Australia, Pierce *et al.* (1987) observed that stressor factors were problematic as a function of type of ward. After identifying seven general stressor factors, (e.g. responsiveness of management, parking, work overload, team status, professional self-esteem, interference with proper-role, training, career prospects), they identified the severity of each according to work area and in terms of moderate or major problems (as indicated by 30 and 50% of the staff respectively). This was intended as a guide for management, in order to direct their attention within specific areas. However, the emergence of common stressor themes in nursing also suggests that some issues could be addressed at recruitment, selection, and/or training phases of the staffing process. Ivancevich and Smith (1982) suggest that an understanding of job difficulty as interpreted by incumbents, is a concept that can be incorporated into the implementation of job re-design, training, performance appraisal and goal setting programmes. 194 registered nurses employed in US medical–surgical units took part in this investigation, which utilized critical incident format interviews, a card sort categorization and questionnaire-response to identify three job-difficulty factors. These included: 1. work overload (such as demanding job requirements, time pressures and physician demands); 2. conflict (i.e. in-patient care, cost control dilemmas and inter-job conflict), and; 3. supervisory or head-nurse practises (i.e. changing work plans, holding up information, no authority delegated). Using multiple regression analysis, it was demonstrated that various job difficulty dimensions were differentially related (i.e. predictors) to job satisfaction, job tension and performance and that job tenure was also a moderating variable. For example, strong relationships existed between workload and job tension for the short and intermediate tenure groups (6 months–1 year and 1–3 years tenure respectively) but was not as strong for the long tenure group (3+ years).

Finally in this section, we report the stressor factors identified by Hingley and Cooper (1986) among nurse managers because the list bears much resemblance to the stressor-elements described in Marshall's (1980) review (Table 6.8):

1. Workload;
2. Relationships with superiors;
3. Role conflict;
4. Death and dying;
5. Home/work conflict, i.e. overspill;
6. Career stress, i.e. poor promotion prospects, low status;
7. Interpersonal relationships:
   a) patients and relatives
   b) colleagues
   c) subordinates
8. Physical resources;
9. Change, i.e. professional developments and new technology.

Indeed, it would seem from these studies that common themes do exist in reported sources of nurse stress, independent of type of unit, type of patient and grade of nursing staff. This observation has important implications for the management of stress, i.e. at what level should intervention take place? It is clear that the pervasiveness of certain stressors demand intervention at the level of the organization (or even higher, for example, through government control of funds which restrict staffing and work conditions). As Dewe (1987) points out; 'when considering the nature of possible intervention strategies, nursing and hospital administrators should be aware of those aspects of the work environment which give rise to the perception of stress.' In the Health Service, work overload and role conflict issues require evaluation of staffing levels, training, career development, systems and structures (e.g. reporting structures, adequate job descriptions, use of career assessment interviews, etc). Interpersonal conflict might require some intervention at a group level in the hospital (e.g. team-building). Evaluation of stress-management programmes have clearly shown that it is ineffective, and of limited use, to simply adopt stress management interventions aimed only at the individual level (i.e. stress inoculation) (Matteson and Invancevich, 1987; DeFrank and Cooper, 1987) because the underlying source of job stress still exists. This is consistent with Marshall's criticism of the literature and research, in that a detailed consideration of coping mechanisms and a focus on intraphysic mechanisms are prevalent, while environmental manipulations as potential mechanisms of intervention are largely ignored. Thus, effective stress control must be approached at three levels, 1. the individual; 2. the group, and; 3. the organization. This is discussed further in Chapter seven.

Observation 3

Nurse-stress literature makes assumptions of inherent stressfulness ... and it omits individual differences as potentially relevant contributing variables (Marshall, 1980).

This is an observation that research has begun to address. However, the complexity of the concept, discussed in Chapter four, provides some insight into the problems of investigating individual moderators in response to stress. Rarely are more than one or two personality variables considered in a research design, which also tends to control for certain demographic differences, such as age, gender, educational attainment or work experience, etc. Thus, although we have started to identify personality charac-teristics as mediators or moderators of the response to stress, very little is understood about the interactive nature of these predis-positions to respond. Since this might be regarded as wanting to run before we can walk, we must, therefore, be content at the moment to examine some of the findings put forward since 1980.

Gray-Toft and Anderson (1981) hypothesized that sources and frequency of stress expressed by nursing staff would be a function of level of training, trait anxiety and sociodemographic characteristics. Therefore, data on age, race, marital status, religious commitment, nursing experience and trait anxiety from 122 nurses were analysed, using analysis of variance, profile analysis and path analysis. These authors found that trait anxiety and level of training were significant predictors of stress. However, the sociodemographic variables were not found to be significant stressor predictors, once the nurse's level of training and trait anxiety were taken into account. Path analysis demonstrated that nurses with high levels of trait anxiety were less satisfied with their work because they experienced stress more frequently in performing their duties than other nurses. High levels of trait anxiety were observed among the staff on the medical unit, whereas hospice nurses evidenced low levels of trait anxiety. It was suggested that nurses with specific personality characteristics are attracted to certain units and these same predispositions may be important factors in accounting for the high levels of stress, job dissatisfaction and turnover observed on the unit (Gray-Toft and Anderson, 1981).

Type A Behaviour (TAB) pattern is an important and well documented moderator of response to stress and is identified as an independent risk factor for CHD. Ivancevich *et al.* (1982) have examined TAB among nurses in the context of a person–environment fit framework. In a comparative study of operating room and medical–surgical nurses ($n = 57$), environmental stressors, including quantitative and qualitative overload, time pressures, role conflict, relationships with supervisor and physician, job satisfaction and certain physiological properties were measured. Medical–surgical ward nurses reported significantly higher levels of quantitative work overload and time pressures but no other differences between the two groups were observed. However, measured TAB was identified as a significant stressor outcome moderator. Type A nurses reported significantly higher levels of stress caused by quantitative work overload, time pressures, and role conflict. They also indicated significantly lower levels of intrinsic job satisfaction and exhibited higher serum cholesterol levels and systolic blood pressure than their Type B counterparts. Correlations between stressors, satisfaction and physiological measures indicated the moderating effects of TAB; and overall these results showed that the Type A–Type B behaviour pattern was a much more significant moderator of associations and differences than was the speciality of the nurse (Ivancevich *et al.*, 1982). Although this study was small and the design was correlational, it does raise points that need to be pursued in more depth. From other studies, it is suggested that Type As also seek to maintain control over their environment, and thus may suffer more than B-Types when faced with a demanding situation over which there is no opportunity for control (the job demand–control model of occupational stress proposed by Karasek (1979) has been discussed in Chapter three). Landsbergis (1988) has considered the variable of control over the environment and the role of job socialization in shaping personality characteristics and coping behaviours among US health care workers, including registered nurses, licensed practical nurses (LPNs), nurses' aides and food service workers ($n = 289$, a 37.5% response rate). His results support the hypothesis that reported job strain (job dissatisfaction, depression and psychosomatic symptoms) and burnout, are significantly higher in jobs that combine high workload demands with low decision latitude (i.e. low control). This association was significant after controlling for the effects of age, gender, education, marital status, children, hours worked per week and type of shift worked. In this investigation, the Job Content Survey was used to identify job titles and/or workplaces at risk for stress related illness (i.e. reported strain and burnout was compared to the occupational average for that group); for example, the nurses' aides were identified as at-risk. Landsbergis (1988) also found that other job characteristics were associated with strain and burnout, and suggests that the job demand–control model should be expanded to include job insecurity, physical exertion, social support and hazard exposure.

Although Landsbergis considers the element of perceived degree of control in the environment as a shaper of behaviour, other researchers have discussed control as a moderator of response to stress and view it as a relatively enduring personality charactertistic and predisposition to respond; for example, locus of control (i.e. internal versus external orientation) (Lefcourt, 1976; 1982), or the hardy personality (Kobasa, 1979; 1982), high on commitment, control and challenge. Although these authors suggest that such characteristics may develop in early life, they are still the product of the socialization process. Yet, they also appear to act as important moderators of the stress response. This research has extended into nursing studies. McCranie *et al.* (1987) have investigated whether personality hardiness moderates the impact of job stressors on burnout among US registered staff nurses; that is, does hardiness promote stress resistance? Data analyses from 107 nurses indicated that burnout scores were not significantly associated with age, years of nursing experience, marital status, type of nursing education or clinical work setting (ICU v. non-ICU). However, rotating-shift-schedule working was associated with burnout scores. Consistent with other studies, this investigation found that nurses who experienced more frequent work-related stress reported greater burnout and nurses who exhibited less personality hardiness reported more burnout. However, hardiness was observed to have a beneficial main effect on reducing burnout, rather than acting in an interactive manner, that is, it did not prevent high levels of job stress from leading to high levels of burnout. This failure to observe a moderating effect for hardiness contrasts with the findings of Kobasa, and the authors suggest that there are perhaps two reasons for this; 1. Kobasa *et al.* used only male subjects (white-collar and professional), whereas this sample was almost entirely female; 2. Kobasa focused on general life-event stressors rather than purely work related stressors and hardiness as a moderator may be less effective in the work setting, because occupational stressors are more impersonal and less controllable than stressors in other life areas. They are less influenced by individual psychological resources and coping efforts (Pearlin and Schooler, 1978). This further endorses the view that effective stress management at the work site demands more than individual-focused strategies alone, with organizational intervention efforts required to prevent burnout among nurses. This includes adequate staffing, flexible scheduling, implementing conflict-management strategies, improving information flow and promoting social support (McCranie *et al.*, 1987). Perceived availability of supervisor support, measured among qualified nurses in the UK ($n = 185$ including charge nurses, staff nurses and enrolled nurses in medical, psychiatric and mental handicap units), was significantly related to reduced emotional exhaustion and depersonalization and fewer thoughts of leaving the job (Firth *et al.*, 1986). Supervisor support in the form of respect and empathy contributed to reduced emotional exhaustion; one dimension of burnout amongst nursing staff. Lack of interpersonal support for nursing students on the ward has repeatedly been identified as a prime factor associated with quitting the profession (i.e. turnover). The problems specific to student nursing are considered in the following section.

Student nursing

In this section, some problems specific to nurse learners are considered. Generally, the literature considers three basic themes:

1. Enhancement of our understanding of the learner; for example, do the reasons given for coming to nursing have an effect on career commitment; what expectations are held by learners? If distress is the outcome of failed expectations or an inability to meet perceived demands, then it would seem to be important to have a clearer understanding of these issues.
2. What happens to the student nurse in the early days of work and training? What changes, if any, take place and are these good or bad?
3. To what extent does environment affect the performance and well-being of trainee nurses?

From the previous section, it was clear that work overload was a pervasive source of stress among qualified nursing staff. Staffing shortages are, in part, the cause of work overload. This situation may arise when inadequate funding restricts staffing levels, when personnel are absent from work (thereby increasing the load for colleagues left to cope) and when the profession is understaffed because it is failing to attract new recruits. Many professional groups are concerned about falling birth rates and their ability to maintain a skilled workforce in the future. Recent and continual change in the Health Service, pay disputes, high media attention on the poor morale of present staff and changes in public and/or social attitudes towards health professionals, all serve to exacerbate this area of concern. Therefore, the costs of stress among nurses may be in terms of 1. a poor or reduced professional image which impacts on the ability to attract individuals into nursing; 2. drop-out, i.e. the distressed student nurse fails to complete training and quits the profession, and; 3. poor performance outcomes and ineffective use of staff resources. It is important, therefore, that we increase our understanding of the experiences and attitudes of learner nurses.

One recent study (Arnold, 1989) provides some insight on these issues. Intakes over a one-year period, at a school of nursing in South West England, were surveyed by questionnaire during initial induction (usually the first day), after four months and again after one year in training (subsequent eight months). All 105 learners (RGN and EN), over four intakes, took part in the survey and in the one year period seven withdrew from their training. The survey sample was predominently young and female; 71% had held a full-time job prior to nurse training and 48% of the learners had worked full-time in a job closely related to nursing (e.g. care assistant, nursing auxiliary). The results show that people who were nurses played a fairly substantial role in the learners decision to become nurses; and the variety in work and the rewards of helping patients were cited by nearly all as important factors in their decision. From the investigation of experiences between the four month and subsequent eight month follow-up, the learners tended to be fairly optimistic about their ability to handle the demands of the work in general (volume and difficulty), but coping clearly sapped the learner's strength. This was manifest in terms of mental and physical exhaustion and worries about being able to handle their academic work. They were more distressed about caring for terminally ill patients and expressed financial worries. These observations are consistent with other findings (Arnold, 1989). Learners were also asked about experiences in the first four months that came as a surprise to them; overall, there was less supervision than expected, concern about the lack of opportunity for learning and training on the wards and other staff (trained nurses) were less friendly than expected. After one year, students most often reported the contact and relationships with patients as the most enjoyable aspect of nursing. Least enjoyable and most often mentioned was the poor relationships with other nurses. In terms of outcomes, the learners became significantly more anxious (social anxiety) in the first four months and this level of anxiety was sustained in the final assessment. However, they also report an increase in confidence, independence and orientation towards people but as Arnold suggests there is evidence of the increasing costs of coping, including less enthusiasm, more anxiety and more frantic attempts to counter the stresses of the work situation. Over the first year, commitment to nursing decreased for 54 of the learners, increased for 29 of them and remained the same for nine students. Overall, commitment levels dropped a small, but statistically significant degree between the four month and one year follow-up measures. Commitment to nursing at four months was predicted by:

1. Worries about living accommodation;
2. Feeling that you are doing a useful job for your patients;
3. Feeling that you have established a really good relationship with a patient.

At one year, six experiences emerged as most prominent:

1. Feeling inadequate or incompetent;
2. Being talked-down to by other staff;
3. Worries about living accommodation;
4. Feeling that you can cope easily enough with your workload;
5. Feeling that you are doing a useful job for your patients;
6. Feeling that you are part of a team.

Commitment was not significantly associated with age, gender, qualification (RGN v. EN), prior exposure to nursing or total amount of surprise after four months. Collectively, the results indicate that commitment is influenced somewhat by day-to-day experiences during nurse training (Arnold, 1989). Although the study is restricted to one unit, it provides some important insights into the experiences and attitudes of learner nurses. It is suggested that studies of this nature should be extended to examine the size of these problems among student nurses in general.

Some support for Arnold's findings were observed in studies reported by Birch (1979) and Parkes (1980a, b, 1982). Birch's study focused in the North of England among students and pupils from four schools of nursing. Over a two-year period, at eight-monthly intervals, four measures of anxiety were taken for each subject ($n = 207$), and a self devised, 56-item questionnaire to identify the pressures of the trainee nurse was administered at the eight month interval and then again after two years of training. The questionnaire examined areas of clinical practice from basic nursing tasks to aspects of death and dying, abortion and the relief of pain (Birch, 1979). During the introductory course, on measures of anxiety, 90 of the learners (43.5%) indicated borderline high anxiety levels (requiring careful follow-up). In fact, of these, 74 individuals could be described as showing signs of definite psychological morbidity, almost certain to have an adverse effect on work and social/emotional adjustment of the individual. Anxiety levels reduced at the eight month and 16 month periods but regained a high level after two years training; perhaps because the pupils in the sample were facing an examination. Anxiety levels were significantly greater than in measures of patients about to undergo surgery. However, as Marshall (1980) points out, the role of anxiety and the prediction from anxiety to behaviour (e.g. performance), is not fully understood. It is also necessary to distinguish between trait and state anxiety and to assess 1. whether nursing attracts the anxious-type and; 2. is this a good or bad thing in terms of outcomes. For example, in Gray-Toft and Anderson's study, nurses with high levels of trait-anxiety reported experiencing high levels of stress, which in turn appeared to result in a significant decrease in job satisfaction and/or an increased turnover rate. Birch also showed that the first 25 items causing stress at the eight month measure had not changed significantly after 24 months in training. Table 6.9 shows the top twelve stressors at eight months and their changing priority after two years of training. Nursing of patients in great pain is top at the eight-month measure but understaffing is the main concern at 24 months. Being disciplined in

Table 6.9 Rank order of top twelve stressors after eight months and twenty-four months of training

Stressor	Rank order	
	8 months	24 months
Nursing of patients in great pain	1	3
Being shown up on the wards in front of other patients and other staff	2	2
Progress test in block study	3	6
Dealing with patients with cancer	4	5
Care of the terminally ill	5	4
Care of the dying	6	6
Dealing with bereaved relatives	7	7
Changing wards	8	13
Your feelings about your own death	9	12
Your feelings about growing old	9	11
Understaffing	10	1
Last offices	11	8
Carrying out procedures before being taught in school	12	15

Source: Birch (1979).

public and the stress of changing wards, where senior staff make no attempt to reduce the levels of stress associated with the change, are very much issues of poor management style and attitudes towards subordinates, and thus can be modified. Birch reports that the majority of pupils and students believed that their training did not prepare them adequately for the care of dying patients and for dealing with bereaved relatives, i.e. not enough attention was paid to the psychological content of nurse training. Only 2% of pupils and 17% of students believed that there was enough psychology taught. Although exposure to death and dying was not reported as a bad experience by Arnold's respondents, it was clear that the experience of distress of caring for terminally-ill patients significantly increased in the first year of nursing, suggesting perhaps that these issues are still not adequately addressed in training (although as Arnold points out, difference between the two studies might also reflect variability in the question and response formats used).

One major source of stress among trainees identified by Birch (1979) was associated with changing wards. Table 6.9 shows that this remained a significant problem even after two years in training. Approximately one-third of the respondents stated that senior staff made no attempt to reduce the stress occurring with ward change. However, the experiment conducted by Parkes (1980 a, b; 1982) is indicative of the importance of the work setting in influencing mental health and well-being. In this investigation, Parkes took advantage of the natural transition of student nurses across different environments during their training programme. Student nurses ($n = 164$) were randomly assigned to one of four possible combinations of ward types, to explore the impact of two potential conditioning variables (i.e. type of nursing (medical/surgical) and sex of patient (male/female) over two ward periods) with each student experiencing both medical and surgical wards and working with both male and female patients. This study allowed systematic built-in subject comparisons of the effects of different work environments in a hospital setting, with initial baseline measures, control for order effects and consistent data-collection techniques (Parkes, 1982). Work satisfaction, psychological effect, sickness absence and work performance were measured. On the basis of previous findings, it was predicted that students would perceive medical wards less favourably than surgical wards and would show higher levels of distress during medical allocations. In addition, it was predicted that a mixed-sex environment in male wards would be more favourable than the single-sex environment of female wards but anxiety levels would be higher in male wards. It was observed that:

1. Medical wards were associated with higher levels of distress and this had adverse impact on work satisfaction and levels of depression.
2. Surgical wards were perceived as significantly higher in job discretion (i.e. they provided more opportunities for the acquisition and use of skills).
3. Medical wards were perceived as lower in social support than surgical wards.
4. Both degree of support and discretion in the job were significantly correlated with lowered anxiety, social dysfunction and depression scores.
5. Male wards were perceived more favourably than female wards, work performance was assessed as significantly better and work satisfaction was higher. However, both anxiety and depression levels were higher — but social support and discretion mitigated these differences between male and female wards.
6. Higher anxiety levels were found to be primarily associated with male medical wards (which included coronary care units and had the highest death rates).
7. Changes in somatic symptoms were positively correlated with changes in sickness absence, but not for the other symptoms (i.e. low and non-significant correlations with anxiety, depression and work satisfaction).

Parkes (1982) states that these results, based on a controlled, counterbalanced and longitudinal study, provide evidence for the causal role of the work setting in influencing mental health and well-being. The work-environment contributed to the observed differences in affective distress between medical and surgical wards, while mitigating differences between male and female wards. It is suggested that inherent differences in the nature of the tasks between the two types of ward means that surgical nursing emphasizes a more cognitive instrumental role (demanding rational, problem solving and technical skills), whereas medical nursing focuses on the affective role, which includes the caring, compassionate and protective aspects of nursing. Furthermore, the type of social climate appears to be crucial, especially factors such as social support, involvement and task orientation. Finally, the physical location of the ward in relation to central facilities (e.g. administration, dining rooms, etc.) is a potential mediator. In the Parkes (1980a, b) studies, it was noted that the surgical wards were much closer to central facilities than were the medical wards. At the initial assessment, this group of students as a whole compared favourably with females in corresponding age groups and were found to be significantly more emotionally stable and extravert than females in the general population (Parkes 1980a, 1982). These observations are important but it is also necessary to continue the monitoring in order to find out what the long-term effect of nursing might be and how these might relate to the deleterious health behaviours and outcomes reported among qualified nurses.

Psychiatric nursing

The decision to allocate a separate section to this occupational category is an acknowledgement that the psychiatric nurse may be exposed to the stressors inherent to general nursing but must also face additional problems:

1. Psychiatric patients are fundamentally different from patients with physical disorders (Powell, 1982). Patients might be dangerous, unpredictable and/or incapable of communication. Expectations and satisfactions for this group must thereby differ from those in general nursing. Arnold (1989) observed that students were attracted to general nursing because it was consistent with images of high levels of variety, happiness when patients are restored to health, demonstrating care and concern and creativity and insight in solving patients' problems. We do not have comparative information for the psychiatric nurse but it seems reasonable to suggest that a different type of nursing would attract a different sort of person with concomitant needs and expectations.
2. Psychiatric nursing has a low status image compared to general nursing. This reflects itself in the recruitment of personnel, in that it is less likely to attract highly educated individuals (Brooking, 1985).

3. Mental health is in a state of change. The transition means that emphasis has moved from custodial charge to community care for many patients. Therefore, the psychiatric nurse must adopt a variety of roles to meet the needs of these patients. Some hospitals are facing closure and/or budget cuts. Thus, the environment is characterized by an atmosphere of change and insecurity. Both are powerful sources of stress.

So, psychiatric nurses may have to face day-to-day stress, lack of resources, job insecurity, change and rumours of change. However, studies of psychiatric nurses are rare and those that do exist tend to be restricted to single hospitals or units, thus, it is not possible to generalize these results. To our knowledge, no large-scale national surveys exist and so it is not possible to comment on the overall health and well-being of the psychiatric nurse or to categorize common stressor themes. It is also likely that differences will exist as a function of specialities within psychiatric nursing. Nevertheless, we are able to consider the literature available, make some comparisons where possible and begin to answer two preliminary questions:

1. What is the state of health among psychiatric nurses?
2. Do unique stressor problems exist for the psychiatric nurse?

The health of the psychiatric nurse

In the mid-80s, Norfolk and Stirton (1985) conducted a survey for the National Union of Public Employees in ten psycho-geriatric wards of a hospital in the North East of England (142 qualified nurses and nursing assistants, both full- and part-time). Personnel were asked to identify the existence of certain stress-symptoms and/or outcomes. A percentage of 23 (all female) were currently undergoing treatment from a doctor, and of those feeling under stress, 73% believed that problems at work were the main contributory factors. Table 6.10 details the incidents of symptoms reported in terms of percentages. Irritability, sleeplessness, tension, aches and pains and low morale are all commonly identified by these respondents. Analysis by gender, age grouping and qualification shows that overall the 18–30 years of age, qualified group of personnel were most at risk, although the unqualified staff in the

Table 6.10 Reported symptoms and outcome experiences among psychiatric nurses—percentages

	%
Irritability	70
Lack of interest in going to work	70
Long periods of tiredness	63
Tension	63
Feeling of Stress	63
Aches in neck muscles	60
Sleeplessness	58
Loss of Temper	58
Recurring Headaches	58
Lack of interest in work	51
Periods of depression	41
Anxiety	33
Recurring indigestion	28
Tendency to leave things to the last minute	26
Skin rashes	23
Migraine	18
High blood pressure	11
Duodenal or stomach ulcers	6
Heart trouble	0

Source: Norfolk and Stirton (1985).

18–30 age group were more likely to report ulcers, skin rashes, high blood pressure and long periods of tiredness. More male nurses than females expressed a lack of interest in work (72 and 47% respectively), and in going to work (72 and 69% respectively). Contrary to popular opinion, recurring headaches were most often reported by young, qualified males; this group were also more prone to loss of temper. Young, qualified female staff were more likely than the males to report depression and feelings of stress, but women in the 30+ age group reported symptoms of anxiety more often. Although these figures project a bleak view, interpretation of the results must be treated with caution because the authors state that the ten wards were chosen for the survey because they had previously initiated the most complaints. Although this type of study suggests that there are areas for concern and points management to specific problems in specific wards, its use is restricted because it failed to identify a random, representative sample, and relied mainly on self-report data.

Jones *et al.* (1987) resolved this problem by involving the whole population of nurses employed within a large Special Hospital in the UK. Replies from 349 respondents (49%) permitted analysis of data by rank and sex but the proportion of returns from the sub-samples varied, and so overall, it was not truly representative of the population in the Hospital and may be biased (in ways difficult to anticipate). In addition, the male/female ratio (73:27) is not typical of nursing, although it reflects the nature of this environment, that is, the care of patients in special and secure conditions. Use of standardized outcome measures for health, well-being and job satisfaction allowed for comparisons with other occupational groups and within sub-samples. They found:

1. No significant differences in measures of general psychological distress (using GHQ/12) between the five nursing ranks (nursing officer and above; charge nurse/sister; staff; SEN; and nursing assistant). Female staff had a marginally poorer level of well-being ($p < 0.06$). Compared to other non-health related occupations, the psychiatric nursing staff in this study reported significantly more psychological distress. However, compared to other samples in the health professions and the unemployed, the obtained mean score of 10.24 is relatively low (Jones, 1987). For example, for medical students the average score was 11.66 (Firth, 1986); for health care workers, 13.30 and for the unemployed, around 15 (reported by Jones, 1987). Separate measures of anxiety and depression were marginally higher, but not statistically different to other occupational groups, and no differences were observed as a function of rank or gender. Staff with a spouse working in the same hospital, reported significantly higher levels of anxiety and psychological distress.

2. Reported job satisfaction was relatively low compared to other occupations. No differences emerged between the ranks but female staff reported significantly more job satisfaction than their male counterparts. Those who lived in hospital accommodation and/or had a spouse working in the hospital also reported lower levels of job satisfaction than those who did not. As expected, job satisfaction was strongly and negatively correlated with measures of psychological distress, anxiety and depression. That is, job dissatisfaction (or low levels of job satisfaction) is associated with high anxiety levels, etc.

205

3. Trait neuroticism measures were significantly lower than for normative sample comparisons. Neuroticism is usually positively associated with reported levels of psychological distress, anxiety and depression. Since trait neuroticism was observed to be low in this sample of psychiatric nurses, the authors suggest that the reported high levels of psychological distress were real and not a reflection of personality predisposition to respond.

Travers and Firth-Cozens (1989) adopted a different approach by investigating sources of stress and job satisfaction experienced by mental health workers within one Mental Health Authority in the UK. Thus, it was possible to examine the impact of major change, cut-backs, threat of closure and/or differences in environmental conditions. Since the majority of respondents were nurses ($n = 254$), the results are worthy of incorporation into this section. 458 personnel from three hospital sites (sites A and B experiencing cut-backs, shortages and eventual closure; and the third, C, was a new psychiatric unit in the General Hospital) returned questionnaires designed to measure sources of stress and stressor outcomes (mental well-being and job satisfaction). This constituted a 32% response rate, average for this type of survey, but limiting in terms of generalizing results to the total population. The final sample included ancillary workers (40), management (24), nurses (254), administrative/clerical officers (52), doctors (26) and non-medical professions (57). A percentage of 65 were women, 81% were full-time workers. Overall, a mean stress score of 12.47 on the GHQ was obtained (a measure of psychological distress/mental well-being). As already noted in the previous study, this score is higher than found in the general population (mean score = 8.67, high score = reduced well-being) but is similar to other client centred or health care workers. However, 30% of respondents scored above three on the GHQ, an estimation of caseness or emotional distress indicative of psychiatric morbidity; and 25% scored above four and are thus identified as at-risk. Thus at least one quarter of these workers were suffering from unacceptably high levels of emotional distress. Personnel at the new unit, 'C', reported significantly greater levels of job satisfaction and significantly lower levels of distress than those in the hospitals experiencing major changes. Indeed, job satisfaction levels overall compared favourably with other workers and health professionals, but 20% of the sample were dissatisfied with staff shortages, the cut-backs and lack of resources; other dissatisfactions were expressed with regard to the lack of feedback and supervision. The opportunity for caring, client contact and social relationships with the patients provided the major source of satisfaction and was highlighted by 61% of respondents. Although mental health work seems to provide the opportunity for a great deal of satisfaction, as a population, many of these workers are suffering from the effects of cut-backs in resources (Travers and Firth-Cozens, 1989). The stressors identified by this group are reported in the next section.

Stress in psychiatric nursing

At the beginning of this section, it was suggested that sources of stress in psychiatric nursing may differ from those engaged in general nursing activities. In a recent review of the descriptive literature, Jones (1987) concludes that two major factors emerge as potential sources of stress for the psychiatric nurse:

1. Patient contact;
2. Administrative and organizational factors.

The psychiatric nurse might work in fear of threat of violence from patients, often in drab, poor environments. Paradoxically, the psychiatric nurse also feels that patient contact provides the greatest potential for satisfaction with the job but contact is inadequate because staff shortages exist. Cut-backs and controls on resources also result in poor training and so the nurse does not feel suitably qualified to cope with certain situations that arise, especially where roles, responsibility, authority and goals are not clearly defined, i.e. often the product of poor organizational and administrative systems and practices. These potential stressor situations are exacerbated when the psychiatric nurse perceives a lack of social support from supervisors, management or organizational sources in the workplace (Jones, 1987).

Nevertheless, an examination of the literature suggests that empirical evidence does not unequivocally support these observations. For example, Norfolk and Stirton (1985) asked respondents in the first phase of their study of ten psycho–geriatric wards to state the main causes of stress in their job. From 54 statements, 92% identified inadequate staffing as the main problem. Over 20% of the staff cite lack of co-operation, interest, support and/or

207

understanding from management as significant sources of stress. Work overload and physical exhaustion was also cited by 20% of staff and was usually linked with the understaffing problems expressed. Other main stressor issues, in order of reported frequency included; poor environment/facilities (15%); and lack of variety, low status, noise and the frustration of not doing enough for patients were each indicated on only two occasions. No mention was made of skill related problems, nurse–patient relationship issues or job insecurity, etc. Thus, this study does not indicate that the psychiatric nurse is experiencing special problems. The limitations of this study have already been expressed, nevertheless, it is also worth mentioning that the study was conducted by a union body. Therefore, it is possible that the staff may have responded in a biased manner in order to fulfil the expectations of the researchers. The replies might be an artifact of the study, in that respondents only presented problems that they believed were of interest to the researchers and, more importantly, ones that they could act upon, that is, the staffing shortage issue and the poor relationships with management.

An American study conducted by Dawkins *et al.* (1985) supports the notion that the main sources of stress among psychiatric nurses are consistent with general nursing situations and are typical of the problems inherent in any large bureaucratic organization. Table 6.11 indicates the 26 high-stressor items expressed by 43 nurses (10% of the nurses at the hospital) working in a large psychiatric hospital. However, the preoccupation with administrative and organizational issues probably reflects the fact that this sample were in supervisory positions (14 staff nurses, 29 nurses in supervisory positions) and so it is not possible to make comparisons across studies. In spite of this, it is interesting to note that when all 78 items were rated and ranked, six themes emerged (independently classified by two raters, 90% inter-rater agreement). These included:

1. Administrative and organizational issues;
2. Staff conflict;
3. Limited resources;
4. Scheduling issues;
5. Negative characteristics of patients;
6. Staff performance.

Note that the first eleven items on Table 6.11 are administrative

Table 6.11 Stress in psychiatric nursing: Items in the high-stress range (indicating factor category)

Items	Geometric mean	Rank	Category*
Not being notified of changes before they occur	125	1	A
Dealing with people in key management positions who are unable to make decisions	95	2	A
Lack of support from administration	88	3	A
Having excessive paperwork	84	4	A
Working for administration that believes in change for the sake of change	81	5	A
Being responsible for too many widely divergent things	72	6	A
Not having suggestions acted on in a timely fashion	65	7	A
Trying to do the job in spite of no one listening or caring	65	8	A
Receiving no recognition for a job well done	64	9	A
Having administrative work interfere with patient care	61	10	A
The 'system' that never listens to suggestions from peers	60	11	A
Lack of adequate staffing in potentially dangerous environments	57	12	R
Working with hostile patients on an inadequately staffed ward	54	13	R
Having a shortage of patient's clothing	51	14	R
A physical threat by a patient	50	15	N
Having an employee reassigned to other units against his wishes	47	16	SC
Working with unskilled, non-professionals who resent new ideas	45	18	SC
Working with poorly motivated staff	45	18	SC
Lack of communication between disciplines	45	19	A
Having a doctor fail to notify staff of changes in patient's order and being held responsible	44	20	SC
Convincing doctors to order adequate medication	43	21	SC
Dealing with the hassle that occurs when you try to take action against incompetent staff	39	22	SP
Finding out that warehouse does not have ward supplies	39	23	R
Having another take credit for an idea or project that I initiated and worked hard on	38	24	SC
Receiving no response from complaints to chief nurse after going through channels	36	25	A
Covering other wards because of unscheduled absences of other RNs	36	26	S

*Key: A = administrative/organizational issues;
   R = limited resources;
   N = negative characteristics of patients;
   SC = staff conflicts;
   SP = staff performance;
   R = limited resources.
Source: Dawkins, Depp and Selzer (1985).

and organizational issues. Dawkins *et al.* (1985) developed their own stressor measure for use in this study. The psychiatric nurses' occupational stress scale (PNOSS) is an item bank developed from communication with psychiatric nurses (described as randomly selected from a computerized staffing list, with a 51% response rate). Since only 14% of the final items were specific to this nursing speciality, it is reasonable to accept this as further confirmation that stress tends to be general to nursing and only a very small proportion of speciality-specific problems exist. This of course does not detract from the understanding that these stressors are potentially of an acute nature. However, it is also necessary to acknowledge that the nurses who did not respond to the request, may perceive stress differently from the responders. To overcome some of the bias that might have existed, the authors sought advice and guidance from a panel of experts in this field of nursing and research before the final questionnaire was administered. However, it is not clear why stratified sampling was not used in order to obtain a representative sample of staff, instead of limiting it to a supervisory population.

Cronin-Stubbs and Brophy (1985) highlight some of the specific problems faced by psychiatric nurses. Although their study focused on the predictors of burnout among nurses ($n = 296$, all female), interview data showed that psychiatric staff were likely to report intense interpersonal involvement and frequent conflict with patients, families, physicians and work colleagues, whereas operating room nurses experienced little involvement with patients, families and colleagues, but conflict with physicians. Intensive care and medical nurses reported moderate amounts of interpersonal involvement with patients and occasional conflicts with families, colleagues and physicians. Other differences were observed as a function of the type of task. For example, it is likely that the psychiatric nurse receives less direct assistance and aid than operating room nurses because they are not usually required to work interdependently, in the same manner as the surgical nurse in the operating theatre. The results also indicate that differences in the levels of feedback (affirmation) observed were a function of nursing speciality; intensive care nurses were more likely to receive continual, concrete and observable confirmation of their actions, whereas the psychiatric nurse was denied this information and often works with a patient without knowledge of specified goals or aims. Cronin-Stubbs and Brophy identify this lack of feedback problem as a predictor of burnout. High burnout scores were associated with the tendency to use prescription drugs to calm down patients and to spend less time in direct contact with them. However, the work of Jones *et al.* (1987) is important because it clearly shows the role of expectation in the relationship between perceived demand and health and well-being outcomes.

Jones *et al.* (1987) developed a questionnaire of perceived job demands, supports and constraints among psychiatric nurses (based on ward visits and discussions with staff). Analysis indicated that job demand consisted of three independent factors (i.e. type of demand): 1. administration; 2. patient supervision, and; 3. aversive demands (e.g. 'undertake work I consider unnecessary' and 'work with patients I am afraid of'). Job demands from patient supervision were the highest perceived demand (mean factor score = 4.26), whereas scores for administrative and aversive demands were lower (mean scores of 2.19 and 1.36, respectively). When the relationships between perceived demands and stress outcomes were examined, the authors found that demand related to patient supervision was not associated with psychological distress, anxiety or depression, whereas administrative demands correlated moderately and positively with health and well-being outcomes (psychological distress and anxiety). However, associations between aversive demands and stress outcomes were strong and highly significant. The authors suggest that; 'patient supervisory demands, although high, are presumably not related to stress because they represent the major function of psychiatric nurses and are expected to be high ... administrative demands are what are probably considered as a subsidiary function of the job ... and may be an unwanted aspect of the job for many of them. Aversive demands, although relatively low, are strongly related to stress for those who do experience them' (Jones *et al.*, 1987).

The final study in this section used a different approach to Jones, concentrating on open-ended questions to investigate:

1. The major sources of stress at work;
2. A stressful event in the past 30 days.

(Travers and Firth-Cozens, 1989)

'Lack of resources and staff shortages' were indicated by 20% of the respondents ($n = 458$) to be the biggest source of stress and a somewhat related 12% of the nurses were stressed by excess demands and overwork. When asked to recall the major stressful event in the last 30 days, 16% cited the stress of violent or disruptive episodes with patients. Poor working relationships were reported by 14% of respondents and lack of resources and staff shortages were reported by 13% of personnel. However, as the authors point out, violence is cited alongside shortages in staff and resources, but it is not clear if; 1. violence is a less acute source of stress of mental health workers if there are adequate staffing levels, or; 2. violent episodes occur more frequently in the light of staff shortages (Travers and Firth-Cozens, 1989), and so more information is needed.

Although many of the problems of psychiatric nursing appear to be common to nursing in general (e.g. work overload due to staffing shortages), the effects may be exacerbated by the nature of the job, that is, the care of the mentally ill. Thus, there are special problems to address. However, none of the studies have focused on the issues of self-selection into psychiatric nursing and/or the personal characteristics of those individuals working in this speciality. If there are aspects of the task that cannot be changed, then it is necessary to pay more attention to the concept of person–environment fit in selection and the training/education of this special group of health professionals.

DOCTORS

The final occupational category considered in this chapter is the doctor. From the literature available, it is acknowledged that stressors among doctors can only be discussed when certain qualifications are established. Differences may be observed as a function of type of medical practice, e.g., surgeon, general practice, etc; speciality; qualification and/or gender. Despite this, certain themes do seem to emerge that have implications for training, career development and the management of stress for those individuals working in medical practice. Nevertheless, research evidence suggests that costs of distress and strain are high among these health professionals.

The costs of stress

According to the job demand–decision latitude model proposed by Karasek (1979) (Chapter 5), employment in medical practice is viewed as an active occupation. That is, high in demand, but with high levels of autonomy and good opportunity for decision making. In fact, consistent with Karasek's hypothesis, Doll and Peto (1979) show that deaths due to cardiovascular disease among physicians and surgeons are lower than in the general population (i.e. lower standardized mortality ratios). Nevertheless, as Payne and Rick (1986) point out; 'because high discretion is part of many highly responsible and professional occupations, it seems unlikely that high discretion alone permits the occupants of such demanding jobs to avoid physical and mental stress totally.' Indeed, some recent studies indicate causes for concern for the health and well-being of both qualified doctors and those individuals still in medical training. For example, a recent large-scale study of general practitioners in England (Cooper et al., 1989; Makin et al., 1988), found that male doctors reported significantly higher levels of anxiety and lower levels of job satisfaction than other normative groups. In addition the Registrar General's mortality figures (1978) indicate that medical practitioners have a higher risk of dying from four causes associated with exposure to stress; suicide (standardized mortality ratio (SMR) = 335), cirrhosis (SMR = 311), accidental poisoning (SMR = 818) and accidents (SMR = 160). However, the overall standardized mortality ratio for male deaths, aged 15–64, is only 81 for medical practitioners compared to 112 for nurses (1970–1972, UK Office of Population Censuses and Surveys).

Alcohol abuse, a behavioural response to stress, seems to be problematic among medical practitioners. Murray (1976) found that the rate of admissions for alcohol dependence was two to seven times higher among doctors in Scotland than among controls of comparable social class. In an investigation of general practitioners (n = 51) between September, 1980 and August, 1981, the General Medical Council reported that 37% were classified as drug addicts or alcoholics. Allibone et al. (1981) estimated that there may be as many as 3000 practising general practitioners who are alcoholics. A follow-up study of medical students in the US, from the classes of 1948 through 1964, reported that suicide was the most frequent cause of premature death (Thomas, 1976). As

213

of November 1, 1975, 49 subjects (3.7%) of the cohort of 1337 subjects had died prematurely (before age 60). Almost half of the deceased subjects died before reaching the age of 40. 17 subjects (34.7%) died by suicide; 9 by accident; 9 with malignant tumour; 5 from myocardial infarction; and 3 were alcohol related deaths. Thomas observed that because the cause of death stated on the death certificate may be inaccurate or deliberately misleading ... it is probable that several deaths included under 'accidents' or 'other deaths' may, in fact, have been additional suicides. However, it is also important to observe that in total, 39 graduates and 10 non-graduates have died and the percentage of deceased non-graduates is 3.6 times as high as that of graduates. Research evidence suggests that sources of stress may be different for male and female doctors (Cartwright, 1987) and the pressures may be greater for women. In Thomas' study, only 9% of the sample were women but of the 17 suicides, four were female deaths (66.7% of the female deaths in total, compared to 30.2% of male premature deaths). In fact, Steppacher and Mausner (1974) report that the suicide rate for female physicians in the US, over a five and a half year study period, was three times that of the overall female population whereas, for male physicians it was only 1.15 times that of the male population.

Typically, descriptive accounts highlight the pressures associated with a high workload, the need to work long hours, time pressures and not having enough free time. This might manifest itself in the form of burnout. By definition, this is a state of physical, mental and/or emotional exhaustion, which frequently occurs in the giving professions. Trubo (1984) suggests that the burned-out physician tends not to leave the profession because career-investment costs are too high, thus, there is a danger that the burned-out doctor becomes detached from patients, cynical and turns to destructive coping mechanisms (alcohol, tranquillizers, etc). Evidence is also available to suggest that the costs of strain and pressure might extend into the private life of those working in medical practice (Cartwright, 1967; Cartwright and Anderson, 1981). Although the divorce rate for male physicians is lower than for many other professional groups, it is higher among female physicians (Rosow and Rose, 1972). This is important because 50% of medical undergraduates are now women. Therefore, it is necessary to consider gender differences in the investigation of stress among doctors.

Various accounts seem to concur that the practice of medicine is generally perceived as being severely stressful (Krakowski, 1982; Bates, 1982). However, it is necessary to differentiate between brief, episodic but acute pressure and less severe but continuous strain. For example, individuals working in cardiothoracic surgery indicate that stress occurred on over 50% of working days (Payne and Rick, 1986). The surgeons monitored in this study perceived significantly higher overall job demands than the anaesthetists and this psychosocial measure of stress was consistent with the measures of vanillylmandelic acid (VMA, a major by-product of catecholamines) and cortisol excretion in urine. Levels of cortisol for both groups were chronically high compared to those found in normal populations. Furthermore, over time, changes in subjective stress associated with change in job responsibilities were reflected in changes in biochemical activity. Although these observations are important, it should be noted that the highest mean stressor rating on a five-point scale was only 1.53 (sd = 1.15). Payne and Rick (1986) also point out that the abnormally high levels of cortisol observed may not be clinically dangerous but simply the result of the body's adaptive response to cope with moderate but bearable levels of job stress. We do not know enough about the significance of this response to stress, especially the long-term consequences. As they observe, both the surgeons and the anaesthetists indicated that they have a high degree of autonomy, are very satisfied with their jobs and perceive their colleagues to be very supportive. Consistent with Payne and Rick's observation, Lin *et al.* (1979) also reported high levels of satisfaction among physicians working in the US, despite the long hours of working and the stress associated with working under time pressures. Lin *et al.* found that this occupational group was as healthy, or healthier than other occupational groups and derived much satisfaction from their work, especially in the mastery of difficult problems and the personal gratification of patient care. Thus, perhaps it is the dissatisfied medical practitioner, who works in a non-supportive environment, who uses maladaptive coping strategies to cope with stress at work. It must be remembered that not all stress is bad (Selye, 1974), but that it is mismanaged stress that is deleterious in its consequences.

Stress among doctors

In recent reviews of stress among medical practitioners presented by Scheiber (1987) and Porter *et al.* (1987), the theme of change features prominently. Change has extended into many aspects of the working lives of the doctor. For example, medicine seems to becoming more of a business venture rather than a profession, thus the medical practitioner is likely to be confronted with the strain of balancing and meeting demands associated with new roles. Within the role itself, changes are evident that alter responsibilities and relationships. Often the medical practitioner must work as a part of a health team, in a group practice and/or in co-operation and conjunction with occupational health workers, counsellors, social workers and psychologists. In addition, more women are entering the profession and this will have an impact on both the culture and the work environment of medical practice. Since many more women are in full-time paid work, spouse–partner roles are changing. This means that the doctor might be exposed to the potential strains of being a dual career couple, changes in the family support network, home and work overspill problems and role conflict issues. Finally, changes in health care systems and the concomitant images of health care held by the general public, suggests that medicine no longer commands such high regard, respect and prestige in contemporary society as in the past. Potential for gratification and satisfaction may thereby be eroded by these changes in image and status. All change necessitates adaptation. If coping is unsuccessful, a state of stress will exist.

This discussion presents the findings of recent studies that: 1. aim to identify sources of stress among medical practitioners; 2. assess the health and well-being of respondents; 3. identify the relationship between stressor agents and outcomes; and 4. highlight differences as a function of gender or qualification level.

The first study presented followed the progress of a group of medical students into their first year as junior house officers, that is, the postgraduate year of medicine (Firth-Cozens and Morrison, 1987). By qualitative methods, it aimed to identify stressors, coping strategies and differences as a function of gender. Doctors were asked to describe a real event in the previous month which had been stressful and rate how stressful they perceived the event to have been. Measures of emotional distress were assessed by using the General Health Questionnaire (GHQ, Goldberg, 1972).

a 72.7% response rate was obtained from 173 men and women (57% male), with an average age of 24.6 years. Table 6.12 shows the most frequently recorded stressors, by number and percentage and the mean stress score allocated on a scale of 1 (slightly stressful) to 4 (extremely stressful). Categories which contained fewer than five counts were omitted. Overwork caused the most extreme distress (a rating of 3.11), but the stress of dealing with death and dying was more commonly reported (by nearly 19% of respondents). No gender differences were observed either for reported sources of stress or for the coping strategies employed, except that more women than men asked for help as a coping strategy. Overall, the strategies included:

1. tackling the situation (29.4 per cent)
2. asked for help (27.6 per cent)
3. rationalised the event (13.5 per cent)
4. failed to cope (11.7 per cent)
5. dismissed the event (6.1 per cent).

The authors found that 22% of the respondents scored in the caseness range on the GHQ on both assessments (over a one-year period). Compared to GHQ low scorers (37.1%), these individuals reported higher mean levels of perceived stress and were significantly more likely to report mistakes as stressful events and dismissal as a coping strategy. Most enjoyable, for this sample was feeling useful and interacting with patients. Least enjoyable was the overwork situation, and having to do trivial tasks (50 and

Table 6.12 Most commonly reported stressors in pre-registration doctors (one month period)

Item	number	%	score	sd
Dealing with death and dying	31	(18.6)	2.90	0.79
Relationships with senior doctors	26	(15.6)	2.85	0.74
Making mistakes	21	(12.6)	2.72	0.58
Over-work	19	(11.4)	3.11	0.86
Relationships with ward staff	16	(9.6)	2.75	0.78
A lack of skills	11	(6.6)	2.73	1.00
Dealing with patients' relatives	9	(5.4)	3.00	0.50
Career decisions	6	(3.6)	2.33	0.52

*4 point scale
Source: Firth-Cozens and Morrison (1987).

16.9%, respectively). As Firth-Cozens and Morrison conclude, this group did not specifically complain about their long hours and lack of sleep as expected but overwork was an extremely stressful situation, reported by over 11% of the group. We do not have any more details on the nature of this complaint, so it is not possible to comment further. However, as already suggested by Marshall (1980), it is an issue that requires further investigation because overwork is a respectable source of stress, which might mask more serious, underlying problems. For example, Payne and Rick (1986) investigated the nature of severity of job demands. They asked about demands from patients, colleagues, relatives, demands on knowledge/skills and on physical capacities and made comparisons between surgeons and anaesthetists. Table 6.13 shows that the surgeons reported higher demands overall and perceived more strain regarding demands on their knowledge than interpersonal relationship issues, but overall, all respondents are reporting relatively low experiences of stress from these circumstances. This type of information is important in assessing the level of intervention for stress management programmes, i.e. to be aimed at the individual, or at change within the organization. Therefore the methodology is not suggested as an alternative, nor is it better than good qualitative data, because in the long-term both are equally useful and necessary.

Firth-Cozens and Morrison (1987) highlight the significance of good relationships at work. Three of the eight most frequently

Table 6.13 Job demands of surgeons and anaesthetists. Mean score ratings based on a five point scale (1 = very mild, 5 = very severe stress)

Variable	Surgeons	Anaesthetists
Demands on knowledge	1.53	1.15
Physical demands	1.35	1.17
Colleagues' demands	1.21	0.96
Demands on skill	1.19	1.11
Demands from other departments	1.19	0.92
Demands from patients	0.88	0.69
Demands from relatives of patients	0.82	0.15
	($n = 108$)	($n = 89$)

Source: Payne and Rick (1986).

mentioned stressors in Table 6.12 describe relationship problems. Stress is experienced from superiors, work colleagues and subordinates, but also from the boundary-role situation, that is, in dealing with patients' relatives. In situations where the quality of interpersonal relationships are poor, it is more likely that inappropriate coping styles might be employed. For example, individuals will be unwilling to ask for help or may try to dismiss an event, if perceived support is lacking and relationships with the boss are not good, especially among young men and women in the establishment phase of their careers (Hall, 1976).

The next two studies focused on the general practitioner. Porter *et al.* (1985) studied the relationship between workload, stress, job performance and quality of care in three group practices in Edinburgh. Eighteen doctors were monitored over three study days, using interview, diary and questionnaire methodologies to assess workload, workflow, perception of pressure experienced and potential stressor-mediating factors such as personality, social support and biographics. This study provides detailed and in-depth information about the allocation of time among general practitioners. The average consultation rate during 66 surgery sessions was 7 patients per hour (range = 3.8 to 11.5 patients per hour). Direct patient care accounted for 83% of the allocated time (excluding night work and weekend working). The findings reported by Porter *et al.* highlight the high degree of individual variability in experienced pressure and variation as a function of difference practices, which questions the value of averages. Some studies overcome this problem by the categorization of respondents as high or low stressed or high, medium or low risk (for example, in the Firth-Cozens and Morrison, 1988 study). By identifying profiles (i.e. strengths and weakness specific to each group), it is possible to tackle stress management from a more positive approach and avoid the problems related to the labelling of stress management intervention in negative, defensive terms. This is discussed in Chapter 7. Although Porter *et al.* observed high variability, they report that almost 50% of the 863 recordings received a pressure rating of 3 on a six-point scale (= optimal/ stimulated), and a quarter were rated 4 and over (4 = stretched, 5 = hurried, 6 = hectic/frantic). Porter *et al.* (1985, 1987) also found that the practice with the slowest consultation rate (5.9 patients per hour) recorded the lowest number of pressure scores (15%) and the practice with the highest consultation rate (8.0 patients per hour) recorded the highest number of pressure scores (32% scored 4 or more). As these authors suggest, it is necessary to understand the behavioural changes that might occur when the doctor is threatened by stress and what the consequences are for the patients.

For example, Morrell *et al.* (1986) found that in over 780 surgery sessions booked at five minute intervals, compared to 7.5 and/or 10 minute intervals, the five principals at a large group practice in the South East of England spent less face-to-face time with patients and identified fewer problems. Patients were also more likely to be less satisfied with the consultation. At this practice, individuals were normally booked in at the rate of nine per hour (6.7 minutes per patient). Under the three experimental conditions, the median times for face-to-face contact were 5.2, 6.7 and 7.4 minutes respectively. The study showed that doctors could not maintain or cope with a five minute interval schedule (i.e. no time for all the other chores, e.g. record keeping, preparing instruments, etc.) but wide variation existed (that is, a range of 0.7–29 minutes per consultation). However, contrary to other evidence there was no indication that patients who attended sessions booked at the shorter intervals received more prescriptions, were referred more often to hospital specialists, or returned more often for further consultation within four weeks. In addition, there was no evidence of more stress as a function of shorter and more frequent consultations, although the doctors complained more of a time shortage. Indeed, other studies have observed associations between degree of job satisfaction and performance, for example, Grol *et al.* (1985) observed 57 general practitioners and found that negative feelings about work; tension, frustration and time pressures, were associated with a tendency not to provide patients with explanations and with a high rate of prescription. However, positive feelings about work (satisfaction and feeling at ease) were associated with a more open approach to patients and more attention to the psychosocial aspects of complaints. Porter *et al.* believe that the way forward in this type of research is in making longitudinal comparisons of stress levels in the one individual and the examination of change in content and style of practice as the general practitioner becomes more stressed, that is, the individual acts as his/her own control. This contrasts with the next study, which is on a large scale and aims to identify the predictors of stress outcomes and symptoms in a national sample. Ultimately, different research designs complement each other and so both are important and necessary.

The objectives for Cooper *et al.* (1989b) were to identify sources of job stress associated with high levels of job dissatisfaction and reduced mental well-being among general practitioners in England — highlighting gender comparisons as well. A questionnaire, based on pilot study findings (Makin *et al.*, 1988), was sent to a random sample of 4000 general practitioners throughout the country, achieving a high response rate (48.2%).

The final sample for analysis ($n = 1817$) comprised 1474 male doctors (81.1%) and 343 women doctors (18.9%). Of these, 91% were in group practice. The demographic picture was typical of this occupational group nationally, except that slightly fewer doctors aged 65 or over responded to the survey. In terms of health behaviour outcomes, 91% of general practitioners did not smoke; 32.5% had an occasional drink, 36.7% had several drinks a week, 18.6% had one or two drinks every day, and nearly 6% had three to six drinks, or more, daily. Male doctors consumed significantly more alcohol than the female respondents.

Potential sources of stress, identified by in-depth interviews in the pilot study, were rated on a five-point scale and the 38 items were analysed to identify common stressor themes or patterns. Table 6.14 lists the items that were grouped statistically into six factors or themes; namely, demands of job and patients' expectations; interruptions; practice administration; work and home interface and social life; dealing with death and dying; and medical responsibilities for friends and relatives.

Many of these sources of stress are the same as those identified by Mawardi (1979) in an American study of private practitioners. The greatest dissatisfaction cited by these 180 physicians, included continuous on-call responsibilities, the demands of the workload and too little personal time.

In terms of outcomes, Cooper *et al.* (1989b) observed that women doctors were significantly more job satisfied than male general practitioners. Satisfactions were greatest with intrinsic features of the job, that is, the amount of freedom, responsibility and variety at work. The lowest levels of satisfaction were the extrinsic factors, such as hours of work and rate of pay. Stepwise regression analysis (used to identify the predictors of outcomes or symptoms), showed that the stressors associated with the demands of the job, the work and home interface, interruptions and practice administration were predictive of job dissatisfaction. Separate

221

Table 6.14 Factor analysis — job stressors identified by general practitioners

---

Stressors

Factor 1 Demands of job and patients' expectations (62.8% of variance)
Fear of assault during night visits
Visiting in extremely adverse weather conditions
Adverse publicity by media
Increased demand by patients and relatives for second
    opinion from hospital specialists
No appreciation of your work by patients
Worrying about patients' complaints
Finding a locum
Twenty four hour responsibility for patients' lives
Taking several samples in a short time
Unrealistically high expectations by others of your role

Factor 2 Interruptions (10.6% of variance)
Coping with phone calls during night and early morning
Night calls
Interruption of family life by telephone
Emergency calls during surgery hours
Home visits
Dealing with problem patients
Remaining alert when on call

Factor 3 Practice administration (8.6% of variance)
Hospital referrals and paperwork
Conducting surgery
Practice administration
Home visits
Arranging admissions
Working environment (surgery set up)
Time pressure

Factor 4 Work: home interface and social life (7.7% of variance)
Demands of your job on family life
Dividing time between spouse and patients
Demands of your job on social life
Lack of emotional support at home, especially from spouse
Interruption of family life by telephone

Factor 5 Dealing with death and dying (5.5% of variance)
Daily contact with dying and chronically ill patients
Dealing with the terminally ill and their relatives

Factor 6 Medical responsibility for friends and relatives (4.8% of variance)
Dealing with friends as patients
Dealing with relatives as patients

Source: Cooper, Rout and Faragher (1989).

analyses for male and female doctors revealed the same predictors but the most significant predictor of job dissatisfaction for male doctors was the stress of the demands of the job; and for women, it was work/home interface stress. This is not surprising, Heins *et al.* (1977) found that women physicians spend 90% as much time in medical practice as male physicians, yet they still assume full responsibility for the home and family and so they have the added burden of trying to balance the demands imposed by both roles.

Three scales of the Crown Crisp Experiential Index were used to measure levels of anxiety, depression and somatic anxiety among this group. Compared to general population norms, the women doctors had significantly lower scores on all three dimensions (high scores = reduced well-being). On the other hand, male general practitioners had significantly higher levels of free-floating anxiety than normative comparison groups, although this emotional anxiety did not reflect in psychosomatic complaints (i.e. low levels of reported somatic anxiety). Stressor predictors of overall mental ill-health included, interruptions at work and home, the stress of practice administration, job demands and patients expectations, and the work/home interface stress (Table 6.14). Again, only slight differences were observed as a function of gender. Although the same predictors were revealed, the strongest predictor of mental ill-health among the women doctors was the stress of the job interfering with family life, whereas interruptions, practice administration and job demands, were again more significant predictor variables for male general practitioners. High TAB pattern was also associated with a reduced level of mental well-being, for example, those who were overly conscious of time, very ambitious, hard driven, and competitive, etc., were more likely to exhibit lower levels of overall mental health. In conclusion, the authors point out that the sources of stress identified as significant predictors of both job dissatisfaction and mental well-being were related to social and managerial skills, rather than technical skills and abilities. These skills can be developed by training. For example, time management, people management and work organization skill development will directly help to reduce the stress associated with these problem areas in work, but might also help indirectly by minimizing the impact of their job on family life. It was also suggested that the provision of a counselling service for general practitioners and other health care workers would be beneficial; 'we cannot expect general practitioners to be supermen

223

and superwomen; as carers they may find that they need to be cared for as well' (Cooper *et al.*, 1989b). Although the well-being of the women doctors in this survey was quite good, they were exposed to the additional burden of trying to balance home and work life demands. In the long-term this might have negative consequences. Thus, perhaps women doctors working in group practices would benefit from some practical help to minimize these pressures. But, as Cartwright (1987) suggests, life stage plays a significant role in the perception of stress. Needs, expectations and responses to stress will vary as a function of age, career stage and other commitments. These issues must be considered in the identification of stress and the subsequent implementation of stress management programmes. Nevertheless, this is equally important for both male and female general practitioners.

CONCLUSION

In this chapter we have considered sources of stress in certain groups of health professionals. The themes common to many of these groups are the issues of understaffing, high levels of demand and the threat of change. It is also clear that response to stress is not invariant and differences exist as a function of individual personality/biographical variations, and/or task and speciality needs and expectations. Some potential sources of stress could be minimized or eliminated by organizational change in systems and practices, or by improved skills training (e.g. social and managerial skills training) but obviously some stress is inherent to the job and cannot be changed. Although we still do not know enough about positive stressors, that is, the stress that motivates, challenges and provides variety and stimulation at work, it is necessary to help the individual cope with distress, i.e. unwanted strain and pressure. The management of stress is the focus of the next and final chapter of this book, and aims to provide self-help information for health professionals, and to increase their understanding of stress management interventions generally. In the long-term, it is hoped that these strategies will be used proactively rather than reactively in patient health and well-being, perhaps in conjunction with occupational and/or environmental health programmes, but also by those individuals working in the health professions.

7

Managing Stress

In the previous chapters, we have seen that stress can create many problems for people. These may be of a physical, psychological or behavioural nature and are the symptoms or outcomes of exposure to a wide range of potential stressor agents. Response to stress is also mediated by a variety of personal characteristics, which may render the individual more or less vulnerable to pressure or strain. Stress and response to stress are multi-faceted concepts, and thus the management of stress also takes many forms. In the first section of this chapter, we will consider some of the ways in which the individual can deal with stress and, hopefully, become more effective at coping with strain and pressure. However, increasingly more organizations are realizing the benefits of the introduction of stress management into the workplace and so these interventions are discussed in the second section of the chapter. Indeed, there is some evidence of the introduction of stress management into the National Health Service (Harvey, *et al.*, 1988), and so this information might be useful for the health professional who finds him/herself recruited into a stress reduction programme, and/or for health-care personnel who are enlisted to implement stress management in the workplace.

COPING WITH STRESS — INDIVIDUAL APPROACHES

From the preceding chapters, many individuals might have begun to identify themselves and can recognize situations, feelings and reactions to stress. Certain personality characteristics and styles of behaviour will sound familiar and stressor situations may painfully describe the circumstances in which you are required to work and live. This is the first principle of stress management; know thyself. It is important to understand what makes us stress prone or stress resistant and when coping changes from adaptive behaviour to maladaptive behaviour. When stimulating pressure changes from debilitating stress we can describe the subsequent strain as distress.

Self-awareness

In this section we will provide some aids and techniques to reduce stress levels but it is our firm belief that any success in dealing with stress must begin with self knowledge. It is important to understand how your high stress is created. For example, whether it stems from personal conflicts within you, from a need to create more balance in your life, or from sources beyond your immediate control. Many researchers and stress management interventionists have criticized organizations for doing too little to reduce stress at work. All too often the blame is placed on the employee, who is encouraged to become stress resistant or more able to cope with stress at work. This is discussed more in the next section. It is relevant here because it is important for the individual to understand that he or she is not necessarily at fault. False acceptance of blame is likely to lead to inappropriate coping strategies. For example, if you believe that you are the only person in the department who cannot cope with the workload, you become unhappy, you might consume more than the occasional drink to relax or unwind or help you get to sleep, until the behaviour becomes a need. For most people, there is no one problem that must be solved; neither is there one answer. As discussed throughout this book, poor coping with stress usually involves many factors, including the individual's personality and coping strategies, life events encountered and degree of social support.

While there are many things an individual cannot control, such as the loss of a loved one, many things most certainly can be managed or at least modified by the individual. Often, self-knowledge brings the awareness that an individual must alter his or her perceptions, behaviour, lifestyle or personal situation in order to cope effectively with stress.

Listed in Table 7.1 are some of the stressor agents discussed in Chapter Three, together with a comparison of adaptive and malad-aptive behaviours. It can be seen that maladaptive behaviour often

Table 7.1

Stress agent	Adaptive behaviour	Maladaptive behaviour
Overwork	Delegates some work	Accepts work overload with result that general performance deteriorates
Lack of awareness of a particular company policy	Finds out what policy is	Guesses inappropriately
Poor working relationship with colleague	Confronts issue with colleague and negotiates better relationship	Attacks colleague indirectly through third party
Underpromotion	Leaves organisation for another	Loses confidence and becomes convinced of own inadequacy
Company versus family demands	Negotiates with boss more 'family time' (e.g., less travel)	Blames company for family discontent
Role ambiguity	Seeks clarification with colleagues or superior	Withdraws from some aspects of work role

Source: Cooper, Cooper & Eaker, *Living with Stress*, Penguin, 1988.

is associated with denial of a problem; it is avoided, or ignored and often becomes aggravated until the situation becomes chronic or acute.

In all the above situations, there is something that the individual and/or the organization can do to transform maladaptive behaviours, which are harmful to the person and those around him or her, into adaptive behaviours. For some people, the changes required may be simple ones but each of these behaviours takes the basic source of the stress and solves it, sometimes temporarily and perhaps permanently. Therefore, it is necessary to recognize the problem. This is not always easy because we often obscure the real reasons behind our problems. We find respectable stressors to blame. For example, overwork is a safe reason to explain our change in behaviour, because everyone is complaining (constantly tired, fatigued/unable to sleep properly, smoking more cigarettes), but in reality, the stress of being passed-over for promotion, the disappointment and the thwarted ambition might be the real

227

reasons for the stress but are much harder to admit to ourselves and others. This could be the real stressor, but of course, it also might make it much harder to cope with the overwork situation. Rarely do we cope with just one situation in isolation. This is what Cooper and Kelly (1984) call the stress-chain, where one situation is linked to another.

To understand those incidents and series of related incidents during the working days, weeks, and months that cause you distress, it might help to keep a stress diary. This should provide you with information about the type of situation, or person, that causes you the most difficulty. An awareness of this should help you to develop an action plan to minimize or eliminate the stress factor, or at the very least, alert you to when a stressful event (in your terms) is about to take place. At the end of each day, for two–four weeks, list all the incidents and the people involved, which caused you distress during the working day. In addition, indicate the actions taken and what you feel, in retrospect, you should have done. It might also be helpful to monitor your response to the stressor. You can soon learn to recognize your own personal stress warning signals — such as headaches, stomach pains, muscle tension, depression, anxiety or a strong desire to escape from a situation. Try to record:

1. Day of week, and time;
2. The incident (what happened);
3. People involved;
4. What you did;
5. Your physical and/or emotional feelings;
6. What you should have done.

At the end of the time allotted, survey the incidents and people involved which caused you the most stress and try to pinpoint particular types of events and specific people who consistently seem to be implicated in stressful work experiences. For example, were your stressors varied, or did they consistently group into a certain type of incident.

1. Were they related to:
   (a) home and work overspill problems (conflicting demands)?
   (b) your work role (clarity, responsibility)?
   (c) overload/time pressures, etc.?
   (d) relationships at work?

(e) being in the organization (very competitive, non-supportive)?
2. Were specific people consistently implicated in the stressful situation? (e.g. the boss, your colleagues, your subordinates, patients, spouse, partner, the family, etc.)?
3. Look through all the types of events and the specific people involved, and begin to make action plans for the future to deal with the problem area.

For example, if you consistently find you had difficulty in dealing with your boss when it came to deadlines, think about the alternative strategies open to you to cope with this type of situation and the particular personality of the boss involved. Each incident and/ or relationship can be managed if you accurately identify the problem and systematically think through the options or alternative methods of coping. Each of the coping strategies should then be ranked in terms of their likelihood of success in achieving your objectives, primarily to minimize future stress and accomplish your work-related tasks and goals. The objective is to devote a space of a few hours to analysing specifically when, where and why you feel tense or stressful. Periodically setting aside time to analyse the sources of stress and balance in your life can become a tremendously rewarding habit. In addition, becoming aware of your body's responses to stress and anxiety can begin to provide valuable clues to what's happening in your life. For some people, actual changes in home or work arrangements may be necessary, others may find that changes are needed in their behaviour; to learn to relax or to become more assertive. Of course, a person can always choose not to make any changes and to continue as usual and hope for the best. The person who refuses to make changes in his or her life is really choosing to endure the present situation, rather than trying to improve things. Change and taking responsibility may be difficult but the rewards, in terms of personal happiness and effectiveness, may be worth the effort involved.

Dyer (1976) describes self-immobilization as the force of resistance to change in our lives; this can range from total inaction to mild indecision and hesitancy. He argues that we must cut through this unhealthy, yet understandable resistance in order to release our potential for happiness. Individuals need to focus on those aspects of lifestyle that may create immobility. A number of possible behaviours reflect this state:

You are immobilized when:

1. You can't talk lovingly to your spouse and children though you want to;
2. You can't work on a project that interests you;
3. You don't make love and would like to;
4. You sit in the house all day and brood;
5. You don't play golf, tennis, or other enjoyable activities, because of a leftover gnawing feeling;
6. You can't introduce yourself to someone who appeals to you;
7. You avoid talking to someone when you realize that a simple gesture would improve your relationship;
8. You can't sleep because something is bothering you;
9. Your anger keeps you from thinking clearly;
10. You say something abusive to someone you love;
11. Your face is twitching, or you are so nervous that you don't function in the way you would prefer.

(Dyer, 1976)

Dyer believes an individual must be able to identify the problem areas or lifestyle patterns that are preventing him or her from achieving life goals and then cut through the lifetime of emotional red tape by changing behaviour and re-designing these patterns. Dyer warns against blaming any circumstance or other person for your failures or an unsatisfying mode of living. People must own up, take responsibility and choose a more satisfying way to live. Part of the processes of know-thyself is deciding how you want to live. Often a stressful lifestyle creeps upon us so insidiously that we fail to recognize its presence until we experience negative consequences. Albrecht (1979) provides cameo descriptions of low stress versus high stress lifestyles among managers, although these patterns are typical for many occupational groups. In Table 7.2, it is possible to compare the differences between reasonable living patterns and the destructive ways of high-stress living. The table shows that many elements of the low-stress lifestyle are ways of living based on common sense, such as eating well and using alcohol sparingly or not at all. Other elements, such as the development of escape routes and a lifestyle with little role-conflict are more creative approaches.

Table 7.2 High-and low-stress lifestyle

Stressful lifestyle	Low-stress lifestyle
Individual experiences chronic, unrelieved stress.	Individual accepts 'creative' stress for distinct periods of challenging activity.
Becomes trapped in one or more continuing stressful situations. Struggles with stressful interpersonal relationships (family, spouse, lover, boss, co-workers, etc.).	Has 'escape routes' allowing occasional detachment and relaxation. Asserts own rights and needs; negotiates low-stress relationships of mutual respect; selects friends carefully and establishes relationships that are nourishing and not harmful.
Engages in distasteful, dull, toxic, or otherwise unpleasant and unrewarding work.	Engages in challenging, satisfying, worthwhile work that offers intrinsic rewards for accomplishment.
Experiences continual time stress: too much to be done in available time.	Maintains a well-balanced and challenging workload; overloads and crises are balanced by 'breather' periods.
Worries about potentially unpleasant up-coming events.	Balances threatening events with worthwhile goals and positive events to look forward to.
Has poor health habits (e.g. eating, smoking, liquor, lack of exercise, poor level of physical fitness). Life activities are 'lopsided' or unbalanced (e.g. preoccupied with one activity such as work, social activities, making money, solitude, or physical activities).	Maintains high level of physical fitness, eats well, uses alcohol and tobacco not at all or sparingly. Life activities are balanced: individual invests energies in a variety of activities, which, in the aggregate, bring feelings of satisfaction (e.g. work, social activities, recreation, solitude, cultural pursuits, family and close relationships).
Finds it difficult to just 'have a good time', relax and enjoy momentary activities. Experiences sexual activities as unpleasant, unrewarding, or socially programmed (e.g. by manipulation, 'one-upping').	Finds pleasure in simple activities, without feeling a need to justify playful behaviour: Enjoys a full and exuberant sex life, with honest expression of sexual appetite.
Sees life as a serious, difficult situation; little sense of humour.	Enjoys life, on the whole; can laugh at him/herself, has a well-developed and well-exercised sense of humour.
Conforms to imprisoning, punishing social roles.	Lives a relatively role-free life; is able to express natural needs, desires, and feelings without apology.
Accepts high-pressure or stressful situations passively; suffers in silence.	Acts assertively to re-engineer pressure situations whenever possible; renegotiates impossible deadlines; avoids being placed in unnecessary pressure situations; manages time effectively.

Source: Karl Albrecht, *Stress and the Manager*, New Jersey: Prentice-Hall, (1979) 107–8.

Managing your lifestyle

Once you have identified what is happening in your life at work or
at home and how you want to live, there are several courses of
action that may help to either remove or reduce stress, or enable
you to cope more effectively with strain and pressure. This requires
making changes which can seem overwhelming at first. However,
as Cooper *et al.* (1988) suggest, stress is not some all-powerful
force in your life that cannot be resisted. By keeping a stress-diary,
you will be able to see more clearly that stress situations can be
altered, managed or balanced with positive experiences, for
example, by rewarding yourself with a relaxing weekend-break
when a difficult and threatening situation has been satisfactorily
finalized. It is also necessary to consider why you might be
resistant to change or insist on clinging on to old ways that seem
safe but in the long-term harmful. Often we can see other's
mistakes more readily than our own, so observe someone close
who seems to be suffering from stress and try and work out how
they could change and improve their situation. Why do they take
on more and more work, instead of saying 'No'? Are you behaving
in the same way? Unfortunately, depressed people tend to find it
difficult to see options and so an outside observer might be willing
to offer alternative ways of behaving. We must avoid being
inflexible to change and be more willing to try out new ways of
behaving in order to reduce or minimize the consequences of
stress.

Being more assertive

Many of the problems individuals face at work are associated with
their own inability to be assertive in their relationships with work
colleagues, bosses and even subordinates. This can reflect itself in
allowing work overload, long hours, frequent travel and a range of
inappropriate activities, which can be individually and organiz-
ationally counterproductive. Alberti and Emmons (1970) describe
the assertive person as open and flexible, genuinely concerned with
the rights of others, yet at the same time able to establish very well
his or her own rights. There are fundamental differences between
assertive, non-assertive and aggressive behaviour. When you are
assertive you are acknowledging your own rights and those of
others; when non-assertive you are denying your own rights; and

232

when aggressive, denying the rights of others. In being assertive we imply certain basic individual rights:

1. The right to make mistakes;
2. The right to set one's own priorities;
3. The right for one's own needs to be considered as important as the needs of other people;
4. The right to refuse requests without having to feel guilty;
5. The right to express oneself as long as one doesn't violate the rights of others;
6. The right to judge one's own behaviour, thoughts and emotions and to take responsibility for the consequences.

Keeping in mind the differences between aggressiveness and assertiveness, many individuals would benefit from assertiveness training. The goal is to help people to learn to solve problems and enable them to say; 'I feel OK about myself. I don't have to make others feel not OK in order for me to get my needs met. I know what I want. I feel good about myself and others. I can think and I have confidence to ask for what I want'. Langrish (1981) provides very detailed help in becoming more assertive. It is necessary to identify those people and activities with which you have difficulty in behaving assertively. Basically, she advocates a five stage approach:

1. Identification of your level of assertiveness. For example, how comfortable do you feel about activities such as asking for help or favours, refusing requests, expressing negative feelings such as annoyance, anger or displeasure, or expressing positive feelings, giving or receiving compliments, initiating and maintaining conversations and standing up for your rights with the people around you at work and at home?
2. Establish a hierarchy of difficulty. This means that you draw up a list to identify problem areas according to the level of difficulty in handling the situation. Once the hierarchy has been constructed, it permits the identification of both short-term and long-term goals, i.e. are anxiety-producing situations always with specific people and/or in certain situations and/or circumstances.
3. Introduce systematic assertiveness training skills. Smith (1975) suggests that these include:

(a) Broken record: a skill that by calm repetition, saying what you want over and over again, teaches persistence, and permits you to ignore manipulative verbal side traps, argumentative baiting and irrelevant logic, while sticking to your desired point. This is particularly effective with persistent salesmen.

(b) Fogging: the acceptance of manipulative criticism by calmly acknowledging to your critic the probability that there may be some truth in what he or she says, yet allows you to remain your own judge of what you do. This allows you to receive criticism comfortably without becoming anxious or defensive.

(c) Negative assertion: acceptance of your errors and faults (without having to apologize), by strongly and sympathetically agreeing with hostile or constructive criticism of your negative qualities. It permits you to look more comfortably at negative elements in your own behaviour without feeling defensive and anxious, or resorting to denial of real errors.

(d) Negative inquiry: the active prompting of criticism in order to use the information (if helpful) or exhaust it (if manipulative), while prompting your critic to be more assertive and less dependent on manipulative ploys. It encourages the other person to express honest negative feelings and improves communication.

(e) Workable compromise: use whenever you feel your self-respect is not in question. Here, you offer a workable compromise to the other person. However, if the end goal involves a matter of your self-worth, there can be no compromise.

(f) Non-verbal communication: when being assertive, a person generally establishes good eye contact, stands or sits comfortably without fidgeting and talks in a strong, steady voice, neither shouting nor mumbling. Assertive words include 'I' statements such as 'I think', 'I feel', 'I want'; co-operative words such as 'let's', or 'we could', and empathic statements of interest such as 'what do you think', 'how do you feel'. A non-assertive response is self-effacing and may be accompanied by such mannerisms as the shifting of weight, downcast eyes, a slumped body posture or a hesitant, giggly or whining voice. Non-assertive words can include qualifiers such as 'maybe', 'I wonder if you could', 'only', 'just', etc.

(g) Avoid aggression: this response is typically expressed by inappropriate anger or hostility which is loudly and explosively uttered. It is characterized by glaring eyes, leaning forward or pointing a finger, and an angry tone of voice. Aggressive words include threats such as 'you'd better' or 'if you don't watch out', put-downs such as 'come on', or 'you must be kidding', and evaluative comments such as 'should', 'I thought you'd know better'. Indirectly aggressive behaviour uses the language of the non-assertive response combined with the non-verbal behaviour of the aggressive mode, concentrating on body posture and angry movements.

4. The fourth stage consists of rehearsal of the appropriate behaviours. This might require formal training, or help from friends and colleagues could be elicited to role play a typical situation. It is important that realistic goals are set, otherwise it will not translate into the performance of assertive behaviour. By starting to be more assertive in a minor problem area, it is possible to build on success, until more difficult situations can gradually be tackled.

5. Finally, transfer the learned behaviour back into the workplace, or home. Keep a daily record of what happened, and how you behaved. It is then possible to evaluate progress and modify future actions in the light of the outcomes of your behaviour, i.e. are you achieving your goals?

Relaxation and exercises

Changing long-lived behaviour patterns are major stress-reduction efforts that take time. Problems are not always simple and rarely does a single answer exist. While you are investing the time and energy needed to sort out the stress factors in your life, there is some more immediate relief available to you — relaxation. A number of excellent books on the subject of stress control and relaxation have been written by stress management consultants who have used their ideas to help individuals and organizations with stress-related problems. The 'purpose of relaxation training is to reduce the individual's arousal level and bring about a calmer

235

state of affairs from both psychological and physiological perspectives. Psychologically, successful relaxation results in enhanced feelings of well-being, peacefulness, a sense of control, and a reduction in felt tension and anxiety: physiologically, decrease in blood pressure, respiration, and heart rate should take place' (Matteson and Invancevich, 1987). Some of the original research on the use of relaxation as a method of stress reduction was pioneered by Benson (1975), although the technique of progressive relaxation was developed by Dr. Edmund Jacobson in the 1920s.

Techniques taught include various forms of meditation, autogenic training (a combination of muscle relaxation and meditation) and relaxation strategies which might consist of breathing exercises, progressive muscle relaxation, self hypnosis, mental imagery and visualization. Carrington *et al.* (1980) incorporated meditation–relaxation techniques in a stress-control programme developed for the New York Telephone Company, and report that the techniques are easily learned and have positive psychological and physical effects on work stress when practised regularly.

The body needs time to relax and recuperate from the effects of everyday stress. Some people can dissipate stress, while others bury it deep within themselves and, for these people life seems to be a series of crises. The chronically up-tight person seems to meet even a small problem as if it were a critical incident, as if somehow his survival were in jeopardy. A sudden call to go and see the boss, a snag in a project schedule, a disagreement with a co-worker, or a problem with a teenage son or daughter all take on the same apparent magnitude for the up-tight person. Such a person meets even the smallest problem situations with an unnecessarily intense reaction (Albrecht, 1979). This kind of stress can reflect itself in a variety of personally damaging behaviours, such as excessive coffee or tea consumption, cigarette smoking, drug-taking and so forth. Most people believe, for example, that the coffee break provides a useful stress-free breathing space, which it can do. It also, however, provides the individual with a further stimulant, as opposed to a relaxant, which can actually adversely affect the biochemical balance in the body. There are a whole range of activities we do during the course of each day which feel right at the time but which can have deterimental effects in the short or medium term. Shaffer's (1983) description of common misguided attempts to relax can be found in his book *Life After Stress*. For example, smoking cigarettes is seen as a pick-me-up or social activity, which also provides increased energy but causes indigestion and poor sleep; drinking wine is a pausing, social activity and muscle relaxant ... but is also a depressant and energy drain; eating sugar or chocolate is seen as a pick-me-up, arousing and a social pause, but is only empty calories and nutritionally poor. Relaxation can combat some of these adverse reactions. The positive bodily outcomes of deep relaxation as a means of coping with peak arousal situations can be found in Table 7.3. This is achieved by the deep relaxation technique. It is a simple technique, which anyone can practise. If you feel somewhat tense about the thought of adding such a technique to your daily life, we suggest you make a commitment to practise relaxation on a daily basis for one month before deciding if you want to continue. Following this technique is a brief description of a shorter relaxation technique, which you may find helpful and more compatible with your lifestyle.

Deep relaxation

For optimal effectiveness, deep relaxation is best done once or twice a day. It can help to assist your body in recovering from distress and prevent the build-up of tension, fatigue, and anxiety.

Table 7.3 The stress response versus the relaxation response

	Peak arousal	Deep relaxation
Adrenalin	More	Less
Respiration	Faster	Slower
Heart	Faster	Slower
Arteries	Constrict	Dilate
Blood pressure	Increase	Decrease
Metabolism	Faster	Slower
Muscle tension	Increase	Decrease
Stomach acid	More	Less
Blood sugar	More	Less
Insulin	More	Less
Cholesterol in blood	More	Less
Brain waves	Beta (i.e. less productive cognitive processes)	Alpha or theta (i.e. more creative cognitive processes)

Source: Nita Catterton (unpublished paper) University of Virginia.

Nita Catterton of the University of Virginia uses the following techniques:

1. Sit in a comfortable position. (Support your upper back, neck and head.) A quiet place where you will not be interrupted is best.
2. Slowly draw in and exhale a deep breath. Check your shoulders for stiffness or tense position. Allow them to fall naturally in a relaxed position. Take in a second deep breath and close your eyes.
3. Complete a body check to locate any areas of tension and tightness. Take each area and relax the involved muscles. Visualize the tension releasing and slipping away as warmth and relaxation flow into the area. You might imagine yourself basking in the sun and feeling the sun warm your area of tension. (If you are having difficulty evaluating whether or not you are relaxing a specific area try increasing the tension in the muscle and hold that tightness for a count of ten, then release.)
4. Starting with your feet, slowly work up through the body, relaxing muscle groups and areas of tightness and tension. Imagine warmth flowing into each area, muscles becoming heavy, and comforting relaxation replacing tightness or tension. Once you've progressed throughout your body, focus on your hands. (You can focus on any area of tension you'd like to work on.) Create a sentence that you can repeat to yourself emphasizing warmth, heaviness, and relaxation, such as; 'My hands are warm, heavy, and relaxed'.
5. Do not be discouraged if at first your mind tends to wander away to other thoughts. Once you are aware that you have wandered to other thoughts simply come back and focus again on the area you are relaxing. Try to notice how good it feels to have some quiet time to yourself and how comfortable it is to let go of any tightness or tension you may have.
6. Deep relaxation is most effective when practised for a length of 20 minutes. If you find that sitting still for that long is more stress-inducing than stress-reducing then start with a period of five or ten minutes and gradually build up to 20 minutes.

7. Always end your relaxation session with several deep breaths. Then, after slowly opening your eyes, maintain your relaxation position for a few minutes before resuming your next activity.

Make a commitment to practise deep relaxation on a daily basis for one month before determining if you want to continue with this stress-reduction technique. Tisdelle *et al.* (1984) used deep muscle relaxation in a stress management programme for dental students. Compared to matched controls, after six sessions (where relaxation, cognitive modification and the usefulness of leisure activities were taught and practised) systolic blood pressure was reduced. After a further three months, the treatment group showed a reduction in trait anxiety and reported that fewer situations caused them stress.

Short relaxation exercise

Shorter relaxation exercises which take a maximum of ten minutes to practise can also be helpful. The following exercise, developed by Dr. Cary McCarthy, is aimed at allowing an individual to evoke a feeling of peace and relaxation whenever desired.

Five to ten minute exercise:

1. Select a comfortable sitting or reclining position.
2. Close your eyes and think about a place that you have been before that represents your ideal place for physical and mental relaxation. (It should be a quiet environment, perhaps the seashore, the mountains, or even your own back garden. If you can't think of an ideal relaxation place, then create one in your mind.)
3. Now imagine that you are actually in your ideal relaxation place. Imagine that you are seeing all the colours, hearing the sounds, smelling the aromas. Just lie back, and enjoy your soothing, rejuvenating environment.
4. Feel the peacefulness, the calmness, and imgine your whole body and mind being renewed and refreshed.
5. After five to ten minutes, slowly open your eyes and stretch. You have the realization that you may instantly return to your relaxation place whenever you desire, and experience a peacefulness and calmness in body and mind.

Momentary relaxation

While the relaxation exercises above require an investment in time, from a few minutes to twenty or more, once you have achieved deep relaxation you can also begin to draw upon your memory of relaxation to achieve partial relaxation during the day. Taking a few deep, slow breaths can often bring on this feeling of relaxation. Albrecht (1979) states that the skill of momentary relaxation should come almost automatically once an individual has mastered a deep relaxation technique. With the following examples he describes the feeling of momentary relaxation:

> The next time you find yourself about to deal with a challenging, stressful situation, simply pause for a few seconds, turn your attention to your body and allow your whole body to relax as much as you can, keeping the situation in mind. You can easily learn to do this 'quickie' relaxation technique in a few seconds and without the slightest outward sign of what you are doing. Anyone looking at you would notice, at most, that you had become silent and that you seemed to be thinking about something for a few seconds. You need not even close your eyes to do this.
>
> If you happen to have a few moments alone before entering the challenge situation, you can relax yourself somewhat more thoroughly. Sit down, if possible, get comfortable, and close your eyes. Use your built-in muscle memory to bring back the feeling of deep relaxation and hold it for about a full minute. Then open your eyes and, as you go about the task at hand, try to retain the feeling of calmness that came with the relaxation. (Albrecht, 1979)

In addition, techniques including meditation, self-hypnosis, biofeedback and autogenic training may be used in order to relax. These usually require the help of experts and/or therapists and require training over a period of time to induce a general feeling of well-being and high coping ability.

Physical fitness and exercise

Research is increasingly giving credence to the idea that exercise is good for the mind as well as the body. For example, Quick and Quick (1984) state that aerobically fit individuals have been shown to have a better interplay between their activating, stress-response sympathetic nervous system and their relaxing, restorative para-sympathetic nervous system. This suggests that fit individuals may be less psychologically reactive in stressful situations. Additional benefits of exercise include improved self-esteem, more restful sleep, a stronger and more attractive body and reduction of anxiety and depression. Anyone considering starting to exercise should begin gradually. In addition, many health promotion bodies recommend that people above the age of 35 have their physician's approval before beginning a new exercise programme.

Exercise is viewed as a coping mechanism which reduces the physiological consequences of stressful situations, alters mood states in the short-term, and personality traits (e.g. anxiety and depression) in the long-term (Falkenberg, 1987). It is suggested that; 1. engaging in long-term aerobic exercise may decrease the level of physiological arousal which occurs during stressful situations; 2. exercising during a stressful event will discharge the physical excitation build-up in the response to stress, i.e. the metabolism of fatty acids released into the blood stream, etc., and 3. exercise activity may induce a state of relaxation. However, the exact psychological and physiological processes which exercise contributes to stress management are not fully understood (Matteson and Ivancevich, 1987). Aerobic exercise has received the most praise as a stress antidote. Through aerobic exercise, the individual's heart rate and respiration rate are sustained at a high level for twenty to thirty minutes. Jogging, brisk walking, aerobic dancing, and swimming are all aerobic exercises. According to Quick and Quick (1984), aerobic exercise is the only form of exercise which can predictably achieve cardio-respiratory fitness. Recreational sports such as squash and tennis can all be excellent ways of releasing tension and frustration but they do not provide the aerobic benefits. Similarly, many people find that a favourite activity or hobby, such as gardening, sewing, listening to music, or soaking in a hot bath, can be tremendously helpful in releasing the build-up of tension. The key to such activities is that they can be done purely for the pleasure they bring. Although such traditional methods of relaxing have received little attention from researchers, many people know that engaging in a favourite activity can help repair the ravages of the day.

'Venting-steam'

In addition to taking advantage of the physical outlet provided by exercise and recreation, you may also find stress relief through talking or writing about your feelings. Venting frustration and anger to an understanding co-worker, friend or family member is one of the most common means of venting steam. Writing down your thoughts can also effectively reduce feelings of conflict or anger. Keeping a regular journal of your feelings or simply dashing off an angry letter that is either thrown away or later revised when emotions have cooled can be therapeutic.

Sleep patterns

'The brain, which controls biological survival, needs rest to maintain its equilibrium ... the brain, without adequate rest and sleep, cannot maintain the biochemical and electrical balances needed for effective functioning ... When the brain is in a state of disequilibrium, a person cannot cope effectively' (Shaffer, 1983). Sleep disturbance affects both functioning and mood states and the body is denied the opportunity for recuperation and repair. Difficulty falling asleep, insomnia, and early morning awakening can all reflect depression or anxiety. Individuals who rely on alcohol to unwind and fall asleep in the evening may often find they awaken in the early morning when their bodies respond to an alcohol-induced adrenalin surge (Quick and Quick, 1984). Individual differences in sleep patterns and needs vary greatly, but we recognize our own particular pattern of behaviour and usually realize that changes may signal strain or pressure. A relaxation exercise, walking the dog or taking a warm bath before retiring to bed may facilitate sleep. Part of our personal action plan for dealing with stress might include resolving to put aside emotional conflicts, or to avoid overeating in the evening hours. Daytime rest periods may also be beneficial. The break must involve a complete withdrawal from the day's activities, but even a brief change in scenery can be refreshing. Shaffer (1983) also suggests that daytime resting or breaks can moderate illness.

A proper diet

While much controversy exists about certain questions on diet and health, most stress researchers appear to agree about the value of eating to maintain level energy reserves through the day and to keep weight at a proper level. The age-old adage, moderation in all things, seems to be sound advice today. Large amounts of sugar, processed foods, alcohol and caffeine have been connected with poor overall health, irregular energy patterns and lowered resistance to illness and stress. Increasing awareness of the possible relationship between certain foods and allergies, delinquent behaviour, anxiety, headache, tension and fatigue are reported. Rippere (1989) describes a wide variety of adult psychiatric problems that have been associated with nutrient deficiencies, food allergies, food addictions and caffeine intake. As she points out, it is pointless to refer an individual to relaxation training while their caffeine intake, from coffee, tea, chocolate and cola, is around one gram per day. However, this form of advice requires specialist help and is recommended when symptoms seem to persist despite the various attempts made to diagnose and treat the problem. For the majority of us, eating patterns should reflect a well-balanced diet that maintains body weight within medical guidelines. This perhaps is easier said than done because we are often controlled by the pressures of society and wooed by media images of how we should look. Again it is necessary to emphasize a need for self-awareness, of what we are and what we can reasonably expect to become. Non-compliance to a diet or an exercise regimen is usually the result of trying to adhere to totally unrealistic goals.

Managing type A behaviour

In Chapter 4, Type A behaviour (TAB) pattern was discussed as a potential moderator of the response to stress. Table 7.4 provides a simple questionnaire (Cooper *et al.*, 1988) based upon the work of Bortner (1969), which can provide a rough idea of the extent of your TAB. The higher the score received on this questionnaire, the more firmly an individual can be classified as Type A. For example, 154 points is the highest score and indicates maximum Type A coronary-prone behaviour. However, it is important to understand that there are no distinct divisions between Type A and Type B. Rather, people fall somewhere on a continuum leaning more towards one type than the other. Eighty-four is an average score and a score above that inclines towards TAB. If you determine that you lean towards TAB, you may want

Table 7.4: Type A Behaviour (TAB)

Circle one number for each of the statements below which best reflects the way you behave in your everyday life. For example, if you are generally on time for appointments, for the first point you would circle a number between 7 and 11. If you are usually casual about appointments you would circle one of the lower numbers between 1 and 5

Casual about appointments	1 2 3 4 5 6 7 8 9 10 11	Never late
Not competitive	1 2 3 4 5 6 7 8 9 10 11	Very competitive
Good listener	1 2 3 4 5 6 7 8 9 10 11	Anticipates what others are going to say (nods, attempts to finish for them)
Never feels rushed (even under pressure)	1 2 3 4 5 6 7 8 9 10 11	Always rushed
Can wait patiently	1 2 3 4 5 6 7 8 9 10 11	Impatient while waiting
Takes things one at a time	1 2 3 4 5 6 7 8 9 10 11	Tries to do many things at once, thinks about what will do next
Slow deliberate talker	1 2 3 4 5 6 7 8 9 10 11	Emphatic in speech fast and forceful
Cares about satisfying him/herself no matter what others may think	1 2 3 4 5 6 7 8 9 10 11	Wants good job recognized by others
Slow doing things	1 2 3 4 5 6 7 8 9 10 11	Fast (eating, walking)
Easy-going	1 2 3 4 5 6 7 8 9 10 11	Hard driving (pushing yourself and others)
Expresses feelings	1 2 3 4 5 6 7 8 9 10 11	Hides feelings
Many outside interests	1 2 3 4 5 6 7 8 9 10 11	Few interests outside work/home
Unambitious	1 2 3 4 5 6 7 8 9 10 11	Ambitious
Casual	1 2 3 4 5 6 7 8 9 10 11	Eager to get things done

Plot total score below:

Type B		Type A
14	84	154

to consider suggestions aimed at managing this behaviour pattern. Friedman and Rosenman, the originators of the link between TAB and high incidences of CHD, do not maintain that this behaviour should be changed but rather managed, to reduce the health-risk implications involved. In addition to the life-prolonging motivation needed to deal with TAB, it should be noted that at least one research project has indicated that successful professional men are more similar to the Type B personality than Type A. In this study, the most successful types were not hard-driving, aggressive and competitive; rather, they were relaxed and possessed a warmth that attracted others (Shaffer, 1983).

Friedman and Rosenman (1974) offer a number of strategies to manage TAB:

1. Try to restrain yourself from being the centre of attention by constantly talking. Force yourself to listen to the conversation of other people. Quit trying to finish their sentences.

2. If you continue to need to talk unnecessarily, perhaps you ought to ask yourself the following questions: (a) Do I really have anything important to say? (b) Does anyone want to hear it? (c) Is this the time to say it?

3. Try to control your obsessional time-directed life by making yourself aware of it and changing the established pattern of behaviour. For example, trying to desperately meet the last post in the office at 4 pm when the letter could wait until tomorrow, in other words, set priorities about what needs to be done and by whom.

4. In order to put some of your TAB into perspective, carry out a number of exercises. Develop reflective periods in your self-created 'hectic programme for life', creating opportunities to assess the causes of your hurry sickness. One of the most important new habits to develop is a weekly review of the original causes of your present hurry sickness. Try to get to the source of your problems and current obsessions. Is your time-dominated behaviour really a need to feel important? Is it designed to avoid some activity or person? Is it really essential to the success of a particular goal? Friedman and Rosenman offer this advice: Never forget when confronted by any task to ask yourself the following questions: (a) Will this matter have importance five years from now? and; (b) Must I do this right now, or do I have enough time to think about the best way to accomplish it?

5. Try to understand that the majority of your work and social life does not really require immediate action, but instead requires a quality end product or a fulfilling relationship.

'Ask yourself, are good judgement and correct decisions best formulated under unhurried circumstances or under deadline pressures?'
6. As part of an effort to broaden yourself and lessen specific aspects of obsessional time-dictated behaviour, indulge in some outside activities: theatre, reading, sewing, and so on.
7. Try not to make unnecessary appointments or deadlines. 'Remember, the more unnecessary deadlines you make for yourself, the worse your "hurry sickness" becomes.'
8. Learn to protect your time and to say, 'No.' 'Try to never forget that if you fail to protect your allotment of time, no one else will. The older you become, the more important this truth is.'
9. Take as many stress-free breathing spaces during the course of an intensive working day as possible. Learn to interrupt long or even shorts sessions of any type of activity that you know or suspect may induce tension and stress before it is finished. Taking the pressure off your stressful task by taking a brief break.
10. Try to create opportunities during the day or night when you can totally relax your body and mind.

Rosenman and Friedman also try to help the Type A person see how his/her behaviour affects relationships with others:

1. Try to make yourself aware of the impact your behaviour has on other people. If you are overtly hostile, certainly one of the most important drill measures you should adopt is that one in which you remind yourself of the fact that you are hostile.
2. Try to reward people for their efforts. Begin to speak your thanks or appreciation to others when they have performed services for you, and not like so many hostile Type A subjects, with merely a grunt of thanks. Such behaviour may seen unnatural at first, but it may help establish a different configuration of behaviours and extinguish the well-rehearsed hostile pattern. Try adopting a more relaxed and positive approach to people, greeting them regularly, taking time off to develop social relationships, and so on.
3. It is often the case that Type As blame other people for not meeting their ideals or find fault in others for their own failures or disappointments. Over and over again, we have

listened to Type As rationalize their hostility as stemming from disappointment over the lack of ideals in their friends. We always have advised such sick people that they should cease trying to be 'idealists' because they are in fact only looking for excuses to be disappointed and hence hostile towards others.

These suggestions may not solve all your Type A generated problems but Rosenman and Friedman are trying to help you manage or modify behaviour patterns which have been established for many years, and may, in the long run, be damaging to your health.

Evaluating the situation

The previously discussed methods of stress management are all aimed at building your stress resiliency and/or lowering your reactivity to stressful events. This section will examine ways of lowering your reactions to stressful events by managing your perceptions of daily events. As we discussed in earlier chapters, the way an individual perceives a situation dramatically affects the stress response experienced. For example, Type A individuals continually set off their stress responses by perceiving life as competitive and time-oriented. People who have an external locus of control perceive that they have little control over the situations which confront them daily. In contrast, the hardy personality perceives he or she has a great deal of control of his life. In the last two cases, it is not so much the actual ability to cope with a situation as the individual's perception of his ability to cope that matters. Other research has shown that coping style is mediated by personality and associated with various health and disease outcomes. For example, in the management of diabetes, Cox (1985) has described the association between personality type and behavioural tendency: 'Introverted diabetics tend to be more careful in balancing food intake to match insulin administration, and are more careful in maintaining sterile precautions. Furthermore, they appear more able to regulate their general lifestyle according to the requirements of the disorder. Extroverted diabetics, on the other hand, tend to hold more 'easy-going' attitudes towards the disorder and tend, partly as a result, to under-rate the importance of careful dieting and to be less

concerned about the accuracy and timing of their insulin injections'
(Cox, 1985). A number of reports in the literature describe cancer
patients as repressive (Bahnson, 1981; Dattore *et al.*, 1980).
Temoshok and Heller (1984) report that defensive, high anxious
subjects had significantly thicker and more invasive melanoma
lesions than patients without these characteristics. Earlier studies
are consistent with this observation. Patients with fast versus slow
growing cancer tended to be more defensive, inhibited, anxious,
overly controlled, with no ability to release tension through motor
or verbal leakage. In addition, in asthma patients, DéAraujo *et al.*
(1976) report that patients with lower coping ability required
higher doses of medication to control their symptoms than did
those who coped well. Therefore, it seems that the perception of
events and/or coping styles may influence the onset or course of
an illness. Several techniques are available to help in the congnitive
reappraisal of stressful situations.

1. Constructive self-talk: This is described as intermittent
   mental monologue that most people conduct about the
   events they experience and their reactions to these events.
   This monologue or self-talk can range from being gently
   positive to harshly condemning. When someone engages in
   negative self-talk, they achieve nothing and just maintain
   the stress, dissipating their emotional energy. If you are
   involved in constructive self-talk, it can achieve more
   positive psychological results. Quick and Quick provide a
   range of examples of situations, mental monologues and
   alternative strategies for constructive self-talk (Quick and
   Quick, 1984). This is shown in Table 7.5.
2. Quick recovery: This is the ability to bounce back from
   upsetting experiences. Learning to recover quickly takes
   little more than an awareness of how you actually do
   recover. As Albrecht describes it, once you begin to think
   about your emotional responses, you can recognize the
   process of returning to emotional equilibrium after a provocation has passed. For example, if you find yourself drawn
   into a personal confrontation, you will very likely experience anger and a full-blown stress response. Your higher
   level mental processes will probably not be functioning very
   well, Albrecht explains. However, at a certain point, your
   emotions will begin to subside and you will realize that you

Table 7.5 Constructive self-talk

Situation	Typical mental monologue	Constructive self-talk alternative
Driving to work on a day which you know will be full of appointments and potentially stressful meetings.	'Oh boy, what a day this will be!' 'It's going to be hell.' 'I'll never get it all done.' 'It'll be exhausting.'	'This looks like a busy day.' 'The day should be very productive.' 'I'll get a lot accomplished today.' 'I'll earn a good night's rest today.'
Anticipation of a seminar presentation or public address.	'What if I blow it?' 'Nobody will laugh at my opening joke.' 'What if they ask about ...?' 'I hate talking to groups.'	'This ought to be a challenge.' 'I'll take a deep breath and relax.' 'They'll enjoy it.' 'Each presentation goes a bit better.'
Recovering from a heart attack.	'I almost died. I'll die soon.' 'I'll never be able to work again.' 'I'll never be able to play sports again.'	'I didn't die. I made it through.' 'The doctor says I'll be able to get back to work soon.' 'I can keep active and gradually get back to most of my old sports.'
Difficulty with a superior at work.	'I hate that person.' 'He makes me feel stupid.' 'We'll never get along.'	'I don't feel comfortable with him.' 'I let myself get on edge when he's around.' 'It will take some effort to get along.'
Flat tyre on a business trip.	'Damn this old car.' (Paces around car, looking at flat tyre.) 'I'll miss all my meetings.' 'It's hopeless.'	'Bad time for a flat.' (Begins to get tools out to start working.) 'I'll call and cancel Jenkins at the next phone. I should make the rest of the appointments.'

Source: J.C. Quick and J.D. Quick, *Organizational Stress and Preventive Management* (New York: McGraw-Hill, 1984), p. 221.

are angry. That is, you will experience your anger as an intellectual concept as well as a physical feeling. Albrecht states that at this point, you have the option to continue and aggravate your angry feelings by rehashing the provocation, rejustifying your position, reopening a new attack on your adversaries, and becoming newly outraged by their unreasonable behaviour. A quick recovery approach would suggest you stop this negative circular approach, become more rational and less conscious of your need to win (Albrecht, 1979).

3. Thought stopping: This means recognizing non-constructive thoughts, attitudes and behaviours and stopping them immediately — by visualizing, for example, a large STOP sign (Quick and Quick, 1984). Then one uses:

4. Mental diversion to divert the topic, issue or crisis to one that is manageable, until one has resources to cope with it. Or as Quick and Quick suggest, one way to stop a thought pattern is to divert yourself to a more positive topic. For instance, once you have prepared yourself adequately for the coming event, such as a presentation or interview, obsessive worry can only drain your emotional resources. Diverting your thoughts to a more pleasant, restful subject can stop a negative thought pattern.

Seeking social support

In addition to the various self-help activities described, it is also important to find the social support that you need. As discussed in Chapter Four, research has found social support a strong buffer against the stresses of work and life generally. A major source of support can be found among family members and friends, but social support and friendships developed at work can be extremely valuable.

Support within the family

It is acknowledged that the workplace creates a greater proportion of stress compared to the home environment. However, much of this stress spills over to adversely affect our partners and the family. Changes in society also combine to put pressures and strains into family life. To minimize these problems and avoid the vicious spiral of stress, the family must work as a unit. According to Shaffer (1983), effective communication in the family unit is the first vital step in providing the foundation for an atmosphere of trust and openness. He advises that family members should speak clearly, both to one another, check out and clarify meanings and ensure that the messages have been understood. In order to develop a closely-bonded unit that is able to deal with problems, all members of the family must be involved in the adoption of strategies which negotiate the issues of roles, boundaries, and conflicts. This should not be a vague session where the individual members explode or are critical of the lack of family support but a constructive, detailed and concise review of the conflict, time commitments, role confusion or whatever is undermining the cohesiveness of the family. This should conclude by developing an action plan which distributes tasks among family members, resolves some conflict, or in some other way follows through to resolution a significant issue for the family or one of its members. For example, if there are time commitment and role problems among family members, the following role negotiation strategy could be followed (Cooper *et al.*, 1988a):

1. Prepare a balance sheet of work and home commitments (listing details of hours spent, tasks undertaken, etc.);
2. Call a formal family meeting to share concerns and discuss the detailed balance sheet;
3. Re-negotiate various family commitments;
4. Create mutual action plans for the next three months which are agreed by all family members;
5. Review success, or otherwise, of action plans at the end of a three-month period;
6. Develop new action plans based on the experience of the previous ones. Continue the process until all parties are adequately satisfied with arrangements.

The family can provide excellent support and a haven against the pressures and strains of work. However, a non-supportive family environment creates a double jeopardy for the individual who also works in a stressful job.

Support at work

In addition to strengthening family ties, individuals can seek support at work. One of the most important sources of social support is through the informal work group. The complicated set of relationships at work and their potential for conflict and ambiguity make it necessary for individuals to seek support from their peers. In this respect, Cooper *et al.* (1988a) suggest a number of different approaches one can take. First, those responsible for people within organizations should create the right atmosphere to encourage social support networks and to provide the most appropriate resources for stress management. Second, the individual can act to create these networks. Below are a number of steps an individual under stress may take to find social support at work:

1. Choose someone at work you feel you can talk to; someone you don't feel threatened by and to whom you can trustfully reveal your feelings. Don't use people who, on reflection, you may be using on an unconscious level as a pawn in a game of organizational politics!
2. Approach this person and explain that you have a particular problem at work or outside work that you would like to discuss. Admit that you need help and that he or she would be the best person to consult because you trust his or her opinion, like him or her as a person, and feel that he or she can usefully identify with your circumstances.
3. Try to maintain and build on this relationship, even at times of no crisis or problems.
4. Review, from time to time, the nature of the relationship, to see if it is still providing you with the emotional support you need to cope with the difficulties that arise. If the relationship is no longer constructive or the nature of your problems have changed (requiring a different peer counsellor), then seek another person for support.

Often, the individual feels that the boss or supervisor does not provide the needed support at work. If this is a problem perceived by the work-group or team it could be tackled at this level. Being more assertive about one's needs and expectations is a potentially difficult situation in such circumstances but the use of open communication patterns and a willingness to change or negotiate can help to improve the social climate at work. It is important for those of us in need of help to own up to our difficulties and not to rely totally on the organization always to be there to resolve them. We must take personal initiatives to seek the kind of professional or peer help that may be necessary, if pressure is experienced at work and we feel unable to adequately cope alone.

Coping with special needs

Many individuals find that they must cope with very specific problems. For example, working women, single parent families, those coping with aged dependants, dual career couples and those facing redundancy, all have special needs and problems. Although self-help strategies can alleviate strain and pressure, there are many ways in which the organization can help to reduce or eliminate stress.

COPING WITH STRESS — WORKPLACE APPROACHES

We constantly hear chief executives, personnel executives, government administrators, hospital administrators, headmasters and others in authority roles extolling the fact that the most important resource they have is people. Yet when it comes right down to it, how often do organizations protect, support and nurture this most valuable asset, the human resource? Not often enough, is the simple answer. Indeed, if we treated human beings as another form of capital asset, the situation might change dramatically, as Handy (1976) suggested; 'salaries and benefits are really regarded as maintenance expenses — something to be kept as low as possible as long as the machine does not break down. There is no capital cost and therefore no need for depreciation. Indeed, the return on investment of most companies would look very strange if their human assets were capitalized at, say, ten times their annual maintenance cost, and depreciated over twenty years. Perhaps, one day, industrial and administrative organizations will start behaving like football clubs and charge realistic transfer fees for their key people assets.'

If human resource professionals or cost accountants in organizations focused more on the financial costs of the human asset, then a more flexible, imaginative, and forward-looking human resource policies would be pursued. At the moment, corporate planners can choose not to concern themselves about this fickle piece of human machinery, discounting or depreciating it at will. Perhaps a partial solution lies with the idea that we encourage organizations to answer a series of questions about their human resources. Flamholtz (1971) has asked a series of revealing questions, together with some of our own, which need to be the focus of organization concern, particularly in the NHS:

1. What is the total value of your organization's human assets?
2. Is it appreciating, remaining constant, or being depleted?
3. How much money was spent last year to recruit and select people?
4. Was this expenditure worth the cost?
5. Does your organization have data on standard costs of recruitment, selection, and placement which are needed to prepare manpower budgets and to control personnel costs?
6. Were the actual costs incurred last year less than, equal to, or greater than standard personnel acquisition and placement costs?
7. How much money was spent last year to train and develop people?
8. What was the return on your investment in training and development?
9. How does this return compare with alternative investment opportunities?
10. How many employees succumbed to illness or premature death?
11. How much does it cost to replace these people?
12. How many young people did you lose due to your promotion and/or mobility policy?
13. What was the wasted future potential (opportunity costs) of losing these people?
14. How many women have you employed, and what has been the cost of their turnover in comparison to their male counterparts?
15. Does the organization really reward managers for increasing the value of their subordinates to the firm?
16. Does your promotion system accurately reflect the manager's value to the organization?
17. Does your firm assess the effects of corporate strategies upon its human resources in quantitative terms?

Planners and personnel policymakers must begin to ask these sorts of questions over the next decade, if they are to make rational decisions about selection, training, and career development, all of which make the best possible use of human resources in the NHS. The long-term payoffs may be as beneficial as the microchip or any other new technological development. There are many ways that organizations can minimize the costs of stress and improve the physical and mental well-being of the workforce.

Stress management and health promotion

With the increase in stress litigation and the escalating costs of employee health care insurance, more and more American companies are providing extensive health care, stress prevention and keep-fit programmes for employees. In the UK and in Europe, however, only a few companies have flirted with stress prevention or counselling programmes. Most companies either have not tackled them seriously, or have abandoned their efforts. In addition, many occupational medics and personnel managers who see the problems of stress at work have found it difficult to implement stress management courses and programmes because senior managers feel that stress is none of their business. However, even if organizations doubt that they bear responsibility for employee health care or stress prevention at work, they should see the cost-saving argument in terms of lost work-days, absenteeism, poor performance, premature death and retraining. In the US, the cost arguments and the legal implications of cumulative trauma cases in court have weighed heavily in favour of primary prevention within companies.

This rapid growth of interest in stress management has produced a wide diversity of programmes. Generally, a package is created to meet the needs of a specific organization. However, five major types of programmes have been used to manage stress and minimize its negative consequences (Jaffe *et al.*, 1986):

1. Education/Awareness building;
2. Assessment-focused;
3. Skill building;
4. Therapeutic counselling;
5. Organizational/Environmental change.

Matteson and Ivancevich (1987) classify stress management in various ways. Some of these strategies are described as preventive interventions, that is, those which focus on eliminating a stressor or neutralizing it in some way before it becomes a source of stress (e.g. job redesign to reduce long hours of working). Others might be categorized as curative, that is, dissipating or relieving stress once it has been experienced. An alternative way of distinguishing between programmes is to identify the level of intervention (i.e. at the individual, the group or organizational level) (DeFrank and Cooper, 1987). Figure 7.1 provides a description of the levels of stress management and their outcomes. Often a combination of programmes is introduced in the form of workshops, personal screening and training, or by self-learning because the individual must be trained to manage the negative effects of stress that cannot be eliminated or reduced by organizational change. Indeed, response to stress is not invariant, and so it is necessary to identify the styles of behaviour or personality characteristics that renders the individual more or less vulnerable to stress.

Educational/awareness building programmes

The aim of this form of intervention is to make the employee aware of the links between stress, illness and personal behaviour. Concepts include:

1. Identification of work and personal stress;
2. Identification of the impact of stress, i.e. symptoms and outcomes;
3. Helping the individual to recognize that strengths and weaknesses, in relation to behavioural style, personality and coping skills, will affect the response to stress and outcomes.

As Jaffe *et al.* (1986) suggest, this form of intervention usually takes the form of a lecture, presentation of written materials distributed to staff, and is often used to initiate and recruit for more intensive interventions. These educational programmes have the advantage of reaching large numbers of people at a time, and are thus cost effective.

Assessment-focused programmes

This type of stress management aims to identify individual stress profiles, that is, to highlight problem areas, skill deficits, strengths and/or the high-risk profile. It can be conducted at a small group

Figure 7.1 Levels of stress management and outcome. Source: DeFrank and Cooper (1987).

INTERVENTIONS

Focus on individual

Relaxation techniques
Cognitive coping strategies
Biofeedback
Meditation
Exercise
Employee Assistance Programmes (EAPs)
Time management

Focus on individual/organizational interface

Relationships at work
Person-environment fit
Role issues
Participation and autonomy

Focus on organization

Organizational structure
Selection and placement
Training
Physical and environmental characteristics
  of job
Health concerns and resources
Job rotation

OUTCOMES

Focus on individual

Mood states (depression, anxiety)
Psychosomatic complaints
Subjectively-experienced stress
Physiological parameters (blood pressure,
  catecholamines, muscle tension)
Sleep disturbances
Life satisfaction

Focus on individual/organizational interface

Job stress
Job satisfaction
Burnout
Productivity and performance
Absenteeism
Turnover
Health care utilization and claims

Focus on organization

Productivity
Turnover
Absenteeism
Health care claims
Recruitment/retention success

level initially, by using a combination of stress diaries, interviews, standardized stress inventories (e.g. the Occupational Stress Indicator, Cooper *et al.*, 1988b), or checklists and group discussions and leading finally to individual consultation. This is more cost effective than a total one-to-one experience. Usually, people want to know how they compare with their peers and work colleagues, or other people generally and so feedback is the vital element of this type of programme. However, much of the information obtained in these sessions is personal and of a sensitive nature, thus strict confidentiality must be observed. In addition, in group work, all individuals must feel completely free and content to share information, or decline without pressure or negative consequences. Unless the group is established to resolve relationship issues, it is generally more productive to limit the group to those of equivalent ranks. For example, it is difficult for a group of middle managers to discuss sources of stress if the boss is present (indeed, it is likely that he/she is the major source of strain for those in the group).

When individual screening is possible, an in-depth interview might include:

1. Relevant history and current status:
   (a) work life, e.g. relocation, goal attainment
   (b) personal life, e.g. marriage/relationship issues, problems/ changes
   (c) is there a specific problem?
2. Life style:
   (a) health status — illness, absenteeism;
   (b) exercise behaviour;
   (c) use of palliatives/drugs;
   (d) changes in sleep pattern;
   (e) nutritional status;
   (f) social support available.
3. Identifying sources of stress. Using Cooper's (1986) model of stress at work (Figure 1.2), as a guideline for semi-structured discussion, six potential sources of stress might be discussed, that is, stressors intrinsic to the job, role stress, career development, relationships at work, the organization structure and climate and finally, the home/work interface.
4. Symptoms of stress:
   (a) behavioural;

(b) physical;

(c) psychological.

Sometimes an individual is defensive and simply does not want to admit being under stress, or finds it difficult to express thoughts and feelings. Certain specific questions may help to stimulate the discussion of sources of stress and outcomes, for example:

1. What are the best/worse things about life/work at the moment?
2. What changes would you make if given the opportunity?
3. What advice would you give to a young person/son/daughter wishing to follow in your footsteps?
4. What changes would you make given your time over again?
5. Tell me about a good/bad day.

Individual screening will also incorporate certain standardised outcome and mediator variable measures, e.g. mental well-being, job satisfaction and personality measures (such a Type A coronary prone behaviour or locus of control). Increasingly this information might be linked with medical details (e.g. blood pressure and assay) or accident or performance data (including absenteeism, sickness records and rating by others, etc.), because it is acknowledged that both subjective and objective data are necessary in successful stress control programmes, particularly when an evaluation of the intervention is required. At the end of an interview, or at a later feedback session, a plan which meets the needs of the individual can be developed. Seamonds (1986) details some of the concepts that might be included as part of a stress control action plan:

1. Clarification of personal and professional goals;
2. Learning to exert control over change by pacing actions;
3. Establishing priorities;
4. Setting realistic goals;
5. Understanding coping skills; adaptive and maladaptive;
6. Developing a flexible style;
7. Developing personal coping skills such as exercise programmes, relaxation methods, proper diet, and social networks;
8. Learning to put things into proper perspective; to play, to relax;
9. Skills building and training — professional help.

Some of these strategies have already been discussed in the previous section on individual coping (pages 225–53). Nevertheless, it is worth mentioning some of the attempts made by organizations who have used these methods toward stress prevention or health promotion. These include the provision of keep-fit facilities on site, dietary control, relaxation and exercise classes. For example, Converse Corporation in Wilmington, USA, provided a voluntary twelve-week relaxation programme for their employees. Over 140 volunteered and were compared to 63 non-volunteers who were selected randomly. The volunteers agreed to keep daily records for twelve weeks and to have their blood pressure measured. In addition, their general health and job performance were assessed during the experimental period. The results indicated that not only was a relaxation training break feasible within normal working hours but that it led to improvements in general health, job performance and well-being. In addition, there was a significant decrease in the blood pressure of managers from the start to the finish of the training.

Physical fitness is the most popular method utilized to deal with stress in the workplace (Rosch and Pelletier, 1987). It is suggested that physical activity is the natural final phase of the stress response which prepares the body for 'fight or flight' (Matteson and Ivancevich, 1987) and so exercise might be viewed as a stress reduction technique. Organizations that support health and fitness programmes believe that returns are in terms of: 1. an increased ability to attract competent employees; 2. a reflection of the company's concern for employees, i.e. a reduction in the impact of stress and by improving the health of the employee; 3. improved fitness and health leads to improved productivity through reduced absenteeism and turnover, and improved attitudes and loyalty. No doubt, the subjective reaction of feeling better, which seems to be consistently reported by those taking part in exercise, enhances its face validity as a stress-reducer and encourages organizations to endorse the practice in the workplace. Activities typically take the form of lunch-hour exercise classes, aerobics, jogging groups, sponsored walking, in-house multi-gym, or in-company team sports, with competitions arranged with other organizations or groups. Pepsico Inc. has created a comprehensive physical fitness programme at its world headquarters at Purchase, New York. Facilities include a fully fitted gymnasium, with a sauna, an electrical treadmill, a striking bag, stationary bicycles, whirlpool baths, showers and massage facilities. In addition, employees have a running track which circles the HQ complex. This programme is under the supervision of a full-time physical therapist and medical physician. Tailor-made exercise programmes are designed for any interested employee by the physical therapist or doctor. Although this facility was originally planned for senior executives, it is now used by all employees on a voluntary basis. The corporate HQ is located in an attractive park-like setting, providing an atmosphere which encourages physical fitness. In addition, regular sessions in aerobic dancing, yoga, as well as diet training to meet the needs of individual employees are provided. It has also been reported that the New York Telephone Company's wellness programme (that is, cardiovascular fitness) saved the organization $2.7 million in absence and treatment costs in one year alone.

In Canada, Canada Life Assurance Co. and North American Life Assurance Co. participated jointly in a research project to see what effects a keep-fit programme would have on their managers. In all, 1125 managers from both companies were enrolled into a systematic physical fitness course in their HQ gymnasium. The companies found several interesting results. First, there was a drop in absenteeism of 22%, which, if translated across the whole company, could mean a saving of some $200,000 a year. Second, they found a 3% rise in productivity in the exercising group as opposed to the unfit one. In addition, they found that the keep-fit managers had a significantly more positive attitude towards work and reported better relationships with their bosses and sub- ordinates. Another study (Cox et al., 1981) of the relationship between participation in a fitness programme and absenteeism indicates a significantly lower rate of absenteeism (22% less) among high participants than either low-level participants or non- participants. Also in a prospective longitudinal study, Browne et al. (1984) found a 20.1% reduction in the average number of disability days from the year prior to entry in the physical fitness programme. Individuals in the combined high and good categories of cardiorespiratory fitness increased from 16.9% to 39.1% and the proportion in the low and fair categories decreased from 56.2% to 33.7%. These results look promising but it is important to remember that there are several reasons why an individual might stay away from work. Illness is just one explanation of absenteeism and so exercise as causal in reduced absenteeism from the workplace is a difficult hypothesis to test. The evaluation of exercise and fitness programmes on organizational outcome variables is difficult and the results may be confounded (that is, the true cause and effect is not established). Rarely is it possible to make comparison between studies because of the variations in methods and designs of the projects (see Falkenberg, 1987, for a review).

This also applies to the association between employee fitness programmes and commitment and turnover in the organization. Tsai *et al.* (1987) used the life table method of analysis, to study the differences in turnover during a four-year period among employees who participated in the Tenneco Health and Fitness Programme and those who did not. Controlling for the effects of age, gender, general job category and duration of employment, continued employment was significantly more likely among the exercisers, especially among the female clerical employees. However, the causal nature of this relationship was not explored, i.e. the differences noted could have been explained by external factors such as the economy or personality or attitudinal factors, and not the exercise regimen *per se*. It is also suggested that the employee might be motivated to stay with their current company because of the attractiveness of the fitness programme facilities (Falkenberg, 1987).

Many organizations might be cautious about the introduction of these fitness programmes, especially if the capital-outlay is high. Emhart Corporation in the USA overcame this problem by gradually building their programme after first surveying the staff about their attitudes towards a scheme. After initially providing a low-cost gym and monitoring its use, they expanded the facilities and hired specialist help and instructors. This step-by-step approach proved very successful. However, the Staywell Programme, introduced by Control Data Corporation is the best researched and most comprehensive intervention. 22 000 personnel with their spouses used this programme as a free corporate benefit; it included five components to encourage people to give up smoking; to improve cardiovascular fitness; control of weight and diet; and to manage stress more effectively. Each employee is provided with a health-risk profile (that is, an intensive screening), an action plan to reduce health risks and then enrolled on an appropriate course (or courses). Management and blue-collar workers participate equally.

The evaluation evidence is most impressive. Control Data

explored the average health care costs claims of their employees, and their hospital stays, and discovered:

1. Employees who were encouraged to quit smoking spent half the number of days in hospital, and had 20% less health care costs, compared with smokers.
2. Those that underwent exercise training had 30% fewer claims, and spent half the number of days in hospital, compared with the sedentary group.
3. Most revealing of all, those employees who entered the cardiovascular fitness programme, and reduced their hypertension levels, had less than half the health care costs of those who did not.
4. In addition, when Control Data checked out the employees they rated 'most at risk' versus those 'least at risk' in terms of health habits (weight, stress, fitness, nutrition and smoking), they found that the high-risk employees were twice as likely to be absent from work due to sickness and to be half as productive, as the low-risk or physically fit group.

Seamonds (1986) suggests that some employees can manage much of their own health care by using available resources. The organization can help by providing facilities and resources in the workplace, and legitimizing stress as a topic for discussion and positive action. They can also help by encouraging individuals to learn the specific skills necessary to cope with stress, and by providing the training as part of personal-development programmes.

Skill-building

Figure 7.1 shows the various, specific skills that help a person to manage stress. Essentially, three types of programmes are available, 1. coping skills; 2. interpersonal skills and; 3. relaxation techniques, already mentioned.

1. Coping skills

Within this category of stress management techniques are all the strategies which deal with the ways that people perceive situations, i.e. cognitive restructuring and behavioural modification. The aim is to help the individual gain control over their reaction to a stressor, by modifying maladaptive patterns of thinking and the faulty premises, beliefs, and assumptions which underlie their cognitions (Matteson and Ivancevich, 1987). The key concept to this approach is accepting that it is not necessarily the situation itself which is harmful, but the way that it is viewed by the person. Therefore, response to stress is mediated by cognitive processes which are the product of beliefs, expectations, past experiences, values and needs, etc. Certain behavioural styles, such as Type A coronary prone behaviour, avoidance, rigid versus flexible, external versus internal locus of control, etc. have been associated with difficulties in managing stress. For example, it is believed that Type As perceive stress in a more exaggerated fashion and so create a more stressful environment for themselves. The rationale of cognitive strategies in stress management is to reappraise, relearn, or re-label the way a situation is perceived by logic and reasoning, rather than by emotional reactions that have been ingrained by past habits (Rosch and Pelletier, 1987). Reappraisal or restructuring often focuses on removing cognitive distortions such as over-generalization, magnifying and personalization (Beech *et al.*, 1984). Cognitive restructuring is an important part of stress inoculation training, rational-emotive therapy and cognitive behaviour modification. These skills include changing the way one perceives and defines stressful events, personal beliefs, expectations, internal conversations and evaluations one has about the pressures one faces (Jaffe *et al.*, 1986).

Behaviour modification is also used to change or reduce an inappropriate or exaggerated response to stress. Techniques include role-play, observation and self-report feedback and can be effectively taught in group sessions (Rosch and Pelletier, 1987). Strategies might take the form of: 1. Assertiveness training, which is designed to provide the individual with more effective control over their activities; 2. Time management; this might include training in skills such as delegating, negotiating, goal setting and confronting; 3. career planning; perhaps to establish more realistic goals or to confront the stressors that arise from the home and work interface, e.g. problems associated with the dual-career family or the need to relocate. Behaviour modification is success-fully used to reduce Type A coronary prone behaviour and in clinical practice is reported to be the most effective method of preventing recurrent heart attacks (Friedman *et al.*, 1974). Suinn and Bloom (1978) have used anxiety management training, which is based mainly on cognitive techniques, in the modification of TAB. Their study showed that at least one component of TAB decreased among the treatment group, compared to a control group who did not receive the training. Blood pressure was also significantly decreased in the treatment group but no effects were observed on biochemical measures (serum cholesterol and tri-glycerides) taken before the training.

Matteson and Ivancevich (1987) suggest that cognitive tech-niques are attractive because they have intuitive appeal, the under-lying assumptions and rationale make sense and possess face validity. They are also applicable to a wide range of situations and stressors, and are relatively inexpensive in terms of time and cost. Evidence from clinical observations suggest that this cognitive approach might be promising, however, evaluation research in the work setting is rare, and thus, it remains to be endorsed as an effective stress management technique.

2. Interpersonal skills

Relationships at work are potential stress-evoking situations. Selye (1974) believed that learning to live with other people is one of the most stressful aspects of life and that, good relationships between members of a group are a key factor in individual and organiz-ational health. Paradoxically it is through contact with others that our needs for affiliation are satisfied. Indeed, Mayo (1945) suggests that a man's desire to be continuously associated in work with his fellows is a strong, if not the strongest human charac-teristic and so the importance of good relationships at work cannot be overstated. At work it is necessary to interact with bosses, peers and subordinates and poor relationships in terms of low trust and low supportiveness are associated with problems which include poor communications, high role ambiguity, job dissatisfaction and job pressure. French and Caplan (1973) found that strong levels of support from co-workers eased job strain. This support also mediated the effects of job strain on cortisone levels, blood pressure, glucose levels and the number of cigarettes smoked. However, as Canning (1987) points out, the emphasis within industry and commerce is for the individual to succeed on their own merits and so there is a tendency not to seek the help of others, or share with others. Canning calls this the 'John Wayne Syndrome'. It leads to the isolation of the individual, with concomitant behaviours such as lack of delegation, inward looking, lack of training and development of subordinates and an over-worked employee who may ultimately break under the strain.

Managing stress involves learning the skills necessary to work with other people, e.g. active listening, effective communication, conflict resolution, team-building and developing and maintaining supportive networks. Many individuals do not realise that their interpersonal style is a source of stress to those around them, for example, the abrasive personality who is hard-driving and achievement oriented, usually has no time to consider working relationships and ignores the interpersonal aspects of feelings and sensibilities of social interaction. Leadership style is also a potential stressor, i.e. the authoritarian, punishing or closed style of management creates considerable stress at work which results in a negative environment of hostility and pressure. The supervisor or boss with a technical or scientific background may regard relationships at work as low priority. Their orientation tends to be towards things and not people (Cooper and Marshall, 1978) and so consideration for working relationships is viewed as trivial, time consuming, petty and an impediment to doing the job well. Interpersonal skills training can be used to avoid or correct these deleterious and/or inappropriate styles of behaviour. In spite of the wide variety of stress management programmes available, which deal with stress in either preventive or curative ways, there is still a need for counselling services for people who react inappropriately to stress, and to prevent more serious problems (Jaffe *et al.*, 1986).

Counselling

Often referred to as employee assistance programmes (EAPs), these interventions typically provide counselling and referral for employee problems. An individual may seek help directly, may be referred by a medical department or attend at the suggestion of a boss or supervisor who senses that problems exist that are beyond the scope of a friendly chat at work. Many companies have incorporated counselling into stress management programmes to cope with problems related to drug and alcohol abuse, work and career problems and family issues. The giant copper corporation, Kennecott Corporation, introduced a counselling programme for employees in distress. This produced a drop in absenteeism of nearly 60% in one year and a 55% reduction in medical costs. Stress counselling has been introduced by the Post Office. The counsellors will not only help individuals cope with stress in the workplace but also identify sources of organizational stress that may be causing the problems. On the basis of any problems identified, they will work with the regional postal authority in planning and initiating organizational change, in redesigning jobs or whatever is necessary to correct the basic or structural problems within the organization. They are also carrying out a simultaneous evaluation of the effectiveness of the counselling, which will help them focus on the most effective aspects of the stress-counselling role. This will enable the Post Office to refine the nature of the role and help in the future introduction of this concept throughout the postal service. Preliminary results to assess the effect of counselling on outcomes such as absenteeism, job satisfaction, work-commitment, depression and anxiety are available (Cooper *et al.*, 1989a). Significant differences between pre- and post-counselling measures were observed for anxiety and depression, but not for job satisfaction or organizational commitment outcomes. Sickness absence showed a decline of 60% from the sixth month period before to the sixth month period after counselling.

There are reservations about in-house counselling services that should be addressed, i.e. confidentially and the degree to which individuals would use the service if offered. For example, in a recent survey in the construction industry, managers were asked about their reactions to stress control programmes. Only 25% said that they would personally use counselling, compared to 81% and 72% of managers who would participate in stress awareness/education and assessment focused programmes respectively, if they were introduced (Sutherland and Davidson, 1989). Establishing links with occupational health clearly reduces the problem of confidentiality. This was seen in the Post Office experience. However, many individuals believe that to admit a need for help of this nature is a sign of weakness and failure, which could jeopardise future career prospects or relationships with others in the organization.

Organizational/environmental change

Some issues exist within the organizational environment, structure and policies which are potential sources of stress for the employee.

For example, the actual physical conditions of the job, hours of working, training, policies and the competitive culture of office politics endorsed by the company, may all be stressor agents. Many of these issues will influence the quality of employees that can be recruited and the ability to retain employees (DeFrank and Cooper, 1987). Increasingly, stress management investigators and practitioners are criticizing organizations because they readily introduce health promotion interventions and stress control aimed at the level of the individual, rather than implement organizational change (although it is accepted that change is not always possible). Thus the stress burden, blame and responsibility are shifted to the employee. As Murphy and Sorensen (1988) declare, individual and group level interventions are straightforward and inexpensive to implement compared to job design or change strategies. They do not disrupt production schedules or create upheaval in the organization's structure or function. However, findings reported from the evaluation of individual or group level stress management interventions suggests that changes in behaviours such as reduced absenteeism or increased productivity may be limited, unless organizational change issues are also addressed to some degree. As already mentioned in the Post Office experience, significant differences between pre- and post-counselling measures were observed for anxiety and depression measures but not for job satisfaction and organizational commitment outcomes (Cooper et al., 1989a). As a primary strategy to reduce employee stress at work, stress management has significant limitations since no attempt is made to alter sources of work stress (Murphy and Sorensen, 1988). An interactive approach must take account of the system and structural elements of the organization, in order to prevent or minimize exposure to potentially stressful organizational stimuli.

A variety of interventions are available to reduce the strains and pressures associated with 'being in the organization' (Cooper and Marshall, 1978). For example, the introduction of Quality Circles increases worker participation and thereby reduces the stress associated with jobs providing poor decision latitude and little or no autonomy. Use of this type of intervention leads to an increase in levels of self-esteem, and greater feelings of control in the workplace. Other strategies might include helping the individual to develop more efficient ways of organizing work, the reassessment of reporting structures, realistic career planning and counselling, the creation of informal support networks, the encouragement of mentoring, or even architectural changes. Some organizations are realizing that they can help to alleviate the stress associated with the home and work interface (e.g. the problems of dual career and single parent families), by introducing job-sharing, flexible work-hours, career sabbaticals, paternity leave, and child care services. Many of the demands and conflicts that are major concerns for the working parent are thus resolved by the introduction of such practices. A lack of these facilities forces the individual to continually try and balance the needs of work and home and usually all three elements suffer in the long-term. Organizations can also help by discouraging individuals from becoming workaholics, with no life outside the job. This means developing a full and satisfying life outside work, including hobbies and leisure interests to help personnel to relax and unwind, and to develop support networks outside the workplace.

From the literature available, certain recommendations have been made specifically for health professionals. Some of these suggestions urge organizational change. For nurses, Baker *et al.* (1987) recommend:

1. Increase effectiveness of staff by introducing more flexibility and more involvement in planning (e.g., use quality circles);
2. Recognize the value of supervision and feedback to encourage professional growth;
3. Provide training and counselling to deal with the trauma of death and dying, and in bereavement counselling;
4. Develop management training in leadership, interpersonal skills, dealing with change and developing teamwork;
5. Provide up-date courses;
6. Develop support structures to erase some of the home/ work/career conflicts;
7. Improve working conditions by providing a stress-free resting place for breaks;
8. Encourage staff support groups; e.g., self-help groups using 'co-counselling' techniques, especially to express and share reactions and emotions;
9. Analyse stress and the workplace and raise awareness of potential risks, i.e. how to recognize stress and deal with it.

Some of these interventions have been initiated in the Health

Service (Baker *et al.*, 1987). However, as Hanlon (1986) suggests, success depends on the long-term support of top management. Interventions have failed without this support and because of inadequate training, little real delegation of authority and/or lack of job security as a reward for increased productivity. Job redesign has been ineffective when attempted in an authoritarian climate, with rigid job descriptions and personnel practices (Kopelman, 1985).

Among dentists, the alleviation of stress might be viewed in a much broader context, that is, a change in social attitudes is necessary. Whilst dentists are viewed as inflictors of pain, this will result in raised anxiety for both the client and the dental practitioner. If these pressures cannot be reduced, dentists must find individual ways to reduce the strain and long-term consequences of exposure to a constant stressor, e.g. by exercise, relaxation and sufficient leisure time or by training which includes role modelling, behaviour modification, systematic desensitization and/or hypnosis. Although many dentists work independently, they also work as part of a team (e.g. nurse, technicians, receptionist, etc.). As team-leader they should perhaps examine their leadership and management skills, to reduce their own stress, and the stress that they unconsciously or inadvertently cause in others. As Furnham (1983) suggests, training in interpersonal and communication skills may be of value as stress reduction strategies.

Tokarz *et al.* (1979) emphasise the importance of introducing stress management as part of postgraduate training in medical schools. This should include skills training to recognize personal needs and the expression of feelings. This advice, of course, serves for all health professionals; it is easier to learn good habits than to learn to break bad habits once they are established. However, if the medical student is not helped to transfer these skills into the surgeries or hospitals, the efforts may be wasted. Many programmes have been introduced to help the individual physician or surgeon cope with stress but rarely are interventions aimed at change in the organization.

Although there are many ways in which the organization can provide a better quality of worklife, implementation is very rare. Until we are able to demonstrate and evaluate an effective stress management programme which addresses all levels of the organization, the authorities are likely to remain cautious and sceptical. Yet, it is important for the future of an effective and less stressful worklife that organizations, in the public as well as the private sector, begin to think about their structures, policies and working practices with regard to their human resources.

Various authors have provided guidelines for the introduction of the ideal stress management programme (see Adams, 1987, for a review). Basically seven points are vital (Adams, 1987; Griffen *et al.*, 1982):

1. Clear, understood and accepted goals are essential. They should be specific, measurable and realistic.
2. A programme should provide both individual and organizational benefits.
3. The support and endorsement of top management is essential.
4. Develop readiness for stress management training; identify areas of concern, co-ordinate with relevant departments, (e.g. medical, personnel), identify target population, formulate objectives, outcomes and expectations, anticipate and address criticism (action for overcoming negative attitudes and resistance to stress-control).
5. Effective overall planning is essential; determine the course content, identify resources available.
6. The focus should be on the acquisition of skills, attitude adjustment and modification of behaviour, that is, a comprehensive approach.
7. Stress management should avoid the preoccupation with stress as a negative concept. A successful programme will emphasize the positive and seek to establish and maintain well-being.

Overall, it is necessary to view employees as individuals who have needs, personalities, and commitments outside the confines of organizational life, and begin to realize (and put into practice) that the performance, efficiency, and satisfaction of an employee is linked to his or her total life experience.

CONCLUSION

Both the individual and the organization must accept some responsibility in the management and control of stress. The first important step is to recognize a need to deal with stress but this must be matched equally with determination and patience, if change is to be effectively introduced and maintained.

References

Adams, J.D. (1987) Creating and maintaining comprehensive stress management training. In *Stress Management in Work Settings* (eds L.R. Murphy and T.F. Schoenborn) NIOSH, May, 1987. 93–107

Akerstedt, T. (1977) Invasion of the sleep-wakefulness pattern: Effects on circadian variation in psychophysiological activation. *Ergonomics, 20,* 459–74

Akerstedt, T. (1987) *Sleep and Stress.* Springer-Verlag, Berlin

Albrecht, K. (1979) *Stress and the Manager. Making it Work For You.* Prentice-Hall, New Jersey

Ahmed, P.I., Kolker, A. and Coelho, G.V. (1979) Toward a new definition of health: An overview. In *Toward a New Definition of Health — Psychosocial Dimensions* (eds P.L. Ahmed and G.V. Coelho) Plenum, New York

Alberti, R.D. and Emmons, M.L. (1970) *Your Perfect Right: A Guide to Assertive Behaviour.* Impact, New York

Alfredsson, L., Karasek, R.A., Theorell, T.G.T., Schwartz, J. and Pieper, C. (1982) Job, psychosocial factors and coronary heart disease. In *Psychological problems before and after myocardial infarction. Advanced Cardiology, Vol. 29* (ed. H. Denolin) Karger, Bale

Allibone, A., Oakes, D. and Shannon, H.S. (1981) The health and health care of doctors. *Journal of the Royal College of General Practitioners, 31,* 328–31

American Cancer Society. (1986) *Cancer Facts and Figures.* New York

American Heart Association. (1986) *Heart Facts.* Dallas

Arndt, S., Feltes, J. and Hanak, J. (1983) Secretarial attitudes towards word processors as a function of familiarity and locus of control. *Behaviour and Information Technology, 2,* 17–22

Arnold, J. (1989) Experiences and attitudes of learner nurses during their first year of training. *Unpublished report,* Manchester School of Management, UMIST, Manchester

Arthur, R.J. and Gunderson, E.K. (1965) Promotion and Mental illness in the Navy. *Journal of Occupational Medicine, 7,* 452–6

Baaker, C.D. (1967) Psychological Factors in Angina Pectoris. *Psychosomatic Medicine, 8,* 43–9

Bacon, C.L., Rennecker, R. and Kutler, M. (1952) Psychosomatic survey of cancer of the breast. *Psychosomatic Medicine, 4,* 453–60

Bahnson, C.B. (1981) Stress and cancer: The state of the art, Part 2. *Psychosomatics, 22,* 207–20

Baker, G.H.B. (1987) Invited review. Psychological factors and immunity. *Journal of Psychosomatic Research, 31* (1), 1–10

Baker, G.H.B. and Brewerton, P. (1981) Rheumatoid arthritis: A psychiatric assessment. *British Medical Journal, 282,* 2014

Baker, R., Dunham, J., Harrison, E., Hingley, P. and Manolias, M. (1987) *Stress in the Public Sector; Nurses, Police, Social Workers and Teachers.* Health Education Authority Report

Bamberg, E., Ruckert, D. and Udris, I. (1986) Interactive effects of social support from wife, non-work activities and blue-collar occupational stress. *International Review of Applied Psychology, 35,* 397–413

Barefoot, J.C., Dahlstrom, G. and Williams, R.B. (1983) Hostility, CHD incidence and total mortality: A 25 year follow-up study of 255 physicians. *Psychosomatic Medicine, 45,* 59–63

Barnes, P.J., Brown, M.J., Silverman, M. and Dollery, C.T. (1983) Circulating catecholamines in exercise and hyperventilation induced asthma. *Thorax, 36,* 435–40

Bass, C. and Akhras, F. (1987) Physical and psychological correlates of severe heart disease in men. *Psychological Medicine, 17,* 695–703

Bass, C. and Wade, C. (1982) Psychological enquiries in patients with normal and abnormal coronary arteries. *Lancet, Nov,* 1147–49

Bates, E. (1982). Doctors and the spouses speak: Stress in medical practice. *Social Health and Illness, 4,* 25–39

Baum, C., Kennedy, D.L., Knapp, D.E. and Faich, G.A. (1984). *Prescription drug use in 1984. Paper presented at the American Public Health Association Annual Meeting. Washington, D.C.* 1985

BDA (1988) Diabetes in the United Kingdom, 1988. A British Diabetic Association Report

Bearham, J. (1976) *The Cost of Accidents Within the Port Industry.* Manpower Development Division, National Ports Council, London

Beech, H.R., Burns, L.E. and Sheffield, B.P. (1984) *A Behavioural Approach to the Management of Stress.* John Wiley & Sons, Chichester

Beehr, T.A. and Newman, J.E. (1978) Job stress, employee health and organisational effectiveness: A facet analysis model and literature review, *Personnel Psychology, 31,* 665–99

Bell, G.H., Enslie-Smith, D. and Patterson, C.R. (1980) *Textbook of Physiology,* 10th ed Churchill Livingstone, UK

Bendig, A.W. (1963) The relation of temperament traits of social extraversion and emotionality to vocational interests. *Journal of General Psychology, 69,* 311–8

Ben-Sira, Z. (1985) Potency: A stress-buffering link in the coping–stress–disease relationship. *Social Science and Medicine, 21* (4), 397–406

Benson, H. (1975) *The Relaxation Response.* William Morrow, New York

Benyon, H., and Blackburn, R.M. (1972) *Perceptions of Work: Variations within a Factory.* University Press, Cambridge

Bhagat, R.S. (1983) Effects of stressful life events upon individual performance effectiveness and work adjustment processes within organisational settings: A research model. *Academy of Management Review, 8,* (4), 660–71

Bieliauskas, L.A. and Garron, D.C. (1982) Psychological Depression and Cancer. *General Hospital Psychiatry, 4,* 56

Bilodeau, L.P., Moody, J.M., Rathburn, J.D. and Krant, R.A. (1983) Evaluation of ECG changes in dentist treating awake patients. *Anaesth. Prog., 30,* 193–6

Birch, J. (1979) The anxious learners. *Nursing Mirror,* Feb 1979, pp. 17–22

274

Bohemier, A. (1985). Mar–Tech, 1985, Montreal. Reported *Lloyds List.* May 23rd, 1985, p. 1

Bortner, R.W. and Rosenman, R.H. (1967) The measurement of pattern A behaviour. *J. Chronic Disorders, 20,* 525–33

Brady, J.V. (1958) Ulcers in 'executive monkeys'. *Scientific American, 199,* 95–100

Brebner, J. and Cooper, C. (1979) Stimulus or response induced excitation: A comparison of behaviour of introverts and extraverts. *Journal of Research into Personality, 12,* 306–11

Breslow, L., and Buell, P. (1960). Mortality from coronary heart disease & physical activity of work in California. *Journal of Chronic Diseases, 11,* 615–26

Brief, A.P., Rude, D.E. & Rabinowitz, S. (1983) The impact of type A behaviour pattern on subjective workload and depression. *Journal of Occupational Behaviour, 4,* 157–64

Brief, A.P., Schuler, R.S. and Van Self, M. (1981) *Managing Job Stress.* Little, Brown & Co., Boston

Brief, P. and Hollenbeck, J.R. (1985). Work and the quality of life. *International Journal of Psychology, 20,* 199–206

British Diabetic Association. (1988) *Diabetes in the United Kingdom — 1998.* BDA Report. London, UK

Broadbent, D.E. (1971) *Decisions and Stress.* Academic Press, London

Broadbent, D.E. and Gath, D. (1981) Symptom levels in assembly line workers. In *Machine Pacing and Occupational Stress* (eds G. Salvendy and M.J. Smith). Taylor and Francis, London

Broadbent, D.E. and Little, F.A. (1960) Effects of noise reduction in a work situation. *Occupational Psychology, 34,* 133–40

Brook, A. (1973) Mental stress at work. *The Practitioner, 210,* 500–06

Brooking, J.I. (1985) Advance in psychiatric nursing education in Britain. *Journal of Advanced Nursing, 10,* 455–68

Brown, B. (1984) Biofeedback for coping with organisational stress. In *Handbook of Organisational Stress Coping Strategies* (eds A.S. Sethi and R.S. Schuler). Ballinger, pp. 191–214, Cambridge, MA

Browne, D.W., Russell, M.L., Morgan, J.L., Optenberg, S.A. and Clarke, A.E. (1984) Reduced disability and health care costs in an industrial fitness program. *J. Occ. Med., 26* (11), 809–16

Buchholz, R.A. (1978) An empirical study of contemporary beliefs about work in American society. *Journal of Applied Psychology, 63,* 225

Buck, P.C. and Coleman, V.P. (1985) Slipping, tripping and falling accidents at work: A national picture. *Ergonomics, 28* (7) 949–58

Buck, V. (1972) *Working Under Pressure.* Staples Press, London

Burke, R.G. (1985) The unseen side of safety training. *Offshore,* August, 1985

Burke, R.J. and Greenglass, E.R. (1987) Work and Family. In *International Review of Industrial and Organisational Psychology* (eds C.L. Cooper and I.T. Robertson). John Wiley, Chichester

Byrne, D.G. (1987) Invited Review. Personality, life events, and cardiovascular disease. *Journal of Psychosomatic Research, 31* (6), 666–71

275

Cakir, A., *et al.* (1979) *Visual Display Terminals.* John Wiley, Chichester, New York

Canning, R. (1987) De-stressing stress management. *Training Officer,* March, 79–84

Cannon, W.B. (1935) Stresses and strain of homeostasisi. *American Journal of Medical Science, 189* (1) 1–14

Caplan, R.D., Cobb, S. and French, J.R.P. (1975a) Relationships of cessation of smoking with job stress, personality and social support. *Journal of Applied Psychology, 60* (2) 211–9

Caplan, R.D., Cobb, S., French, J.R.P., Van Harrison, R. and Pinneau, S.R. (1975b). Job Demands and Worker Health: Main Effects and Occupational Differences. *NIOSH Research Report*

Carrington, P., Collings, G. and Benson, H. (1980) The use of meditation — relaxation for the management of stress in a working population. *Journal of Occupational Medicine, 22* (4) 221–31

Carruthers, M.E. (1976) Risk Factor Control, *conference paper* at Stress of Air Traffic Control Officers, April, 1976, Manchester

Carter, F.A. and Corlett, E.N. (1981) Shiftwork and Accidents. *Report to the European Foundation for the Improvement of Living and Working Conditions.* Shanklin, Ireland, 1982

Cartwright, A. (1967) *Patients and Their Doctors.* Routledge & Kegan Paul, London

Cartwright, A. and Anderson, R. (1981) *General Practice Revisited.* Tavistock, London

Cartwright, L.K. (1987) Occupational Stress in Women Physicians. In *Stress in Health Professionals* (eds R. Payne and J. Firth-Cozens). John Wiley, UK

Chan, K.B. (1977) Individual Differences in Reactions to Stress and their Personality and Situational Determinants. *Social Science and Medicine, 11,* 89–103

Cheliout, F. (1979) Rythme thêta postérieur au cour de la veille active chez l'homme. *Reveue EEC en neuropsychologie, 9,* 52–7

Cherry, M. (1974) *On High Steel: The Education of an Iron Worker.* Ballantine, New York

Chisholm, R.F., Kasl, S.V. and Mueller, L. (1986) The effects of social support on nuclear worker responses to the Three Mile Island accident. *Journal of Occupational Behaviour, 7,* 179–93

Chissick, S.S., and Derricott, R. (eds) (1981) *Occupational Health & Safety Management,* John Wiley, UK

Christian, P. and Lolas, F. (1985) The stress concept as a problem for a theoretical pathology. *Social Science and Medicine, 21* (12), 1363–5

Clark, J. (1975) *Time Out? — A Study of Absenteeism.* Royal College of Nursing, London

Clegg, C.W. and Wall, T.D. (1981) A note on some new scales for measuring aspects of psychological well-being at work. *Journal of Occupational Psychology, 54,* 221–5

Cobb, S. (1976) Social support as a moderator of life stress. *Psychosomatic Medicine, 38,* 301–14

Cobb, S. and Kasl, S.V. (1977) *Termination — The Consequences of Job*

Loss. H.E.W. Publications, pp. 77–224, NIOSH, USA

Cobb, S. and Rose, R.H. (1973) Hypertension, peptic ulcer and diabetes in air traffic controllers. *Journal of the Australian Medical Association,* *224,* 489–92

Coch, L. and French, J.R.P. (1948) Overcoming resistance to change. *Human Relations, 1,* 512–32

Cohen, A. (1974) Industrial noise, medical absence and accident record data on exposed workers. In Proceedings of the International Congress on Noise as a Public Health Problem. (ed W.D. Ward), *U.S. Environmental Protection Agency,* Washington

Cohen, A. (1976) The influence of a company hearing conservation program on extra-auditory problems in workers. *Journal of Safety Research, 8,* 146–62

Cohen, S. and Syme, L. (1985) Issues in the study and application of social support. In *Social Support and Health* (eds S. Cohen and L. Syme). Academic Press, Orlando, Florida

Cooper, C.L. (1974) Executive Stress: A Ten Country Comparison. *Human Resource Management, 23,* 395–407

Cooper, C.L. (1980) Dentists under pressure. In *White Collar and Professional Stress* (eds C.L. Cooper and J. Marshall). John Wiley, UK

Cooper, C.L. (1981) *The Stress Check.* Prentice Hall, USA

Cooper, C.L. (1986) Job distress: recent research and the emerging role of the clinical occupational psychologist. *Bulletin of the British Psychological Society. 39,* 325–31

Cooper, C.L. (1988) Personality, Life Stress and Cancerous Disease. In *Handbook of Life Stress, Cognition and Health* (eds S. Fisher and J. Reason). John Wiley, UK

Cooper, C.L., Cooper, R.D., Eaker, L.H. (1988a). *Living with Stress.* Penguin, Harmondsworth

Cooper, C.L. and Davidson, M.J. (1982) The high cost of stress on women managers. *Organisational Dynamics,* Spring, 1982, 44–53

Cooper, C.L. and Davies-Cooper, R. (1983) Occupational stress among international interpreters. *Journal of Occupational Medicine, 25,* 889–95

Cooper, C.L., Davies-Cooper, R. and Faragher, E.B. (1985) Stress and Life Event Methodology. *Stress Medicine, 1,* 287–9

Cooper, C.L., Davies-Cooper, R. and Faragher, E.B. (1986) A prospective study of the relationship between breast cancer and life events, Type A behaviour, social support and coping skills. *Stress Medicine, 2* 271–7

Cooper, C.L. and Kelly, M. (1984) Stress among crane operators. *Journal of Occupational Medicine, 26,* 8, 575–8

Cooper, C.L., Mallinger, M. and Kahn, R. (1978) Identifying sources of occupational stress among dentists. *Journal of Occupational Psychology, 51,* 227–34

Cooper, C.L., and Marshall, J. (1978) *Understanding Executive Stress.* Macmillan, UK

Cooper, C.L. and Melhuish, A. (1980) Occupational stress and the manager. *Journal of Occupational Medicine, 22* (9) 588–92

277

Cooper, C.L. and Roden, J. (1985) Mental health and satisfaction among tax officers. *Social Science and Medicine, 21* (7) 747–51

Cooper, R. and Payne, R. (1967) Extraversion and some aspects of work behaviour. *Personnel Psychology, 20,* 45–7

Cooper, C.L., Reynolds, P. and Sadri, G. (1989a) Stress counselling in industry: The Post Office experience. *Paper presented at The Annual Conference of the British Psychological Society,* March, 1989, St. Andrews

Cooper, C.L., Rout, U. and Faragher, B. (1989b) Mental health, job satisfaction and job stress among general practitioners. *British Medical Journal, 298,* 366–70

Cooper, C.L., Sloan, S.J. and Williams, S. (1988b) *Occupational Stress Indicator.* NFER Nelson, UK

Cooper, C.L., Watts, J., Baglioni, Jr., A.J. and Kelly, M. (1988c) Occupational stress among general practice dentists. *Journal of Occupational Psychology, 61,* 163–74

Cooper, C.L., Watts, J. and Kelly, M. (1987) Job satisfaction, mental health, and job stressors among general dental practitioners in the UK. *British Dental Journal,* Jan. 24, 1987, 77–81

Copper, A.J. and Metcalfe, M. (1963) Cancer and extraversion. *British Medical Journal, 20,* 18–9

Corah, N.L., O'Shea, R.M. and Skeels, D.K. (1982) Dentists' perceptions of problem behaviours in patients. *Journal of the American Dental Association, 104,* 829–33

Cox, D.J., Taylor, A.G. and Nowacek, G. (1984) The relationship between psychological stress and insulin-dependent diabetic blood glucose control: preliminary investigations. *Health Psychology, 3,* 63–75

Cox, M., Shephard, R.J. and Corey, P. (1981) Influence of an employee fitness programme upon fitness, productivity and absenteeism. *Ergonomics, 24,* 795–806

Cox, T. (1985) *Stress.* Macmillan, London

Cox, V.C., Paulus, P.B., McCain, G., Karlovac, M. (1982) The relationship between crowding and health. In *Advances in Experimental Psychology, Vol 4* (eds A. Baum and J. Singer), Lawrence Erlbaum, USA

Christian, P. and Lolas, F. (1985) The stress concept as a problem for a 'theoretical pathology'. *Social Science and Medicine, 21* 1363–5

Craig, T.J. and Abeloff. (1974) Psychiatric symptomology among hospitalised cancer patients. *American Journal of Psychiatry, 131,* 1323–7

Craske, S. (1968) A study of the relation between personality and accident history. *British Journal of Medical Psychology, 41,* 399–404

Cronin-Stubbs, D. and Brophy, E.B. (1985) Burnout: can social support save the psychiatric nurse? *Journal of Psychosocial Nursing and Mental Health, 23* (7) 8–13

Crown, S., Crisp, A.H. (1979) *Manual of the Crown-Crisp Experiential Index.* Hodder & Stoughton, London

Crump, J.H., Cooper, C.L. and Smith, M. (1980) Investigating occupational stress: A methodological approach. *Journal of Occupational Behaviour, 1* (3) 191–204

Cypress, B.K. (1984) Patterns of ambulatory care in international medicine in the national ambulatory medical care survey. USA January 1980–December 1981. *Vital and Health Statistics* Series 13, *80.* DHHS Pub. No. (PHS). 1984. pp. 84–1741, Washington, DC

Danowski, T.S. (1963) Emotional stress as a cause of diabetes mellitus. *Diabetes, 12,* 183

Dattore, P., Shontz, F. and Coyne, L. (1980) Premorbid personality differentiation of cancer and non-cancer groups. *Journal of Consulting and Clinical Psychology, 48* (3) 388–94

Davidson, M.J. (1987) Women and Employment. In *Psychology at Work* (ed. P. Warr). Penguin, UK

Davidson, M.J. and Cooper, C.L. (1981) Occupational stress in female managers — a review of the literature. *Journal of Enterprise Management, 3,* 115–38

Davidson, M.J. and Cooper, C.L. (1983) *Stress and the Woman Manager.* Blackwell, Oxford

Davidson, M.J. and Veno, A. (1980) Stress and the Policeman. In *White Collar & Professional Stress* (eds C.L. Cooper & J. Marshall). John Wiley, London

Dawkins, J.E., Depp, F.C. and Selzer, N.E. (1985) Stress and the psychiatric nurse. *Journal of Psychosocial Nursing and Mental Health Services, 23* (11) 9–15

DeAraujo, G., Dudley, D.L. and Van Asdel, P.P. Jr. (1972) Psychological assets and severity of chronic asthma. *Journal of Allergy and Clinical Immunology, 50,* 257

DeFrank, R.S. and Cooper, C.L. (1987) Worksite stress management interventions: Their effectiveness and conceptualisation. *Journal of Managerial Psychology, 2* (1) 4–10

Dembroski, T.M., MacDougal, J.M., Williams, R.B., Haney, T.L. and Blumenthal, J.A, (1985) Components of Type A, hostility and anger-in relationship to angiographic findings. *Psychosomatic Medicine, 47,* 219–33

Department of Health and Social Security. (1981) *Drinking Sensibly.* HMSO, London

Dewe, P.J. (1987) Identifying the causes of nurses' stress. *Work and Stress, 1* (1), Jan–March 15–24

DHSS (1981) *Drinking Sensibly.* HMSO, London

Dirken, J.M. (1966) Industrial shift work: Decrease in well-being and specific effects. *Ergonomics, 9,* 115–24

Dohrenwend, B.S., and Dohrenwend, B.P. (1974) *Stressful Life Events.* Wiley, New York

Doll, R. and Jones, A.F. (1951) *Occupational factors in the aetiology of gastric and duodenal ulcers.* Medical Research Council Special Report Series. No. 276. HMSO, London

Doll, R. and Peto, R. (1979) Mortality among doctors in different occupations. *British Medical Journal, 1,* 1433–6

Dončević, S., Theorell, T. and Scalia-Tomba, G. (1988) The psychosocial work-environment of district nurses in Sweden. *Work and Stress, 2* (4) 341–51

Dooley, D., Rook, K. and Catalano, R. (1987) Job and non-job stressors and their moderators. *Journal of Occupational Psychology, 60*, 115–32

Dubos, R. (1959) *Mirage of Health*. Harper and Row, New York

Dunbar, F. (1943) *Psychosomatic Medicine*. Hoeber, New York

Dunkel-Schetter, C., Folkman, S. and Lazarus, R.S. (1987) Correlates of social support receipt, *Journal of Personality and Social Psychology, 53* (1), 71–80

Durkheim, E. (1951) *Suicide*. Free Press, New York

Dyer, W.W. (1976) *Your Erroneous Zones*. Avon Books, New York

Edelwich, J. and Brodsky, A. (1980) *Burnout*. Human Sciences Press, New York

Elliott, D.H. (1985) The offshore worker. *The Practitioner, 229*, June, 565–71

Evans, E. (1926) *A Psychosocial Study of Cancer*. Dodd-Mead, New York

Evans, G.W. (1979) Behavioural & physiological consequences of crowding in humans. *Journal of Applied Social Psychology, 9* (1) 27–46

Evans, G.W., Palsane, M.N. and Carrere, S. (1987) Type A behaviour and occupational stress: A cross cultural study of blue collar workers. *Journal of Personality and Social Psychology, 52* (5) 1002–7

Evans, P. and Bartolomé, F. (1980) The relationship between professional and private life. In *Work, Family and Career* (ed. C.B. Derr). Praeger, New York, 281–317

Evans, P. and Bartolomé, F. (1984) The changing picture of the relationship between between career and family. *Journal of Occupational Behaviour, 5*, pp. 9–21

Evans, P.D. and Fearn, J.M. (1985) Type A behaviour, choice of active coping strategy and cardiovascular activity in relation to threat of shock. *British Journal of Medical Psychology, 58*, 95–9

Eysenck, H.J. (1965) *Smoking, Health and Personality*. Weidenfeld and Nicholson, UK

Eysenck, H.J. (1967) *Biological Basis of Personality*. Charles C. Thomas, Springfield, Illinois.

Eysenck, H.J. (1980) *The Causes and Effects of Smoking*. Maurice Temple Smith, London

Eysenck, H.J. (1984) Lung cancer and the stress–personality inventory. In *Psychosocial Stress and Cancer* (ed. C.L. Cooper). John Wiley, UK

Eysenck, H.J. (1988) Personality, stress and cancer: Prediction and prophylaxis. *British Journal of Medical Psychology, 61*, 57–75

Eysenck, H.J. and Eysenck, M.W. (1985) *Personality and Individual Differences. A Natural Science Approach*. Plenum, London

Eysenck, H.J. and Eysenck, S.B.G. (1969) *Personality Structure and Measurement*. Routledge & Kegan Paul, London

Eysenck, H and Fulker, D. (1983) The components of Type A behaviour and its genetic determinants. *Pesonality and Individual Differences, 4*, (5) 499–505

Eysenck, M.W. (1982) *Attention and Arousal. Cognition and Performance*. Springer, Berlin

Falkenberg, L.E. (1987) Employee fitness programmes: Their impact on the employee and the organisation. *Academy of Management Review,* *12* (3) 511–22

Feldman, M.P. (1971) *Psychology in the Industrial Environment.* Butterworths, London

Fine, B.J. (1963) Introversion, extraversion and motor driver behaviour. *Perceptual and Motor Skills, 16,* 95–100

Fink, D.J. (1978) More on cancer. *Business Week,* November 27, p. 66

Finn, F.N., Hickey, N., and O'Doherty, E.F. (1969) The psychological profiles of male and famale patients with CHD. *Irish Journal of Medical Science, 2,* 339–41

Firth, J. (1986) Levels and sources of stress in medical students. *British Medical Journal, 292,* 1177–80

Firth, H. and Britton, P. (1989) Burnout, absence and turnover among British nursing staff. *Journal of Occupational Psychology, 62,* 55–9

Firth, H., McInere, J., McKeown, P. and Britton, P. (1986) Interpersonal support among nurses at work. *Journal of Advanced Nursing, 11,* 273–82

Firth, J. and Morrison, L. (1986) What stresses health professionals? A coding system for their answers. *British Journal of Clinical Psychology, 25,* 309–10

Firth-Cozens, J. and Morrison, L.A. (1987) Sources of stress and ways of coping in junior house officers. *Research report,* SAPU, No. 873. University of Sheffield, Sheffield

Fisher, S. (1988) Methodological factors in the investigation of stress and health at work: The development of the epidemiological problem analysis approach. In *Occupational Stress, Issues and Developments in Research* (eds J.J. Hurrell, L.R. Murphy, S.L. Sauter and C.L. Cooper). Taylor Francis, New York

Flamholtz, E. (1971) Should your organisation attempt to value its human resources? *California Management Review 10,* 82–6

Fleming, T.C. (1986) Alcohol and other mood changing drugs. In *Occupational Stress. Health and Performance at Work* (eds S.G. Wolf and A.J. Finestone. P.S.G. Littleton, Massachusetts

Flores, T. and Valdés, M. (1986) Behaviour pattern A. Reward, fight or punishment. *Personality and Individual Differences, 7* (3) 319–26

Folkman, S., Lazarus, R.S., Dunkel-Schetter, C., DeLongis, A. and Gruen, R. (1986) The dynamics of a stressful encounter: Cognitive appraisal, coping and encounter outcomes. *Journal of Personality and Social Psychology, 50,* 992–1003

Folsom, A.R. (1985) Do Type A men drink more frequently than Type B men? Findings in the multiple risk factor intervention trial (MRFIT). *Journal of Behavioural Medicine, 8* (3) 227–35

Foque, E. (1931) Le Probleme au cancer dans les aspects psychiques. *Hospital Gazette* (Paris), *104,* 827

Fox, B.H. (1978) Premorbid psychological factors as related to cancer incidence. *Journal of Behavioural Medicine, 1* (1) 45–133

Frankenhaeuser, M. (1975) Experimental approaches to the study of catecholamines and emotion. In *Emotions: Their Parameters and Measurement* (ed. L. Levi). Raven Press, New York

Frankenhaeuser, M., and Johansson, G. (1986) Stress at work: psychobiological and psychosocial aspects. *International Review of Applied
Psychology, 35*, 287–99

French, J.R.P. (1973) Person-role fit. *Occupational Mental Health, 3*, 1

French, J.R.P. and Caplan, R.D. (1970) Psychosocial Factors in Coronary
Heart Disease. *Industrial Medicine, 39*, 383–97

French, J.R.P. and Caplan, R.D. (1973) Organisational Stress and
Individual Strain. In *The Failure of Success* (ed. A.J. Marrow).
Amacon, New York pp. 30–66

Friedlander, F. and Greenburg, S. (1971) Effect of job attitudes, training
and organisational climate on performance of the hard core
unemployed. *Journal of Applied Psychology, 55*, 287–95

Friedman, M. and Rosenman, R.H. (1974) *Type A: Your Behaviour and
Your Heart.* Knopf, New York

Fryer, D. and Payne, R. (1986) Being Unemployed. In C.L. Cooper and
I.T. Robertson (Eds) *International Review of Industrial and Organisational Psychology.* John Wiley, Chichester

Fuller, J.H., Elford, J., Goldblatt, P. and Adelstein, A.M. (1983) Diabetes
Mortality. A new light on an underestimated public health problem.
Diabetologia, 24, 336–41

Furnham, A. (1981) Personality and activity preference. *British Journal of
Social Psychology, 20*, 57–68

Furnham, A. (1983) Social skills and dentistry. *British Dental Journal,
154*, 404–11

Gale, A. (1987) Reviews and Appraisal. In *Personality Dimensions and
Arousal* (eds J. Strelau and H.J. Eysenck). Plenum, London

Ganster, D.C. and Victor, B. (1988) The impact of social support on
mental and physical health. *British Journal of Medical Psychology, 61*,
17–36

Geller, A. (1983) *Alcohol and Anxiety.* Johnson Institute Inc.,
Minneapolis

Gerhart, B. (1987) How important are dispositional factors as determinants of job satisfaction? Implications for job design and other personnel
programmes. *Journal of Applied Psychology, 72* (3) 366–73

Gertman, D.I. and Haney, L.N. (1985) Personality and Stress — What
impact on decision making? In: *Contemporary Ergonomics* (ed. D.J.
Oborne). Proceedings of the Ergonomics Society's Annual Conference.
Nottingham, 1985. Taylor Francis, London

Gil, K.M., Keefe, F.J., Sampson, H.A., McCaskill, C.C., Rodin, J. and
Crisson, J.E. (1987) The relation of stress and family environment to
atopic dermatitis symptoms in children. *Journal of Psychosomatic
Research, 31* (6) 673–84

Gillespie, C. and Gillespie, V. (1986) Reading the danger signs. *Nursing
Times,* 30 July, 24–7

Gilligan, I., Fung, L., Piper, D.W. and Tennant, C. (1987) Life event stress
and chronic difficulties in duodenal ulcer: A case control study. *Journal
of Psychosomatic Research, 31* (1) 117–23

Glaser, B.G. and Strauss, A.L. (1968) *Time For Dying.* Aldine, Illinois.

Glowinkowski, S.P. (1985) *Managerial Stress: A Longitudinal Study.*

Unpublished doctoral thesis. UMIST, Manchester, UK

Goldberg, D.P. (1972) *The Detection of Psychiatric Illness by Questionnaire.* Oxford University Press, London

Golding, J.F., Harpur, T. and Brent-Smith, H. (1983) Personality, drinking and drug taking correlates of cigarette smoking. *Personality and Individual Differences, 4* (6) 703–6

Goldmeier, D., Johnson, A., Jeffries, D., Walker, G.D., Underhill, G., Robinson, G. and Ribbans, H. (1986) *Psychological Aspects of Psychosomatic Research, 30* (5) 601–8

Goodell, H., Wolf, S. and Rogers, F.B. (1986) Historical Perspective, Chapter 2. In *Occupational Stress. Health and Performance at Work* (eds S. Wolf and A.J. Finestone. PSG Inc., Littleton, Massachusetts

Goodkin, K., Antoni, M.H. and Blaney, P.H. (1986) Stress and hopelessness in the promotion of cervical intraepithelial neoplasia to invasive squamous cell carcinoma of the cervix. *Journal of Psychosomatic Research, 30* (1) 67–76

Gore, S. (1978) The effects of social supports in moderating the health consequences of unemployment. *Journal of Health and Social Behaviour, 19,* 157–65

Gowler, D. and Legge, K. (1975) Stress and external relationships: The 'hidden' contract. In *Managerial Stress* (eds D. Gowler and K. Legge). Gower, UK

Grant, I., Kyle, G.C. Teichman, A. and Mendels, J. (1974) Recent Life events and diabetes in adults. *Psychosomatic Medicine, 36,* 121

Gray-Toft, P. and Anderson, J.G. (1981) Stress among hospital nursing staff, its causes and effects. *Social Science and Medicine, 15A* (5) 639–647

Greene, W.A. (1962) The psychosocial setting of the development of leukaemia and lymphoma. *Annual New York Academy of Sciences, 125,* 794–802

Greene, W.A. and Swisher, S.N. (1969) Psychological and somatic variables associated with the development and course of monozygotic twins discordant for leukaemia. *Annual New York Academy of Sciences, 164,* 394–408

Griffen, D., Everly, G. and Fuhrman, C. (1982) Designing an effective stress management training program. *Training/HRD,* September, 44–47

Grigsby, D.W. and McKnew, M.A. (1988) Work-stress Burnout among Paramedics. *Unpublished report,* Department of Management, Clemson University, USA

Groen, J.J. (1971) Psychosocial influences in bronchia asthma. In *Society, Stress and Disease, Vol. 1* (ed. L. Levi). Oxford University Press, Oxford

Grol, R., Mokkink, H., Smits, A., Van Eijk, J., Beek, M., Mesker, P. and Mesker-Niesten, J. (1985) Work satisfaction of general practitioners and the quality of patient care. *Family Practice, 2,* 128–35

Gruneberg, M.M. and Oborne, D.J. (1982) *Industrial Productivity. A Psychological Perspective.* Macmillan, London

Guest, D. and Williams, R. (1973) How home affects work. *New Society, 23,* 114–7

283

Hagnell, O. (1966) The premorbid personality of persons who develop cancer in a total population investigated in 1947 and 1957. In *Psychophysiological Aspects of Cancer.* Annals of the New York Academy of Science, *846*

Hall, D.T. (1976) *Careers in Organisations.* Goodyear Publishing Co., Santa Monica

Hall, D.T., and Hall, F.S. (1980) Stress and the two-career couple. In *Current Concerns in Occupational Stress* (eds C.L.Cooper and R. Payne), Wiley, New York pp. 243–66

Hall, L. and Torrington, D. (1986) Why not use the computer? The use and lack of use of computers in personnel. *Personnel Review, 15* (1) 3–7

Handy, C. (1976) *Understanding Organisations,* Penguin, Harmondsworth

Handy, C. (1978) The family: Help or Hindrance. In *Stress at Work* (eds C.L. Cooper and R. Payne). New York: Wiley. pp. 107–123

Haney, C.A. (1977) Illness behaviour and psychosocial correlates of cancer. *Journal of Social Science and Medicine, 11* (4) 223–8

Hanlon, M.D. (1986) Reducing hospital costs through employee involvement strategies. *National Productivity Review, 5* (1) 22–31

Hanson, S.L. and Pichert, J.W. (1986) Perceived stress and diabetes control in adolescents. *Health Psychology, 5,* 439–52

Hartman, E.A. and Pearlman, B. (1982) Burnout: Summary and future research. *Human Relations, 35* (4) 283–305

Harvey, J., Durbin, J. and Elson, J. *et al.* (1988) Stress in the NHS: Sagging and Sapping. *The Occupational Psychologist,* BPS, UK, (Dec) (6), 8–11

Hawkins, L., White, M. and Morris, L. (1983) Smoking, stress and nurses. *Nursing Mirror,* 13 Oct. 1983

Haynes, S.G., Levine, S., Scotch, N., Feinleib, M. and Kannel, W.B. (1978a). The relationship of psychosocial factors to coronary heart disease in the Framingham Study I. Methods and risk factors. *American Journal of Epidemiology, 107,* 362–83

Haynes, S.G., Feinleib, M., Levine, S., Scotch, N., and Kannel, W.B. (1978b). The relationship of psychosocial factors to coronary heart disease in the Framingham Study II. Prevelance of coronary heart disease. *American Journal of Epidemiology, 107,* 384–402

Haynes, S.G., Feinleib, M. and Kannel, W.B. (1980) The relationship of psychosocial factors to coronary heart disease in the Framingham Study III. Eight-year incidence of coronary heart disease. *American Journal of Epidemiology, 111,* 37–58

Haynes, S.G., Feinleib, M., and Eaker, E.D. (1981) Type A behaviour and the ten year incidence of coronary heart disease in the Framingham Heart Study. In *Psychosomatic Risk Factors and Coronary Heart Disease: Indication for Specific Preventitive Therapy* (ed. Rosenman, R.H.). Hans Huber, Bern, Switzerland

Health Education Authority. (1987) Look after your heart. Campaign Strategy. London: Department of Health and Social Security. *Publication No. 1,* April, 1987

Health and Safety Executive (HSE) (1982) *Health and Safety Statistics 1980.* HMSO, Norwich

Hecker, H.L., Chesney, M.A., Black, G.W. and Frautschi, N. (1988) Coronary prone behaviours in the Western Collaborative Group study. *Psychosomatic Medicine, 50,* 153–64

Heinrich, H.W. (1979) *Industrial Accident Prevention: A Scientific Approach.* 4th Edn. McGraw Hill, New York

Heins, M., Smock, M. and Martindale, L. *et al.* (1977) A profile of the women physician. *Journal of the American Medical Association, 32,* 21–6

Hellesøy, Odd, H. (1985) (ed.) Work Environment Statfjord Field. Universitetsforlaget, Bergen

Henne, D. and Locke, E.A. (1985) Job dissatisfaction: What are the consequences? *International Journal of Psychology, 20,* 221–40. (North Holland)

Hennigan, J.K., and Wortham, A.W. (1975) Analysis of workday stress on industrial managers using heart rate as a criterion. *Ergonomics, 18,* 675–81

Herd, J.A. (1988) Physiological Indices of Job Stress. In *Occupational Stress Issues and Developments in Research* (eds J.J. Hurrell, L.R. Murphy, S.L. Sauter and C.L. Cooper). Taylor Francis, London

Hertz, R.P. and Emmett, E.A. (1986) Risk factors for occupational hand injury. *Journal of Occupational Medicine, 28* (1) 37–41

Herzberg, F. (1966) *Work and the Nature of Man.* Staples Press, London

Hingley, P. and Cooper, C.L. (1986) *Stress and the Nurse Manager.* John Wiley, London

Hingley, P., Harris, P. and Cooper, C.L. (1988) *Nurse Stress Index.* Resource Assessment and Development, Thirsk, UK

Hinkle, L.E. (1973) The concept of stress in the biological and social sciences. *Science, Medicine and Man, 1,* 31–48

Hinkle, L.E. (1987) Stress and disease: The concept after 50 years. *Social Science and Medicine, 25* (6) 561–6

Hirschfeld, A.H. and Behan, R.C. (1963) The accident process: I. Etiological considerations of industrial injuries. *Journal of the American Medical Association, 186,* 193–9

Hirschfeld, A.H. and Behan, R.C. (1966) The accident process. III. Disability: Acceptable and unacceptable. *Journal of the American Medical Association, 197,* 125–9

HMSO (1981) *Offshore Safety.* Report of the Committee Chairman: J.H. Burgoyne

Hockey, G.R. (1970) Effect of loud noise on attentional selectivity. *Quarterly Journal of Experimental Psychology, 22,* 28–36

Hoiberg, A. (1980). Sex and occupational differences in hospitalization rates among navy enlisted personnel. *Journal of Occupational Medicine, 22* (10) 685–90

Hoiberg, A. (1982) Occupational stress and illness incidence. *Journal of Occupational Medicine, 24,* 445–51

Horne, R.L. and Picard, R.S. (1980) Psychosocial risk factors for lung cancer. *Psychosomatic Medicine, 41,* 503–14

House, J.S. (1981) *Work Stress and Social Support.* Addison-Wesley, USA

House, J.S., McMichael, A.J., Wells, J.A., Kaplan, B.N. and Landerman, L.R. (1979) Occupational stress and health among factory workers. *Journal of Health and Social Behaviour, 20,* 139–60

Howard, J.H., Cunningham, D.A. and Rechnitzer, P.A. (1976) Health patterns associated with Type A behaviour; A managerial population. *Journal of Human Stress, 2,* 24–31

Howard, J.H., Cunningham, D.A., Rechnitzer, P.A. and Goode, R.C. (1976) Stress on the job and career of a dentist. *Journal of the American Dental Association, 93,* 630–6

Howard, J.H., Cunningham, D.A. and Rechnitzer, P.A. (1986) Role ambiguity, Type A behaviour, job satisfaction: Moderating effects on cardiovascular and biochemical response associated with coronary risk. *Journal of Applied Psychology, 71* (1) 95–101

Hurrell, J.J. and Kroes, W.W. (1975) *Stress Awareness.* National Institute for Occupational Safety and Health. Ohio, Cincinnati

ILO (1986) *Psychosocial factors at work: Recognition and control.* Report of the Joint ILO/WHO Committee on Occupational Health. Ninth Session. 1984. Geneva: International Labour Office

Innes, J.M. (1981) Social Psychological Approaches to the Study of the Induction and Alleviation of Stress: Influences upon health & Illness. In *Progress in Applied Social Psychology. Vol. 1* (eds. G.M. Stephenson and J.M. Davies). John Wiley, UK

Irwin, J. and Anisman, H. (1984) Stress and pathology: Immunological and central nervous system interations. In *Psychosocial Stress and Cancer* (ed. C.L. Cooper). John Wiley, UK

Ivancevich, J.M. and Matteson, M.T. (1980) *Stress at Work.* USA, Foresman, Scott

Ivancevich, J.M., Matteson, M.T. and Preston, C. (1982) Occupational stress, Type A behaviour and physical well-being. *Academy of Management Journal, 25* (2) 373–91

Ivancevich, J.M. and Matteson, M.T. (1984) A Type A–B person-work environment interaction model for examining occupational stress and consequences. *Human Relations, 37* (7) 491–513

Ivancevich, J.M. and Matteson, M.T. (1988) Type A behaviour and the healthy individual. *British Journal of Medical Psychology, 61,* 37–56

Ivancevich, J.M. and Smith, S.V. (1982) Job difficulty as interpreted by incumbents: A study of nurses and engineers. *Human Relations, 35* (5) 391–412

Jacobson, B. (1981) *The Ladykillers: Why Smoking is a Feminist Issue.* Pluto Press, New York

Jacobson, E. (1958) *Progressive Relaxation.* University of Chicago Press, Chicago

Jacobson, S.P. (1978) Stressful situations for neonatal intensive care nurses. *American Journal of Maternal Child Nursing, 3* (3) 144–50

Jaffe, D.T., Scott, C.D. and Orioli, E.M. (1986) Stress management: Programs and prospects. *American Journal of Health Promotion, 1* (1) 29–37

Jahoda, M. (1979) The impact of unemployment in the 1930s and the

1970s. *Bulletin of the British Psychological Society, 32,* 309–14

James, A. (1988) Perceptions of stress in British ambulance personnel. *Work and Stress, 2* (4) 319–26

James, D.W.B. (1983) *A Safe Place of Work.* Butterworths, London

James, S.A., Harnett, S.A. and Kalsbeck, W. (1983) John Henryism and blood pressure differences among black men. *Journal of Behavioural Medicine, 6,* 259–78

Jenkins, C.D. (1971) Psychologic and social precursors of coronary disease. *New England Journal of Medicine, 284* (5) 244–55

Jenkins, C.D. (1983) Psychosocial and behavioural factors. In *Prevention of Coronary Heart Disease* (eds N. Kaplan and J. Stamler). Saunders, Philadelphia

Joe, V.C. (1971) Review of the internal–external control construct as a personality variable. *Psychological Reports, 28,* 619–40

Johansson, G. (1972) Sex differences in the catecholamine output of children. *Acta Physiologie Scandanavia, 85,* 569

Johnston, D.W. (1989) The prevention of cardiovascular disease by psychological factors. Health Psychology Section: British Psychology Conference. Annual Conference, July, 1988. Birmingham

Johnston, D.W., Cook, D.G. and Shaper, A.G. (1987) *Type A behaviour and ischaemic heart disease in middle-aged British men.* Paper presented at the Society of Behavioural Medicine, Washington, D.C. March, 1987

Jones, D.M. (1983) Noise. In *Stress and Fatigue in Human Performance* (ed. R. Hockey). John Wiley, UK

Jones, J.G. (1987) Stress in Psychiatric Nursing. In *Stress in Health Professionals* (eds R. Payne and J. Firth-Cozens). John Wiley, UK

Jones, J.G., Janman, K., Payne, R.L. and Rick, T.J. (1987) Some determinants of stress in psychiatric nurses. *International Journal of Nursing Studies, 24,* 129–44

Jones, J.W. (1980) *Preliminary test manual: The Staff Burnout Scale for Health Professionals (SBS–HP).* Park Ridge, Il: London House Press

Kagan, A. and Levi, L. (1971) Adaptations of the psychosocial environment to man's abilities and needs. In *Society Stress and Disease, Vol. 1* (ed. L. Levi). Oxford University Press, Oxford

Kahn, R.L., Wolfe, D.M., Quinn, R.P., Snoek, J.D., Rosenthal, R.A. (1964) *Organisational Stress: Studies in Role Conflict & Ambiguity.* John Wiley, UK. p. 41

Kalimo, R. (1980) Stress in work: 'Conceptual analysis and a study on prison personnel'. *Scandinavian Journal of Work Environment Health, 6* (3) p. 148

Kalimo, R. and Mejman, T. (1987) Psychological and behavioural response to stress at work. In *Psychosocial Factors at Work* (eds R. Kalimo, M.A. El-Batawi and C.L. Cooper). WHO, Geneva

Karasek, R.A. (1979) Job demands, job decision latitude and mental strain. Implications for job redesign. *Administrative Science Quarterly, 24,* 285–306

Karasek, R., Gardell, B. and Lindell, J. (1987) Work and non-work correlates of illness and behaviour in male and female Swedish white

287

collar workers. *Journal of Occupational Behaviour, 8,* 187–207

Kasl, S.V. (1978) Epidemiological Contributions to the Study of Work Stress. In *Stress at Work* (eds C.L. Cooper and R. Payne). John Wiley, UK

Kasl, S.V. and Cobb, S. (1970) Blood Pressure changes in men undergoing job loss: A preliminary report. *Psychosomatic Medicine, 32* 19–38

Katz, D. and Kahn, R.L. (1978) *The Social Psychology of Organisations.* 2nd edn, Wiley, New York

Keenan, V., Kerr, W. (1951) Psychological climate and accidents in an automotive plant. *Journal of Applied Psychology, 35* (2) 108–11

Kelly, M. and Cooper, C.L. (1981). Stress among blue collar workers. A case study of the steel industry. *Employee Relations, 3* (2) 6–9

Kennedy, S., Kiecolt-Glaser, J.K. and Glaser, R. (1988) Immunological consequences of acute and chronic stressors: Mediating role of interpersonal relationships. *British Journal of Medical Psychology, 61,* 77–85

Kent, G. (1987) Stress among Dentists. In *Stress in Health Professionals* (eds R. Payne and J. Firth-Cozens). John Wiley, UK

Kerr, W.A. (1950) Accident proneness of factory departments. *Journal of Applied Psychology, 34,* 167–70

Kessler, R.C. (1982) Life events, social supports and mental health. In *Deviance and Mental Illness* (ed. W.G. Grove), Sage, Beverly Hill California, pp. 247–71

Kissen, D.M. (1963) Personality characteristics in males conducive to lung cancer. *British Journal of Medical Psychology, 36,* 27–36

Kissen, D.M. and Eysenck, H.J. (1962) Personality in male lung cancer patients. *Journal of Psychosomatic Research, 6,* 123–37

Kline, P. (1983) *Personality: Measurement and Theory.* Hutchinson, London

Kline, P. (1987) Factor analysis and personality theory. *European Journal of Personality, 1,* 21–36

Knauth, P., and Rutenfranz, J. (1982) Development of criteria for the design of shiftwork systems. *Journal of Human Ergology, 11,* Suppl. 337–67

Knowles, J.H. (1977) *Doing Better and Feeling Worse: Health in the United States.* Norton, New York

Knox, S.S., Theorell, T., Svensson, J. and Waller, D. (1985) The relation of social support and working environment to medical variables associated with elevated blood pressure in young males: A structural model. *Social Science and Medicine, 21* (5) 525–31

Kobasa, S. (1979) Stressful life events, personality, health: An enquiry into hardiness. *Journal of Personality and Social Psychology, 37* (1) 1–11

Kobasa, S.C. (1982) The hardy personality: toward a social psychology of stress and health. In *The Social Psychology of Health and Illness* (eds G.S. Sanders and J. Suls). Lawrence Erlbaum, Hillsdale, New Jersey

Kobasa, S.C.O., Maddi, S.R., Puccetti, M.C. and Zola, M.A. (1985) Effectiveness of hardiness, exercise and social support as resources against illness. *Journal of Psychosomatic Research, 29* (5) 525–33

Kohler, P.F. and Vaughan, J. (1982) The autoimmune diseases. *Journal of American Medical Association, 248,* 2646–57

Kopelman, R.E. (1985) Job redesign and productivity: A review of the evidence. *National Productivity Review, 4* (3) 237–55

Kornhauser, A. (1965) *Mental Health of the Industrial Worker.* Wiley, New York

Krakowski, A.J. (1982) Stress and the practice of medicine. *Journal of Psychosomatic Research, 26,* 91–8

Krantz, D.S., Grunberg, N.E. and Baum, A. (1985) Health Psychology. *Annual Review of Psychology, 36,* 349–83

Kritsikis, S.P., Heinemann, A.L. and Eitner, S. (1968) Die Angina Pectoris in Aspeckt Ihrer Korrelation mit Biologischer Disposition, Psychologischen und Soziologischem Emflussfaktoren. *Deutsch Gasundh, 23,* 1878–85

Kummer, R. (1983) Noise in oil and gas extractive industries. *International Symposium — Luxembourg. Op cit.*

Lachman, V.D. (1983) *Stress Management: A Manual for Nurses.* Grune and Stratton, New York

LaCroix, A.Z. and Haynes, S.G. (1986) Gender differences in the stressfulness of workplace roles: A focus on work and health. In *Gender and Stress* (eds R. Barnett, G. Baruch and L. Biener). Free Press, New York

Lader, M.H. (1971) Response to repetitive stimulation. In *Society, Stress and Disease, Vol. 1* (ed. L. Levi). Oxford University Press, Oxford

Laing, R.D. (1971) *The Politics of the Family and other Essays.* Pantheon, New York

Landsbergis, P.A. (1988) Occupational stress among health care workers: A test of the job demands-control model. *Journal of Occupational Behaviour, 9,* 217–39

Landy, F.J. and Trumbo, D.A. (1980) *Psychology of Work Behaviour.* Dorsey Press, Homewood, Illinois

Langeluddecke, P., Goulston, K. and Tennant, C. (1987) Type A behaviour and other psychological factors in peptic ulcer disease. *Journal of Psychosomatic Research, 31* (3) 335–40

Langford, V. (1988) Stress, satisfaction and managers in the construction industry. *The Occupational Psychologist, 6,* Dec. 1988. The British Psychological Society

Langrish, S. (1981) Assertiveness Training. In *Improving Interpersonal Relations* (ed. C.L. Cooper). Gower Press, Epping

Larbi, E.B., Cooper, R.S. and Stamler, J. (1983) Alcohol and hypertension. *Archives of Internal Medicine, 143,* 28–9

LaRocco, J.M. and Jones, A.P. (1978) Co-worker and leader support as moderators of stress-strain relationships in work situations. *Journal of Applied Psychology, 63* (5) 629–34

Larsen, R.J. (1985) Individual differences in circadian activity rhythm and personality. *Personality and Individual Differences, 6* (3) 305–11

Lavie, P., Kremerman, S. and Wiel, M. (1982) Sleep disorders and safety at work in industry workers. *Accident Analysis and Prevention, 14* (4) 311–4

Lawler, E.E. (1971) *Pay and Organisational Effectiveness.* McGraw-Hill, New York

Lazarus, R.S. (1966) *Psychological Stress and the Coping Process.* McGraw-Hill, New York

Leatt, P. and Schneck, P. (1985) Sources and management of organisational stress in nursing sub-units in Canada. *Organisational Studies, 6* (1) 55–79

Lebovits, B.Z., Shekelle, R.B. and Ostfeld, A.M. (1967). Prospective and retrospective studies of CHD. *Psychosomatic Medicine, 19,* 265–72

Lefcourt, H.M. (1976) *Locus of Control.* Wiley, UK

Lefcourt, H.M. (1982) *Locus of Control. Current Trends in theory and research, 2nd edn.* Lawrence Erlbaum, London, New Jersey

LeShan, L. (1959) Psychological states as factors in the development of malignant disease: A critical review. *Journal of the National Cancer Institute, 22,* 1–8

Levi, L. (1987) Definitions and the conceptual aspects of health in relation to work. In *Psychosocial Factors at Work and Their Relation to Health* (eds R. Kalimo, M.A. El-Batawi and C.L. Cooper). WHO, Geneva

Levinson, D.J. (1978a) *The Seasons of a Man's Life.* Alfred A Knopf, USA

Levinson, H. (1978b) The abrasive personality. *The Harvard Business Review, 56,* May–June, 86–94

Lewin, K., Lippitt, R. and White, R.K. (1939) Patterns of aggressive behaviour in experimentally created social climates. *Journal of Social Psychology, 10,* 271–99

Lin, N., Ensel, W.M., Simeone, R.S. and Kuo, W. (1979) Social support, stressful life events and illness. A model and an empirical test. *Journal of Health and Social Behaviour, 20,* 108–19

Lindenthal, J., Myers, J. and Pepper, M.P. (1972) Smoking, psychological status and stress. *Social Science and Medicine, 6,* 583–91

Livy, B. and Vant, J. (1979) Formula for selecting roughnecks and roustabouts. *Personnel Management,* February, 1979

Llorente, M. (1986) Neuroticism, extraversion, and the Type A behaviour pattern. *Personality and Individual Differences, 7* (3) 427–9

Locke, E.A. (1976) The nature and causes of job satisfaction. In *Handbook of Industrial and Organizational Psychology* (ed. M.D. Dunnette). Rand McNally, Illinois. pp. 1297–349

Lunn, J.A. (1975) *The Health of Staff in Hospitals.* Heinemann, London

Maes, S., Vingerhoets, A. and Van Heck, G. (1987) The study of stress and disease: Some developments and requirements. *Social Science and Medicine, 25* (6) 567–78

Makin, P.J., Rout, U. and Cooper, C.L. (1988) Job satisfaction and occupational stress among general practitioners — A pilot study. *Journal of the Royal College of General Practitioners, 38,* 303–6

Mann, A.H. and Brennan, P.J. (1987) Type A behaviour score and the incidence of cardiovascular disease: A failure to replicate the claimed associations. *Journal of Psychosomatic Research, 31* (6) 685–92

Margolis, B., Kroes, W. and Quinn, R. (1974) Job stress and unlisted occupational hazard. *Journal of Occupational Medicine, 1* (16) 659–61

Marmot, M.G. (1983) Stress, social and cultural variations in heart disease. *Journal of Psychosomatic Research, 27,* 377

Marshall, J. (1980) Stress among Nurses. In *White Collar and Professional Stress* (eds C.L. Cooper and J. Marshall). John Wiley, UK

Marshall, J. and Cooper, C.L. (1979) *Executives Under Pressure.* Macmillan, London

Martin, P. (1987) Psychology and the Immune System. *New Scientist, 9* April 1987, 46–50

Maslach, C. and Jackson, S.E. (1981) The measurement of experienced burnout. *Journal of Occupational Behaviour, 2,* 99–113

Masuda, M., Perko, K.P. and Johnson, R.G. (1972) Physiological activity and illness history. *Journal of Psychosomatic Research, 16* (2), 129–36

Matarazzo, J.D. (1980) Behavioural health and behavioural medicine: Frontiers for a new health psychology. *American Psychologist, 35,* 807–17

Matteson, M.T. and Ivancevich, J.M. (1987) Individual stress management interventions: Evaluation of techniques. *Journal of Managerial Psychology, 2* (1) 24–30

Mawardi, B.H. (1979) Satisfactions and dissatisfactions and causes of stress in medical practice. *Journal of the American Medical Association, 241,* 1483–6

Mayo, E. (1945) *The Social Problems of an Industrial Society.* Harvard University, Boston

McClelland, D.C., Alexander, C. and Marks, E. (1982) The need for power, stress, immune function and illness among male prisoners. *Journal of Abnormal Psychology, 91,* 61–70

McCrae, R.R. and Costa, P.T. Jr. (1985) Comparison of EPI and psychoticism scales with measures of the five-factor model of personality. *Personality and Individual Differences, 6* (5) 587–97

McCrae, R.R., Costa, P.T. and Bosse, R. (1978) Anxiety, extraversion and smoking. *British Journal of Social and Clinical Psychology, 17,* 269–73

McCranie, E.W., Lambert, V.A. and Lambert, C.E. (1987). Work stress, hardiness, and burnout among hospital staff nurses. *Nursing Research, 36* (6) 374–9

McGrath, J.E. (1970) A conceptual formulation for research on stress. In *Social and Psychological Factors in Stress* (ed. J.E. McGrath). Holt, Rinehart & Winston, New York, pp. 10–21

McGrath, J.E. (1976) Stress and behaviour in organisations. In *Handbook of Industrial and Organisational Psychology* (ed. M.D. Dunnette). Rand McNally, Chicago

McKenna, E.F. (1987) *Psychology in Business: Theory and Applications.* Lawrence Erlbaum, London

McLean, A.A. (1979) *Work Stress.* Addison-Wesley, USA

McMichael, A.J. (1978) Personality, Behavioural & Situational Modifiers of Work Stressors. In *Stress at Work* (eds C.L. Cooper and R. Payne). John Wiley, UK

Mead, G.H. (1934) *Mind, Self and Society,* University of Chicago Press, Chicago

Medalie, J., Synder, M. and Groen, J.J. (1973) Angina pectoris among 10000 men: Five year incidence and univariate analysis. *American Journal of Medicine, 55,* 583–94

Melhuish, A. (1978) *Executive Health.* Business Books, London

Melhuish, A. (1987) Dangers of the Bottle. *Director.* UK, July, 1987

Metts, A.P.H. (1982) The relationship between work injuries and smoking habits among a group of cotton textile workers. *Dissertation Abstracts International, 42* (11) May, 4373–B

Miles, R.H. and Perreault, W.D. (1976) Organisational role conflicts: Its antecedants and consequences. *Organisational Behaviour and Human Performance, 17,* 19–44

Miller, D.P. and Swain, A.D. (1987) Human Error and Human Reliability. In G. Salvendy, *Handbook of Human Factors.* John Wiley, New York

Miner, J.B. and Anderson, J.K. (1958) Intelligence and emotional disturbance: Evidence from army and veterans administration records. *Journal of Abnormal and Social Psychology, 56,* 75–81

Miner, J.B. and Brewer, J.F. (1976) Management of ineffective performance. In *Handbook of Industrial and Organizational Psychology* (ed. M.D. Dunnette). John Wiley, New York

Mischel, W. (1976) *Introduction to Personality,* 2nd Edn. Holt Rinehart Winston, New York

Mitchell, S.J.F. (1988) An investigation into the stressors reported by nurses of the terminally and critically ill: Hospice and hospital nurses compared. Unpublished dissertation: Manchester School of Management. UMIST, UK

Mitchell, J.T. (1984) The 600–run limit. *Journal of Emergency Medical Services, 9* (1) 52–4

Monk, T.H. and Folkard, S. (1983) Circadian rhythms and shiftwork. In *Stress and Fatigue in Human Performance* (ed. R. Hockey). John Wiley, UK

Monk, T.M., and Tepas, D.I. (1985). Shift Work. In *Job Stress and Blue Collar Work* (eds C.L. Cooper and M.J. Smith). John Wiley, UK

Morgan, P. and Davies, N. (1981) Costs of occupational accidents and disease in GB. *Employment Gazette,* Nov. 1981, 477–85

Morrell, D.C., Evans, M.E., Morris, R.W. and Roland, M.O. (1986) The five minute consultation; effect of time constraint on clinical context and patient satisfaction. *British Medical Journal, 292,* 870–3

Muchinsky, P.M. (1977) Employee absenteeism: A review of the literature. *Journal of Vocational Behaviour, 10,* 316–40

Mueller, E.F. (1965) Psychological and physiological correlates of work overload among university professors, unpublished doctoral dissertation. Ann Arbor, University of Michigan

The Multiple Risk Factor Intervention Trial Group (1979) The MRFIT behaviour pattern. Study I. Study design, procedures and reproductibility of behaviour pattern judgements. *Journal of Chronic Diseases, 32,* 293–305

Munsterberg, H. (1913) *Psychology and Industrial Efficiency.* Houghton-Mifflin, New York

Murphy, L.R. (1985) Individual Coping Strategies. In *Job Stress and Blue Collar Work* (eds C.L. Cooper and M.J. Smith). John Wiley, UK

Murphy, L.R. and Sorenson, S. (1988) Employee behaviours before and after stress management. *Journal of Organisational Behaviour, 9,* 173–82

Murray, R.M. (1976) Alcoholism amongst male doctors in Scotland. *Lancet, ii*, 729–33

National Cancer Institute (1985) Cancer Rates and Risks. US Dept. of Health & Human Services

National Institute on Alcohol Abuse and Alcoholism. *Alcohol World Health and Research*, 9 (2) 1984/5

Newbold, E.M. (1926) *A Contribution to the study of the human factor in the causation of accidents.* Report 34. Industrial Health Research Board

Nichols, K.A., Springford, V. and Searle, J. (1981) An investigation of distress and discontent in various types of nursing. *Journal of Advanced Nursing, 6,* 311–8

Nicholson, J.H., Donaldson, M.S. and Oh, J.E. (1983) H.M.O. Members and Clinicians Rank Health Education Needs. *Public Health Reports, 98,* 222–6

NIOSH (1986) *National Strategy on the Prevention of Work-Related Psychological Disorders.* NIOSH, Cincinnati. October 1986

Norfolk, B. and Stirton, J. (1985) Stress at work. A survey conducted on ten psycho-geriatric wards at High Royds Hospital. National Union of Public Employees — Preliminary Report

Noweir, M.H. (1984) Noise exposure as related to productivity, disciplinary actions, absenteeism, and accidents among textile workers. *Journal of Safety Research, 15,* 163–74

O'Brien, C., Smith, W.S., Goldsmith, R., Fordham, M. and Tan, G.L. (1979) A study of the strains associated with medical nursing and vehicle assembly. In *Response to Stress: Occupational Aspect* (eds C. Mackay and T. Cox). IPC Science and Technology Press, London

O'Connor, K. (1985) A model of situational preference amongst smokers. *Personality and Individual Differences, 6* (2) 151–60

Office of Population Census and Surveys. (1986) HMSO, London

Ojesjo, L. (1980) The relationship to alcoholism of occupation, class, and employment. *Journal of Occupational Medicine, 22,* (10) 657–66

Opbroek, H.A. (1983) *Men and Materials Handling in Offshore Operations* International Symposium, Luxembourg. *Op cit.*

Opdyke, A.P. and Thayer, J.M. (1987) The work environment. A social and technical response to injury and illness losses. *Personnel Journal.* Feb. 37–42

Osler, W. (1910) Angina pectoris. *Lancet, i,* 839

Packard, V. (1972) *A Nation of Strangers.* McKay, New York

Paffenbarger, R.S., Wolf, P.A. and Notkin, J. (1966) Chronic disease in former college students. *American Journal of Epidemiology, 83,* 314–28

Pahl, J.M. and Pahl, R.E. (1971) *Managers and their Wives.* Allen Lane, London

Parkes, K.R. (1980a) Occupational stress among nurses. 1. A comparison of medical and surgical wards. *Nursing Times, 30,* 113–6

Parkes, K.R. (1980b) Occupational stress among nurses. 2. A comparison of male and female wards. *Nursing Times, 6,* 117–9

Parkes, K.R. (1982) Occupational stress among student nurses: A natural experiment. *Journal of Applied Psychology, 67* (6) 784–96

Paykel, E.S. (1982) Life events and early environment. In *Handbook of Affective Disorders* (ed. E.S. Paykel). Churchill Livingstone, Edinburgh

Paykel, E.S. and Rao, B.M. (1984) Methodology in studies of life events and cancer. In *Psychosocial Stress and Cancer* (ed. C.L. Cooper). John Wiley & Sons, Chichester and New York

Payne, R. (1981) The relationship between affect and description: A neglected area in the stress field. Unpublished working paper.

Payne, R.L. and Rick, J.T. (1986) Psychosological markers of stress in surgeons and anaesthetists. In *Biological and Psychological Factors in Cardiovascular Disease* (eds. T.H. Schmidt, T.M. Dembroski and G. Blümchen). Springer-Verlag, Berlin

Pearlin, L.I., Lieberman, M.A., Menaghan, E.G. and Mullan, J.T. (1981) The stress process. *Journal of Health & Social Behaviour, 22,* 337–56

Pearlin, L.I. and Schooler, C. (1978) The structure of coping. *Journal of Health and Social Behaviour, 19,* 2–21

Pestonjee, D.M., Singh, A.P. and Ahmad, N. (1977) Job satisfaction and accidents. *Indian Journal of Industrial Relations, 13,* 65–71

Phares, E.J. (1984) *Introduction to Personality.* Columbus, Ohio: Charles E. Merrill Publishing Co., Columbus, Ohio

Philbert, M., Frère, J.J. et Emmanueli, X. (1975) Working, Living and Medical Conditions Aboard an Oil Barge in the North Sea. *Archives de maladies professionnelles de medécine due travail et de Sécurité Sociale (Paris), 36* (3) 137–44

Pickering, T.G. (1988) The study of the blood pressure in everyday life. In *Behavioural Medicine in Cardiovascular Disorders* (eds T. Elbert, W. Langosch, A. Steptoe and D. Vaitl). John Wiley & Sons, Chichester and New York

Pierce, J.P., Linder-Pelz, S., Minslow, M., Mock, P. and Broch, K. (1987) Stress and Occupational Stressors in Nursing: Information for Management. Unpublished Report. Royal North Shore Hospital, Sydney, Australia

Pincherle, G. (1972) Fitness for Work. *Proceedings of the Royal Society of Medicine, 65* (4) 321–4

Plant, M.A. (1979) Occupations, Drinking Patterns and Alcohol-Related Problems: Conclusions from a follow-up study. *British Journal of Addiction, 74* (3) 267–73

Porter, A.M.D., Howie, J.G.R. and Levinson, A. (1985) Measurement of stress as it affects the work of the general practitioner. *Family Practice, 2* (3) 136–46

Porter, A.M.D., Howie, J.G.R. and Levinson, A. (1987) Stress and the General Practitioner. In *Stress in Health Professionals* (eds R. Payne, and J. Firth-Cozens). John Wiley & Sons, Chichester and New York

Porter, L.W. and Steers, R.M. (1973) Organisational, work and personal factors in employee turnover and absenteeism. *Psychological Bulletin. 80,* 151–76

Poulton, E.C. (1978) Blue Collar Stressors. In *Stress at Work* (eds C.L. Cooper and R. Payne). John Wiley & Sons, Chichester and New York

Powell, D. (1982) Learning to relate? A study of student psychiatric nurses' views of their preparation and training. *Royal College of Nursing*, London

Powell, P.I., Hale, M., Martin, J. and Simon, M. (1971) *2000 Accidents. A Shop Floor Study of the Causes.* NIIP Report No. 21. NIIP, London

Quick, J.C. and Quick, J.D. (1984) *Organisational Stress & Preventive Management.* McGraw-Hill USA

Ramsey, J.D. (1983) Heat & Cold. In *Stress & Fatigue in Human Performance* (ed. Robert Hockey). John Wiley & Sons, Chichester and New York

Ray, J.S. (1973) Alcoholism and Insurance. Labour-Management Newsletter. National Council on Alcoholism, Washington, DC, 1–8

Registrar General (1978) *Decennial Supplement for England and Wales.* HMSO, London

Richardson, C.T. (1983) Gastric ulcer in gastrointestinal disease. In *Pathophysiology, Diagnosis and Management* (eds M.H. Sleisenger and J.S. Fordtran). *Vol. 1*, 3rd Edn W.B. Saunders, Philadelphia

Rippere, V. (1989) Nutrition and adult psychiatric problems. Paper presented at the Annual Conference, the British Psychological Society, St. Andrews, March, 1989

Rizzo, J., House, R.E. and Lirtzman, J. (1970) Role conflict and ambiguity in complex organisations. *Administrative Science Quarterly, 15,* 150–63

The Robens Report. (1972) *Safety and Health at Work.* HMSO, London

Robinson, D.A. (1976) *From Drinking to Alcoholism.* John Wiley, New York

Roethlisberger, F. and Dickson, J.J. (1939) *Management and the Worker.* Harvard University Press, Cambridge, Massachusetts

Rogers, M.P., Dubrey, D. and Reich, P. (1979) The influence of the psyche and the brain on immunity and disease susceptibility. *Psychosomatic Medicine, 41,* 147–64

Rosch, P.J. (1984) Stress and Cancer. In *Psychosocial Stress and Cancer* (ed C.L. Cooper). John Wiley & Sons, Chichester and New York

Rosch, P.J. and Pelletier, K.R. (1987) Designing worksite stress management programmes. In *Stress management in Work Settings* (eds L.R. Murphy and T.F. Schoenborn). NIOSH, May, 1987, p. 69–91

Rose, G. and Marmot A. (1981) Social class and coronary heart disease. *British Heart Journal, 45,* 13–19

Rosenmann, R.H., Friedman, M. and Strauss, R. (1964) A predictive study of C.H.D. The W.C.G.S. *Journal of the American Medical Association, 189,* 15–22

Rosenmann, R.H., Friedman, M. and Strauss, R. (1966) C.H.D. in the Western Collaborative Group Study. *Journal of the American Medical Association, 195,* 86–92

Rosenmann, R.H., Brand, R.H., Jenkins, D., Friedman, M., Strauss, R., and Wurm, M. (1975) Coronary heart disease in the Western Collaborative Group Study. Final follow up experience of 8.5 years. *Journal of the American Medical Association, 233,* 875–7

Rosow, I. and Rose, K.D. (1972) Divorce among doctors. *Journal of Marriage and Family, 34,* 587–598.

Rotter, J.B. (1966). Generalized expectancies for internal versus external control of reinforcement. *Psychological Monographs, 80* (1) (whole no. 609), 1966, 1–28

Rowland, K.R., Ferris, G.R., Fried, Y. and Sutton, C.D. (1988) An Assessment of the Physiological Measurement of Work Stress. In *Occupational Stress — Issues and Developments in Research* (eds J.J. Hurrell, L.R. Murphy, S.L. Sauter and C.L. Cooper). Taylor Francis, UK

Ruberman, W., Weinblatt, E., Goldberg, J.D. and Chaudhary, B. (1984) Psychosocial influences on mortality after myocardial infarction. *New England Journal of Medicine, 311,* 552

Russek, H.I. (1962) Emotional stress and coronary heart disease in American physicians, dentists and lawyers. *American Journal of Medical Science, 243,* 716–25

Russek, H. (1965) Stress, tobacco and coronary heart disease in North American professional groups. *Journal of the American Medical Association. 192,* 189–94

Russek, H.I. and Zohman, B.L. (1958) Relative significance of heredity, diet and occupational stress in C.H.D. of young adults. *American Journal of Medical Sciences, 235,* 266–75

Rutenfranz, J., Colquhoun, W., Knauth, P. and Ghata, J. (1977) Biomedical and psychosocial aspects of shift work. *Scandinavian Journal of Work Environment and Health, 3,* 165–82

Sales, S.M. (1970) Some effects of role overload and role underload. *Organizational Behaviour & Human Performance, 5,* 592–608

Sales, S.M. and House, J. (1971) Job dissatisfaction as a possible risk factor in coronary heart disease. *Journal of Chronic Diseases, 23,* 861–73

Sallis, J.F., Trevorrow, T.R., Johnson, C.C., Hovell, M.F. and Kaplan, R.M. (1987). Worksite stress management: A comparison of programmes. *Psychology and Health, 1* (3) 237–55

Salvendy, G. and Knight, J. (1983) Circulatory responses to machine paced and self-paced work. An industrial study. *Ergonomics, 26,* 713–7

Sarason, I.G. and Sarason, B.R. (1981) The importance of cognition and moderator variables in stress. In *Toward a Psychology of Situations: An Interactional Prospective* (ed. D. Magnusson). Lawrence Erlbaum, Hillsdale, New Jersey, 195–210

Sarason, I. and Johnson, J. (1979) Life events, organisational stress and job satisfaction. *Psychological Reports, 44,* 75–9

Sartre, J.P. (1944) *Huis Clos.* Theatre Gallimard, Paris

SAUS (1985) Alcohol Education Programme — Regional Profile. University of Bristol, Bristol

Scheiber, S.C. (1987) Stress in Physicians. In *Stress in Health Professionals* (eds R. Payne and J. Firth-Cozens). John Wiley & Sons, Chichester and New York

Scheier, M.F. and Carver, C.S. (1985) Optimism, coping and health: Assessment and implications of generalized outcome expectancies. *Health Psychology, 4,* 219–49

Schmale, A.H. and Iker, H.D. (1971) Hopelessness as a predictor of cervical cancer. *Social Science and Medicine*, 5, 95–100

School for Advanced Urban Studies (SAUS) (1985) *Alcohol Education Programme Regional Profile*. Bristol: University of Bristol

Schuler, R.S. (1980) Definition and conceptualization of stress in organisations. *Organizational Behaviour & Human Performance*, 25, 184–215

Schwartz, G.E. (1982) Testing the biopsychosocial model: The ultimate challenge facing behavioural medicine. *Journal of Consulting and Clinical Psychology*, 50, 1040–53

Seamonds, B.C. (1983) Extension of research into stress factors and their effect on illness absenteeism. *Journal of Occupational Medicine*, 25, 821–2

Seamonds, B.C. (1986) The concept and practice of stress management. In *Occupational Stress. Health and Performance at Work* (eds S. Wolf and A.J. Finestone). PSG Publishing, Littleton, Masschusetts

Selye, H. (1956) *The Stress of Life*. McGraw-Hill, USA

Selye, H. (1974) *Stress without Distress*. J.B. Lippincott, Philadelphia

Selye, H. (1976) *Stress in Health & Disease*. Butterworths, London

Selye, H. (1979) Correlating Stress and Cancer. *American Journal of Proctology, Gastroenterology, Colon and Rectal Surgery*, 30 (4) 18–28

Selye, H. (1983) The Stress Concept: Past, Present and Future. In *Stress Research* (ed. C.L. Cooper). John Wiley, UK

Selye, J. and Bajusz, E. (1959) Conditioning by corticoids for the production of cardiac lesions with noradrenaline. *Acta Endocrinology*, 30, 183

Sergean, R. (1971) *Managing Shiftwork*. Gower Press, London

Shaffer, M. (1983) *Life after Stress*. Contemporary Books, Chicago

Shaw, L. and Sichel, H.S. (1971) *Accident Proneness: research in the occurence, causation and prevention of road accidents*. Pergamon, Oxford

Sheehy, N.P. and Chapman, A.J. (1987) Industrial Accidents. In *International Review of Industrial Pychology, 1987* (eds C.L. Cooper and I.T. Robertson). John Wiley, UK

Shekelle, R.B., Gayle, M., Ostfeld, A.M. and Paul, O. (1983) Hostility, risk of coronary heart disease and mortality. *Psychosomatic Medicine*, 45, 109–14

Shekelle, R.B., Raynor, W.J., Osterfeld, A.M., Garron, D.C., Bieliauskas, L.A., Liu, S.C., Maliza, C. and Paul, O. (1981) Psychological depression and 17 year risk of death from cancer. *Psychosomatic Medicine*, 43, 117–25

Shillitoe, R.W. (1988) *Psychology and Diabetes. Psychosocial Factors in Management and Control*. Chapman and Hall, London

Shimmen, S. (1962) Extra-mural factors influencing work behaviour at work. *Journal of Occupational Psychology*, 36 (3) 124–31

Shimmen, S., McNally, J. and Liff, S. (1981) Pressure on women engaged in factory work. *Employment Gazette*, August, 1981, 344–9

Shirom, A., Eden, D., Silberwasser, S. and Kellerman, J.J. (1973) Job stress and risk factors in coronary heart disease among occupational categories in Kibbutzim. *Social Science & Medicine*, 7, 875–92

Shostak, A.B. (1980) *Blue-Collar Stress*. Addison-Wesley, USA

Siegman, A.W., Dembrokski, T.M. and Ringel, N. (1987) Components of hostility and the severity of coronary artery disease. *Psychosomatic Medicine*, 49, 127–35

Singer, G. (1985) New Approaches to Social Factors in Shiftwork. In *Shiftwork and Health* (ed. M. Wallace). Brain Behaviour Research Institute, Bundoora, Australia

Sjobring, H. (1963) *La Personality, structure et development.* Doin, Paris

Sloan, S. and Cooper, C.L. (1986) *Pilots Under Stress.* Routledge & Kegan Paul, London

Smith, M.J. (1975) *When I Say No, I Feel Guilty.* Bantam Books, New York

Smith, M.J., Cohen, B.G., Stammerjohn, L.W. and Happ, A. (1981) An investigation of health complaints and job stress in video display operations. *Human Factors*, 23, 389–400

Smith, M.J., Cohen, H.H., Cleveland, R., and Cohen, A. (1978) Characteristics of successful safety programs. *Journal of Safety Research*, 10, 5–15

Smith, M.J., Colligan, M.J. and Tasto, D.L. (1982) Health and safety consequences of shift work in the food processing industry. *Ergonomics*, 25, 133–44

Smith, T., Houston, B., Kent, A. and Stucky, R.J. (1984) Type A behaviour, irritability and cardiovascular response. *Motivation and Emotion*, 8 (3) 221–30

Smith, W.R. and Sebastian, H. (1976). Emotional history and pathogenesis of cancer. *Journal of Clinical Psychology*, 32 (4) 63–6

Social Trends 17 (1987) Central Statistics Office, HMSO, London

Sorenson, G., Jacobs, D.R., Pirie, P., Folsom, A., Luepker, R. and Gillum, R. (1987). Relationships among Type A behaviour, employment experiences and gender: The Minnesota Heart Survey. *Journal of Behavioural Medicine*, 10 (4) 323–36

Stagner, R., Flebbe, D.R. and Wood, E.F. (1952) Working on a railroad: A study of job satisfaction. *Personnel Psychology*, 5, 293–306

Staw, B.M., Bell, N.E. and Clausen, J.A. (1986) The dispositional approach to job attitudes: A lifetime longitudinal test. *Administrative Science*, 31, 56–77

Steers, R.M. and Rhodes, S.R. (1978) Major influences on employee attendance: A process model. *Journal of Applied Psychology*, 63, 391–407

Steppacher, R.C. and Mausner, J.S. (1974) Suicide in male and female physicians. *Journal of the American Medical Association*, 228, 323–8

Studenski, R. (1981) Level of anxiety and work accidents. *Przeglad Psychologiczny*, 24, 137–45

Suchman, E.A. (1961) A conceptual analysis of the accident phenomenon. *Social Problems*, 8, 241–53

Suinn, R.M. (1976) How to break the vicious cycle of stress. *Psychology Today*, 59–60

Suinn, R.M. and Bloom, L.J. (1978) Anxiety management training for pattern A behaviour. *Journal of Behavioural Medicine*, 1, 22–35

Surry, J. (1968) *Industrial Accident Research: A Human Engineering Appraisal.* Ontario Department of Labour, Canada

Surwit, R.S. and Feinglos, M.N. (1984) Relaxation-induced improvement in glucose tolerance is associated with decreased plasma cortisol. *Diabetes Care*, 7, 203–4

Sutherland, V.J. and Cooper, C.L. (1986) *Man & Accidents Offshore: the costs of stress among workers on oil and gas rigs*. Lloyd's List/ Dietsmann (International) NV, London

Sutherland, V.J. and Davidson, M.J. (1989) Stress among Construction Site Managers: A Preliminary Study. *Stress Medicine*, 5, 221–35

Swinburne, P. (1981) The psychological impact of unemployment on managers and professional staff. *Journal of Occupational Psychology*, 54, 47–64

Tasto, D.L. and Colligan, M.J. (1978) Health consequences of shift work. *Stanford Research Technical Report. URU 4426*. Mento Park, California

Temoshok, L. & Heller, B.W. (1984) On comparing apples, oranges and fruit salad: A methodological overview of medical outcome studies in psychosocial oncology. In *Psychosocial Stress and Cancer* (ed. C.L. Cooper). John Wiley & Sons, Chichester and New York

Theorell, T. (1976) Selected illness and somatic factors in relation to two psychosocial stress indices — a prospective study on middle aged construction building workers. *Journal of Psychosomatic Research*, 20, 7–20

Theorell, T. (1986) Characteristics of employment that modify the risk of coronary heart disease. Chapter 8. In *Occupational Stress. Health and Performance at Work* (eds S. Wolf and A. Finestone). PSG, Littleton, Massachusetts

Thomas, C.B. (1976) What becomes of medical students: The dark side. *The John Hopkins Medical Journal*, 138, 185–95

Thomas, C.B. (1977) Habits of nervous tension: Clues to the human condition. The precursors study. 725 N. Wolfe Street, Baltimore, MD.

Thomas, C.B. and Greenstreet, R.L. (1973) Psychobiological characteristics in youth as predictors of five disease states: Suicide, mental illness, hypertension, coronary heart disease and tumor. *John Hopkins Medical Journal*, 132, 16–43

Thoits, P.A. (1982) Conceptual, methodological and theoretical problems in studying social support as a buffer against life stress. *Journal of Health and Social Behaviour*, 23, 145–9

Thoits, P.A. (1986) Social support as coping assistance. *Journal of Consulting and Clinical Psychology*, 54 (4) 416–23

Thorensen, C.E. & Eagleston, J.R. (1984) Counselling, health and psychology. In *Handbook of Counselling Psychology* (eds S.D. Brown and R.W. Lent)

Tilley, A.J., Wilkinson, R.T., Warren, P.S.G., Watson, B. and Drud, M. (1982) The sleep and performance of shift workers. *Human Factors*, 24 (6) 629–41

Tisdelle, D.A., Hansen, D.J., St. Lawrence, J.S. and Brown, J.C. (1984) Stress management training for dental students. *Journal of Dental Education*, 48, 196–201

Tokarz, P., Bremer, W. and Peters, K. (1979) *Beyond Survival*, American Medical Association, Chicago

Travers, C. and Firth-Cozens, J. (1989) Experiences of mental health work, hospital closure, stress and social support. Paper presented at the British Psychological Society, Annual Occupational Psychology Conference, Bowness-on-Windermere, January, 1989

Trubo, R. (1984) Burnout. When the doctor's bag gets heavy. *Medical World News*, March, 38–55

Tsai, S.P., Baun, W.B. and Bernacki, E.J. (1987) Relationship of employee turnover to exercise adherence in a corporate fitness program. *Journal of Occupational Medicine, 29* (7) 572–5

Tsuang, Ming, T. and Vandermey, R. (1980) *Genes and the Mind. Inheritance of Mental Illness.* University Press, Oxford

Van Sell, M., Brief, A.P. and Schuler, R.S. (1981) Role conflict and role ambiguity: Integration of the literature and directions for future research. *Human Relations, 34* (1) 43–71

Wallack, L. and Winkleby, M. (1987) Primary prevention: A new look at basic concepts. *Social Science and Medicine, 25* (8) 923–30

Wallick, F. (1972) *The American Worker: An Endangered Species.* Ballantine, New York

Ward, C.H. and Eisler, R.M. (1987) Type A behaviour, achievement striving and a dysfunctional self-evaluation system. *Journal of Personality and Social Psychology, 53* (2) 318–26

Wardwell, W.I., Hyman, M. and Bahnson, C.B. (1964) Stress and coronary disease in three field studies. *Journal of Chronic Diseases, 17,* 73–84

Warr, P. and Wall, T. (1975) *Work and Well Being.* Penguin, Harmondsworth. pp. 197–205

Warshaw, L.J. (1979) *Managing Stress.* Addison Wesley, Reading, Massachusetts

Weeks, H. (1978) Dealing with stress. *Maternal Child Nursing, 3* (3) 151–2

Weiner, H. (1977) *Psychobiology and Human Disease.* Elsevier, New York and Holland

Wethington, E. and Kessler, R.C. (1986) Perceived support, received support and adjustment to stressful life events. *Journal of Health and Social Behaviour, 27,* 78–89

Whitlock, F.A., Stoll, J.R. and Rekhdahl, R.J. (1977) Crises, life events and accidents. *Australian & New Zealand Journal of Psychiatry, 11,* p. 127

WHO (1984) *Psychosocial factors and health: Monitoring the psychosocial work environment and workers' health.* World Health Organisation, Geneva

Williams, R.B., Barefoot, J.C. and Skekelle, R.B. (1985) The health consequences of hostility. In *Anger, Hostility and Behavioural Medicine* (eds M.A. Chesney and R.H. Roseman). Hemisphere/McGraw-Hill, New York

Williams, R.B., Barefoot, J.C., Honey, T.L., Hurrell, F.E., Blumenthal, J.A., Pryor, D.B. and Peterson, B. (1988) Type A behaviour and angiographically documented coronary atherosclerosis in a sample of 2289 patients. *Psychosomatic Medicine, 50,* 139–52

Wilson, E. (1857) *Diseases of the Skin.* Churchill, London

Witzel, L. (1970) Anamese and zweiterkrankungen bei patienten mit bosartigen neubildungen. (Medical histories of patients with malignant tumors compared with patients with other diseases). *Medizinische Klinik, 65,* 876–9

Wolf, S. (1971) Psychosocial forces in myocardial infarction and sudden death. In *Society Stress and Disease, Vol. 1* (ed. L. Levi). Oxford University Press, New York

Wolf, S. (1986) *Common and Grave Disorders Identified with Occupational Stress* — Wolf and Finestone (op cit.)

Wolf, S. and Wolff, H.G. (1943) *Gastric Function: An experimental study of a man and his stomach.* Oxford University Press, New York

Wolff, H.G. (1953) *Stress and Disease.* Charles C. Thomas, USA

Woods, S.C. & Porter, D. (1974) Neural control of the endocrine pancreas. *Physiological Review, 54,* 596–619

Yerkes, R.M. and Dodson, J.D. (1908). The relation to the strength of the stimulus to the rapidity of habit formation. *Journal of Comparative Neurology & Psychology, 18,* 459–82

Index